Of all the letters in the Pauline corpus, the letter to the Romans has attracted the greatest degree of scholarly attention. Yet surprisingly scant consideration has been given to the question of its literary genre. Taking up the comparatively brief suggestions of previous scholars, Dr Guerra argues that the letter belongs to the protreptic genre – the class of writing in antiquity which urges the adoption of a particular way of life (or a deeper commitment to it), setting out its advantages, replying to objections, and demonstrating its superiority. Working through each chapter of the letter in turn, he indicates how Paul provides a critique of non-Christian ways of life (both Jewish and Gentile) and affirms the superiority of Christian gospel. It becomes apparent that the Pauline apologetics of Romans stand between the hellenistic Jewish tradition and the later Greek Christian apologists, and may have influenced the latter. In addition, Dr Guerra shows convincingly that the understanding of Romans as protreptic in character reveals its underlying logical unity, and also that the letter may be firmly located within the particular situation of the Roman church.

SOCIETY FOR NEW TESTAMENT STUDIES

MONOGRAPH SERIES

General Editor: Margaret E. Thrall

81

ROMANS AND THE APOLOGETIC TRADITION

Romans and the apologetic tradition

The purpose, genre and audience of Paul's letter

ANTHONY J. GUERRA

Associate Professor of Humanities,
University of Bridgeport, Connecticut

CAMBRIDGE
UNIVERSITY PRESS

Published by the Press Syndicate of the University of Cambridge
The Pitt Building, Trumpington Street, Cambridge CB2 1RP
40 West 20th Street, New York, NY 10011–4211, USA
10 Stamford Road, Oakleigh, Melbourne 3166, Australia

First published 1995

Printed in Great Britain at the University Press, Cambridge

A catalogue record for this book is available from the British Library

Library of Congress cataloguing in publication data
Guerra, Anthony, J.
Romans and the apologetic tradition: the purpose, genre and audience
of Paul's letter / Anthony J. Guerra.
    p.   cm. – (Society for New Testament Studies monograph series: 81)
Includes bibliographical references and index.
ISBN 0 521 47126 5 (hardback)
1. Bible. N.T. Romans – Criticism, interpretation, etc.
2. Apologetics – Early church, ca. 30–600.   I. Title.
II. Series: Monograph series (Society for New Testament Studies); 81.
BS2665.2.G84 1995 227′.106 – dc20 94–9612   CIP

ISBN 0 521 47126 5 hardback

CE

CONTENTS

PREFACE

An interpretive hypothesis must be judged finally according to its explanatory power with respect to the parts as well as the whole of a given literary work. I argue that Romans is a protreptic writing seeking to affirm Paul's ministry and the gospel which he preached. In recent years, sections of the genuine Pauline epistles (especially 1 and 2 Cor.),[1] and even entire epistles have been considered to be self-apologies wherein Paul defends his apostleship.[2] This restriction of the use of the term apology to a self-defense, however, is not justified by the ancient sources for the most characteristic Jewish Hellenistic apologies were propaganda on behalf of the Law rather than the author's defense against personal accusations.[3] Further, the undisputed Christian apologetic writings of the second century are not primarily defenses but positive propagandistic appeals to win converts to the new movement.[4] These writings fulfill the same function as do philosophical Protreptics.[5] Genre criticism, albeit important, should be complemented by analysis of content. In considering the material content of Romans, I have employed motif analysis as the primary method. This approach was chosen over, on the one hand, word analysis which is often too restrictive and may as readily obfuscate as elucidate an author's intent; and on the other hand, a thematic analysis that may promote sweeping conceptual

---

[1] E.g. N. A. Dahl, "Paul and the Church at Corinth According to I Corinthians 1:10–4:21" in *Studies in Paul: Theology for the Early Christian Mission* (Minneapolis, Augusburg, 1977), pp. 51–3; and J. Bradley Chance, "Paul's Apology to The Corinthians," *Perspectives in Religious Studies*, pp. 145–55; E. Richard, "Polemics, Old Testament, and Theology: A Study of II Cor:3:1–4:6," 340–67).

[2] Most significantly in Hans Dieter Betz, *Galatians* (Hermeneia, Philadelphia, Fortress, 1979).

[3] See Helmut Koester on the definition of an apology, *Introduction to the New Testament*, vol. 2 (Philadelphia, Fortress, 1982), pp. 338–440.

[4] See Appendix.

[5] Mark D. Jordan, "Ancient Philosophical Protreptic and the Problem of Persuasive Genres," *Rhetorica*, 4 (1986), 309–33.

generalizations which however intriguing may again have little to do with an author's intended meaning. Motif analysis, in my view, represents a middle way between these two and allows for confrontation of an author's conceptual universe while remaining attentive to specific verbal formulations. Motif analysis has been applied to the apologetic texts used in establishing the data base for apologetic theology and in the exegesis of Romans. Finally, in terms of this investigation, there was a persistent effort to recognize the significance of the historical context and circumstances of Romans. Thus, genre, motif, and historical criticism are all central to this work.

A guiding presupposition of this investigation has been that Paul seeks to communicate intelligibly and effectively to the audience which he is addressing. Thus the question of the image of this audience with which Paul operates in writing Romans is of some importance. The proposal made here is that Paul's image is of a dual audience: Jewish and Gentile Christians. Because of the theological distance and the past history of conflict between the apostle and the former, Paul attempts in Romans to present his teaching and ministry in the most inviting manner and to respond to typical objections of Jewish Christians. This primary image of Paul's audience must be brought into clearer focus by reference to the "Roman factor": that is Paul's attention to the locale of his addressees, their special sensibilities and proximity to the seat of imperial power.

My thinking about the protreptic character of Romans began at Harvard Divinity School in 1984 under the guidance of Helmut Koester and eventuated in a dissertation: "Romans 3.29–30 and the Apologetic Tradition." Chapters 2 and 3 of the present work incorporate material, with revision, from the earlier writing. While at Harvard, I received valuable assistance from several other members of the faculty including Dieter Georgi, George MacRae, Bernadette Brooten, and Krister Stendahl. The present investigation continues the analysis of the remaining twelve chapters of Romans and also considers the question of the audience of Romans which was not raised in the earlier work. I am grateful to the National Endowment for the Humanities for the opportunity to study with Professor Louis H. Feldman in his 1989 summer seminar: "The Greek Encounter with Judaism." During that period my thinking with respect to Paul's purpose and audience in Romans was crystalized. I would like to thank the Society of Biblical Literature for the privilege of chairing the consultation on "Apologetic Literature in the

Graeco-Roman World" during 1987–8. These sessions provided a context for a serious and fruitful exchange of views on ancient apologetic literature. I am also grateful to William R. Schoedel, Eugene Gallagher, and Robert M. Grant, as well as to David E. Aune, who shared his monograph on Romans before publication, and to whom, as the notes testify, I am much indebted.

I also wish to express my appreciation to Bard College for a semester sabbatical in which I was able to complete the writing of this manuscript. I am especially grateful to the Bard history department for the opportunity to teach courses in Roman history that allowed me to re-read and, yes, read for the first time much literature that New Testament scholars know they "ought" to have read. I am also much indebted to both William C. Mullen and Christopher Callanan of the Bard classics department. It is with affection that I recognize the support and encouragement from my colleagues in the Bard religion department, David Pierce, Fritz Shafer, Laurie Patton, as well as Bruce Chilton, who has read and commented on more than one draft of this work. A special note of gratitude is due to Annette Reed, my Bard student assistant who helped prepare the indices, proof read the manuscript as well as type major portions of the text. Lastly, I feel most indebted to Dr. Margaret E. Thrall in whom I have enjoyed the rare blessing of working with an editor who possesses not merely general competence on the primary text under consideration but special expertise. Her editorial comments have been consistently perceptive and have immeasurably enhanced the present work. I am, of course, entirely responsible for any shortcomings which remain.

ABBREVIATIONS

AJSL	*American Journal of Semitic Languages and Literature*
ANRW	*Aufstieg und Niedergang des roemische Welt*
APOT	*The Apocrypha and Pseudepigrapha of the Old Testament*
ASNU	*Acta Seminarii Neotestamentici Upsaliensis*
BAG	*A Greek–English Lexicon of the New Testament and other early Christian Literature*
BAGD	Ibid. 2nd edn revised
BDB	F. Brown, S. R. Driver and A. Briggs, *A Hebrew and English Lexicon of the Old Testament*, Oxford
BFCTh	Beitraege zur Foederung Christlicher Theologie
BHTh	Beitraege zur historischen Theologie
BZ	*Biblische Zeitschrift*
CAT	Commentaire de l'Ancien Testament
CBQ	*Catholic Biblical Quarterly*
CNT	Commentaire du Nouveau Testament
EKKNT	Evangelisch-Katholischer Kommentar zum Neuen Testament
ET	English translation
EvTh	*Evangelische Theologie*
FRALNT	Forschungen zur Religion und Literatur des Alten und Neuen Testaments
HDR	Harvard Dissertations in Religion
HNT	Handbuch zum Neuen Testament
HTR	*Harvard Theological Review*
HThKNT	Herders theologischer Kommentar zum Neuen Testament

HUT	Hermeneutische Untersuchungen zur Theologie
ICC	International Critical Commentary
IDB	*Interpreter's Dictionary of the Bible*
JBC	R. E. Brown et al. (eds.), *The Jerome Biblical Commentary*
JBL	*Journal of Biblical Literature*
JJS	*Journal of Jewish Studies*
JQR	*Jewish Quarterly Review*
KAT	E. Sellin (ed.), Kommentar zum A.T.
LD	Lectio Divina
LEC	Library of Early Christianity
LSJ	*A Greek–English Lexicon*, Rev.
MNTC	Moffatt New Testament Commentary
NTS	*New Testament Studies*
NovT	*Novum Testamentum*
RB	*Revue Biblique*
SBLDS	Society for Biblical Literature Dissertation Series
SBT	Studies in Biblical Theology
SJLA	Studies in Judaism in Late Antiquity
SNTSMS	Society for New Testament Studies Monograph Series
StudNeot	Studia Neotestamentica
TDNT	*Theological Dictionary of the New Testament*
VC	*Vigilae Christianae*
VS	Verbum Salutis
VT	*Vetus Testamentum*
WBC	Word Biblical Commentary
WUNT	Wissenschaftliche Untersuchungen zum Neuen Testament
ZThK	*Zeitschrift Für Theologie und Kirche*
ZNW	*Zeitschrift für die neutestamentliche Wissenschaft*

1

APOLOGETIC AND AUDIENCE: MAKING THE MESSAGE MEET

In this chapter, two interrelated interpretive hypotheses concerning Paul's letter to the Romans are presented, namely that the letter is a Προτρεπτικὸς Λόγος or a Protreptic, and that this Protreptic is directed to an audience comprised in significant part of Jewish Christians. The denial of a significant presence of Jewish Christians in Paul's Roman audience has been argued on both textual and circumstantial grounds and both rationales will be shown to be seriously deficient. Moreover there is a reigning theory among commentators, to the effect that Paul wrote the letter to the Romans as a dress rehearsal for the speech which he intended to give on his upcoming visit to Jerusalem. This proposal has plausibility mainly because the contents of the letter strongly suggest that Paul is addressing Jewish Christians, yet such are excluded from the Roman community by many commentators.[1] Once the reasons for denying that Jewish Christians are part of Paul's audience are found wanting, then the Jerusalem speech hypothesis is readily seen to be untenable. As to the protreptic character of the letter to the Romans, there has generally been surprisingly scant attention paid to the question of the genre of Romans in the history of Romans scholarship. In his revised and expanded *The Romans Debate*, Karl Donfried seems to be correct in asserting that it is too early to celebrate a consensus concerning the rhetorical character of Romans.[2] Even the emerging consensus that Romans is epideictic – one of three broad classifications of rhetoric (see glossary) – may be

[1] A. J. M. Wedderburn, *The Reasons for Romans* (Edinburgh, T. & T. Clark, 1988), pp. 18–19. Wedderburn names Ernst Fuchs, Jack Suggs, Ulrich Wilckens and Jacob Jervell as among the proponents of this theory. See James D. G. Dunn, *Romans*, WBC, 38 (Dallas, Word Books, 1988) p. lvi who is the latest exegete of Romans to adopt the Jerusalem speech theory. Dunn does not seem to be aware that this theory is incompatible with his assumption that Paul was informed about the Roman situation, as e.g. at 13.1–7. See also below chapter 6.
[2] Donfried, *The Romans Debate*, p. lxxi.

complicated by the initial results of genre criticism (see glossary), as literary genres such as the Protreptic employ more than one kind of rhetoric. Momentarily, we shall review the most significant writings on the ancient protreptic genre and the few attempts to relate the genre to Paul's letter to the Romans.

The appropriation of the protreptic genre by second-century Greek–Christian apologists will provide the context in which to understand the pivotal role that Romans played in the literary and theological development of early Christianity. Several commentators on Romans have noted the element of "apology" in Romans but it has not been observed that there is a more fundamental relationship between Romans and Christian apologetic literature arising from their use of a common literary genre: Protreptic. One of the most commonplace misunderstandings of ancient Christian apologies is that they are primarily reactive or defensive writings. The etymology of the term (ἀπολογία = defense) itself abets this misunderstanding. However, much of early Christian apologetic literature has primarily a protreptic thrust. The terms "apology" and "apologetic" are used widely in scholarly literature on early Christianity.[3] In addition to sporadic use in commentaries and journal articles, one finds that standard introductions to the New Testament, histories of early Christianity, and manuals of early Christian and Patristic literature regularly employ the terms "apology" and "apologetic." However, these terms, unlike "Wisdom" and most recently "Apocalyptic,"[4] have not been given precise definition. One must begin by distinguishing between the terms "apology" and "apologetic."[5] "Apology" is the designation for several ancient literary works such as Justin's two apologies. The word "apology" may also be used to indicate a genre designation

[3] See *inter alia*: W. H. C. Frend, *The Rise of Christianity* (Philadelphia, Fortress, 1984); Edgar J. Goodspeed, *A History of Early Christian Literature*, rev. Robert M. Grant (Chicago, University of Chicago Press, 1966); Helmut Koester, *Introduction to the New Testament* (2 vols., Philadelphia, Fortress, 1982), vols. I & II; Johannes Quasten, *Patrology, Vol. I: The Beginnings of Patristic Literature* (Utrecht–Antwerp, Spectrum Publishers, 1975); Berthald Altaner, *Patrologie* (Freiburg, Herder, 1978).

[4] Above all the work of John J. Collins is to be admired for its clarity; see his *The Sibylline Oracles of Egyptian Judaism*, SBLDS, 13 (Missoula, Mt., Scholars Press, 1974); *Apocalypse: The Morphology of a Genre*, Semeia 14 (Missoula, Mt., Scholars Press, 1979); and *The Apocalyptic Imagination: An Introduction to the Jewish Matrix of Christianity* (New York, Crossroads, 1984).

[5] Paul D. Hanson in an early stage of the work of defining apocalypse made a similar distinction between apocalypse and apocalyptic. See Hanson, "Apocalypticism," *IDB Supp.*, 29.

for literature whose central function is to adduce arguments contradicting charges that are being made. While explicit themes of such apology are to be found in the so-called Christian apologies, with the possible exception of Athenagoras' work, they are not predominant either quantitatively or structurally in these second-century apologetic writings. From the perspective of literary genre, many if not most of them cannot be adequately or even primarily construed as apologies but are imitative of philosophical Protreptic.[6] "Apologetic," on the other hand, denotes a certain mode of theological argumentation, the features of which will be outlined after discussion of the secondary literature on the protreptic genre.[7]

ROMANS AND THE PROTREPTIC

The *protreptikos logos* as a classical genre

Paul Hartlich attempted the first explicit investigation of ancient protreptic literature in his 1889 doctoral dissertation entitled *Exhortationum (Προτρεπτικων) a Graecis Romanisque Scriptarum Historia et Indole*.[8] Hartlich oberved that Protreptics could serve either of two purposes: (1) to urge others to take up a particular profession ranging from the military to medicine, or (2) to encourage students to progress further in their chosen disciplines.[9] Hartlich lamented the loss of the most famous examples of protreptic literature, notably Aristotle's *Protrepticus* and Cicero's *Hortensius*. Following the lead of other German classical scholars of the nineteenth century who recognized that Iamblichus' writings preserve substantial portions of Aristotle's lost work, Hartlich remarks sardonically that the former's greatest value derives from his slavish use of the latter. Although Hartlich's work never rises to the

---

[6] On philosophical Protreptic see Mark D. Jordan, "Ancient Philosophic Protreptic." The position that ancient Christian apologies are Protreptic in genre has been previously proposed; see M. Pellegrini, *Studi Su L'Antica Apologetica* (Rome, 1947), pp. 12–23, and Koester, *History and Literature*, pp. 338, 340. I have demonstrated that Justin's *First Apology* is a *logos protreptikos* in Anthony J. Guerra, "The Conversion of Marcus Aurelius and Justin Martyr: The Purpose, Genre, and Content of the First Apology," *The Second Century*, 9:3 (1992).

[7] For a synoptic view of recurrent motifs in second-century Greek Christian apologetic writings, see Appendix.

[8] Paul Hartlich, *Exhortationum (Προτρεπτικων)* a Graecis Romanisque Scriptarum Historia et Indole, Leipziger Studien II (1889).

[9] Ibid., pp. 221–3.

4 Apologetic and audience

demands of genre criticism to provide a definitive description of the purpose, form, and content of a kind of literature, his comments on Aristotle's work as derived from Iamblichus are still valuable and offer sound leads as to the general characterization of the Προτρεπτικὸς Λόγος. Both Iamblichus and Proclus were interested in Aristotle's *Protrepticus* because of the latter's defense of philosophy against prevalent criticism.[10] In responding to the objection that philosophers are both impractical and contentious, Aristotle describes the philosopher's task as initially concentrating on the practical concerns of living and only afterwards embracing the arts designed to make human life more cultivated and pleasant.[11] Thus, Aristotle argues that philosophy is to be approved because it takes into account the entirety of human life, proceeding from material concerns to the highest endeavor, the contemplation of the divine, and furthermore, it is this intrinsic value of philosophy that has enabled it to persist throughout the ages. Most importantly, Hartlich described the overall structure of the *Protrepticus* as "something akin to a dialogue" (*aliquid dialogi simile*),[12] consisting of three parts: (1) the opponents of philosophy speak; (2) Aristotle refutes them; and (3) Aristotle exhorts to the pursuit of philosophy. Hartlich proposes that Cicero also responded to stated objections to philosophy in the *Hortensius*, first by explicitly refuting the stated objections, and second by praising philosophy and urging others to commit to study it.[13]

In his general survey of epideictic literature, Theodore Burgess includes an important discussion of the Προτρεπτικὸς Λόγος despite the fact he agrees with Menander's judgment that the genre is a union of the symboleutic and epideictic rhetorical styles,[14] as exhortatory genres readily transcend the distinctions of rhetorical taxonomy. Originated by the Sophists,[15] and widely used by promoters of philosophy and of rhetoric, the Προτρεπτικὸς Λόγος is a genre of literature that attempts to persuade students to pursue a

[10] Ibid., p. 260.
[11] Ibid., p. 267.
[12] Ibid., p. 270.
[13] Ibid., p. 293. Hartlich refers respectively to these two parts by the Greek rhetorical terms: λόγος ἀπελεγκτικός and λόγος ἐνδεικτικός.
[14] Theodore Burgess, "Epideictic Literature," *University of Chicago Studies in Classical Philology*, 3 (1902), 112–13. Recall that Aristotle distinguished between the two rhetorical styles on the basis of the attitude of the hearer who is either a κριτής (judge) or a θεωρός (spectator). Burgess excuses himself from a full treatment of the genre on the grounds that Hartlich has already provided one.
[15] Ibid., 229–30.

proposed way-of-life. Burgess also points to the use of the genre to exhort athletes and soldiers as they were about to engage in their respective contests.[16] Because of the common function to recruit students, the philosophical Protreptics employ rhetorical modes indistinguishable from those of the rival schools of rhetoricians. As the Προτρεπτικὸς Λόγος is an exhortation to some general way of life inclusive of thought and conduct, the genre could serve a number of professions and thus Protreptics were written to encourage others to adopt, practice, or advance in medicine, the military and athletics as well as rhetoric and philosophy. In passing, Burgess makes the intriguing suggestion that the Προτρεπτικὸς Λόγος represents a continuation of the paranetic and moralizing elements in Homer, Pindar, and especially the gnomic poets.[17] He characterizes the genre in a broad way as a "union of philosophy and rhetoric."[18] He relies heavily on Hartlich's work but does disagree with him that the terms παραίνεσις (paranesis) and προτρεπτικὸς λόγος can be clearly differentiated, for they are often used interchangeably and "in a loose, indefinite way."[19] Burgess allows a distinctive technical meaning for the two terms, albeit rarely observed. Technically, the προτρεπτικὸς λόγος is an exhortation to a general course – philosophy, rhetoric, virtue – articulating a comprehensive view setting forth the advantages and replying to the objections with respect to it, whereas παραίνεσις has a more restricted and personal application, presenting a "series of precepts which will serve as a guide of conduct under fixed conditions."[20] Isocrates' several Protreptics demonstrate how readily the genre can embrace paranesis-exhortation to follow conventional moral precepts appropriate to common life situations (cf. e.g. James); Προτρεπτικός and Παραίνεσις in practice are often used interchangeably despite their distinctions as technical terms.[21]

More recently, Abraham Malherbe has advanced our understanding of the internal logic of protreptic discourse.[22] The protreptic goal to win someone over to a particular enterprise or way of

[16] Ibid., 209–10.
[17] Ibid., 173.
[18] Ibid., 229–30.
[19] Ibid., 230.
[20] Ibid., 230.
[21] So Pseudo-Justin's *Cohortatio*, a Λόγος Προτρεπτικὸς which bears the title Λόγος Παραινετικὸς Πρὸς Ἕλληνας.
[22] Abraham J. Malherbe, *Moral Exhortation, A Greco-Roman Sourcebook*, LEC, 4 (Philadelphia, Westminster, 1986).

life is achieved by demonstrating its superiority and exposing the flaws of all competing alternatives. Malherbe has pointed to Epictetus' description of the philosopher's burden of "protrepsis" to reveal the inner inconsistencies in his hearers' lives in order to bring them to conversion:

> I invite you to come and hear that you are in a bad way, and that you are concerned with anything rather than what you should be concerned with, and that you are ignorant of the good and the evil, and are wretched and miserable. That's a fine invitation! And yet if the philosopher's discourse does not produce this effect, it is lifeless and so is the speaker.[23]

Epictetus likens the philosopher to a physician who diagnoses a patient's illness and then removes cancerous growths, that is, the listener's moral failings:[24]

> Wherefore he (Rufus) spoke in such a way that each of us as we sat there fancied someone had gone to Rufus and told him of our faults; so effective was his grasp of what men actually do, so vividly did he set before each man's eyes his wickedness.

The protreptic writer/speaker points out the self-defeating as well as contradictory way of life which his/her audience is pursuing:

> Well! But isn't there such a thing as the right style for exhortation (Protrepsis)? ... Why, what is the style of exhortation? The ability to show to this individual, as well as to the crowd, the warring inconsistencies in which they are floundering about and how they are paying attention to anything rather than what they truly want. For they want the things that conduce to happiness, but they are looking for them in the wrong place.

---

[23] Malherbe, p. 122. I am following Malherbe's translation here and in the subsequent quotations of Epictetus.

[24] In discussing Protreptic, Philo of Larissa makes this explicit comparison between the philosopher and the physician. He comments that as a physician first offers therapy for illness and second refutes the false remedies of charlatans, so in fulfilling his protreptic task, the philosopher should also expose misleading advice and commend the proper treatment. Stobaeus, *Anth.* 2.7.2 as pointed out by Mark Jordan, "Philosophical Protreptic," 316.

In Protreptic, the rhetoric of blame or censure serves the positive purpose of exhortation: to encourage the hearer to change his/her life and proceed on a new course or to progress in one already engaged. Negative examples are presented and criticized so as to make the positive models more appealing to the hearer. Evidence for Malherbe's characterization of Protreptic is to be found in Plato's *Euthydemus* (278e–282d; 288b–307c).[25] Therein, Socrates offers a protreptic speech in which he exhorts his hearers to wisdom in part by exposing to ridicule the pair Euthydemus and Dionysdorus who are convinced they possess perfect knowledge. The aim of the Protreptic is to bring the hearer to the realization of the need for a teacher and his/her teaching. However, Euthydemus (along with his brother), who serves as the negative exemplum, insists on teaching Socrates that not only he but everyone is omniscient and in the course of this attempt Euthydemus exposes his own foolishness. Socrates represents the exemplary philosopher who understands the limits of his own knowledge and is also capable and worthy of leading others to wisdom and virtue. The processes of censure or indictment exposing error and moral weaknesses, and of praise recommending the good and right way, are complementary in advancing the protreptic purpose to persuade the hearer to turn to the latter. In addition to providing positive reasons for choosing the recommended course and negative reasons for turning away from inferior and/or evil paths, Aristotle's *Protrepticus* and other writings of the genre presume a general atmosphere of hostility and consequently respond explicitly to objections leveled against their espoused worldview.

In his 1986 article, Mark D. Jordan helps to explain the nature of ancient philosophical Protreptic and also examines the extant material that comments upon the protreptic genre.[26] Jordan bases his analysis on four Protreptics by philosophers and while noting the existence of Protreptics in other fields is explicitly concerned with defining the genre of philosophical Protreptic. One ancient commentator on the structure of the philosophical Protreptic, Stobaeus, after defining the philosophical Protreptic as an "urging towards virtue," suggests a two part division for Protreptics: one part "shows the great good of philosophy" and another "refutes

---

[25] A. J. Festugière, *Les Protreptiques de Platon: Euthydeme, Phedon, Epinomis* (Paris, J. Vrin, 1973).
[26] Mark D. Jordan, "Ancient Philosophic Protreptic and the Problem of Persuasive Genres," *Rhetorica*, 4 (1986), 309–33.

(*apelegkei*) the attacks, accusations and other malicious assaults against philosophy."[27] Iamblichus is reported by Proclus to have divided Protreptic into three parts following his analysis of the *First Alcibiades* of Plato: refutation to overcome ignorance, persuasion to take up the way of virtue and "midwifery" to help recover our original nature.[28] Proclus expresses a reservation, however, that such analysis may be confusing means with ends and for him such divisions are only functional headings that subserve the philosopher's given ends.[29] Jordan attempts to move beyond the Procline ends analysis and proposes that it is the "rhetorical situation," the hearer's moment of existential choice before ways-of-life which defines the Protreptic: "Protreptics are just those works that aim to bring about the fit choice of a lived way of wisdom – however different the form of these works and their notions of wisdom might be."[30] For Jordan, it is this desired effect that the hearer commit her/his whole self to an "on-going pedagogy" that is the primary characteristic of philosophical Protreptic. Jordan's identification of this focal motivation generative of philosophical Protreptic is perceptive but it is unfortunate that he retreated from the task of determining the characteristic generic structure of the Protreptic.

Προτρεπτικὸς Λόγος and Romans

The possible relationship between the protreptic genre and Paul's letter to the Romans was first noticed by Klaus Berger in the course of his comprehensive genre investigations of New Testament writings. Berger suggested in two writings in 1984 that Romans 1–11 is unique in the New Testament as representing the only sustained piece of protreptic discourse to be found therein.[31] All other protreptic passages of the New Testament, among which he includes Matthew 11.25–30; 7.13–27; John 3.1–21 etc., are relatively brief. In neither work does Berger argue for his judgment about Romans, as his purpose is to present in both cases a comprehensive review of Hellenistic genres and their appropriation by New Testament writers. He considers the Λόγος Προτρεπτικός in his discussion

---

[27] Ibid., 317.
[28] Ibid., 317–18.
[29] Ibid., 318.
[30] Ibid., 330.
[31] Klaus Berger, *Formgeshichte des Neuen Testament* (Heidelberg, Quelle & Meyer, 1984) p. 217; "Hellenistische Gattungen im Neuen Testament", in *ANRW*, Part II, vol. 25/2 (Berlin and New York, de Gruyter, 1984), 1140.

of symboleutic rhetoric although he acknowledges that it could also be assigned to epideictic.[32] A primary feature of the Protreptic, according to Berger, is the use of the "Two Ways of Life and Death" schema such as in the Wisdom of Solomon 1–5 and the Didache I–VI. Romans 1–11 presents the way of Christianity as surpassing the otherwise pre-eminent way of Judaism.[33] Berger notes that it is this general characteristic of Protreptic to recommend a way to its audience contrasted with an alternative path shown to be inferior that is the key to its use by later Christian authors such as Melito of Sardis and Clement of Alexandria.[34] Unfortunately, he does not elaborate these seminal ideas.

In 1986, Stanley Stowers devoted one paragraph to a description of Romans as a protreptic letter in his *Letter Writing in Greco-Roman Antiquity*. As his title indicates, he intends in this monograph to provide a typology of letter writing in antiquity. According to Stowers, ancient letter writing theory classified letters according to the "typical purposes" that letter writers hope to accomplish.[35] He defines the purposes of protreptic works as: "to urge the reader to convert to a way of life, join a school, or accept a set of teachings as normative for the reader's life."[36] Stowers likens Aristotle's *Protrepticus* to a letter because, in his view, it is actually "addressed to Aristotle's royal friend rather than, as is often said, merely dedicated to him."[37] As for Romans, Stowers states that it is in both "form and function" a protreptic letter.[38] Stowers understands that, while both answering objections to his teachings throughout Romans 3–11 and censuring the attitudes that prevent Jews and Gentiles from accepting these teachings, Paul recommends his gospel to the Romans and presents himself as a master teacher.

David Aune's recent article is to date the most serious attempt to argue that Romans is a Λόγος Προτρεπτικός.[39] Whereas Jordan suggests that the Λόγος Προτρεπτικός can be either an exoteric

---

[32] Berger, *ANWR*, 1139.
[33] Berger, *Formgeschichte*, 218; *ANWR*, 1140.
[34] Berger, *ANWR*, 1139–41.
[35] Stowers, *Letter Writing in Greco-Roman Antiquity*, p. 23.
[36] Ibid., p. 113.
[37] Ibid., p. 91.
[38] Ibid., p. 114.
[39] David Aune, "Romans as a Logos Protreptikos in the Context of Ancient Religious and Philosophical Propaganda" in Martin Hengel and Ulrich Heckel (eds.), *Paulus und das antike Judentum* (Tübingen, Mohr/Siebeck, 1992), pp. 91–121. Also published in Karl P. Donfried (ed.), *The Romans Debate: Revised and Expanded Edition* (Peabody, Hendrickson, 1991), pp. 278–96.

literary genre directed at the conversion of the outsider or an esoteric genre seeking to strengthen or deepen an insider's commitment to the way already adopted, Aune describes the genre as exclusively exoteric aimed at conversion of the outsider.[40] Aune notes that the Λόγος Προτρεπτικός includes also a strong element of dissuasion (ἀποτρέπειν) or censure (ἐλεγχειν) that seeks to liberate individuals from erroneous beliefs that would presumably impede conversion.[41] Agreeing with classical sources cited by Jordan that ancient Protreptic reveals a tri-partite structure,[42] he delineates three basic structural elements of the genre: (1) a negative section centering on the critique of rival sources of knowledge, ways of living, or schools of thought which reject philosophy; (2) a positive section in which the truth claims and ways of living of the philosophical school are presented, praised and defended; followed by (3) an optional section, προτρεπτικός, consisting of a personal appeal to the hearer, inviting the immediate acceptance of the exhortation.[43]

With respect to Romans, Aune proposes that the main section (Rom. 1.16–15.13) is a Λόγος Προτρεπτικός in an epistolary frame (1.1–15; 15.24–16.27).[44] Paul, Aune states, is seeking to convince Roman Christians that his gospel is the truth and to explain the lifestyle and commitment that it enjoins. He believes that Paul is contending for his brand of Christianity over other "competing schools of Christian thought,"[45] but unfortunately does not specify them. Aune attempts to straddle both sides of the debate as to whether Paul writes to address an actual situation in Rome or whether he intends a statement of timeless truths.[46] He does, however, seem to concur with Robert Karris in rejecting "any supposedly concrete situation to be teased out of the concluding

---

[40] Aune, p. 95; Jordan's formulation may better account for the range of ancient protreptic writings and may, incidentally, be more congenial to its instance in Romans.

[41] Aune, p. 96.

[42] Despite these observations, Jordan himself resists conclusive judgments on the structure of Protreptic, preferring an exclusive existentialist approach to defining the genre. See above.

[43] See David E. Aune, p. 101. Aune notes further that the rhetorical strategy of σύγκρισις is frequently employed.

[44] This distinction between the epistolary frame and the main protreptic section is somewhat undercut by Aune's own admission that "since ancient authors often framed discourses with formal epistolary features, there is no great distance between the Λόγος Προτρεπτικός and the ἐπιστολὴ Προτρεπτική." Aune, p. 97.

[45] Aune, p. 92.

[46] Ibid., p. 112.

section (especially 14.1–15.13)."⁴⁷ Aune's indecisiveness over the question of the audience and purpose of Romans hinders his argument for reading the work as a Protreptic, particularly with respect to Romans 9–11.

Romans 1.16–4.25 constitutes, for Aune, a major textual unit that functions as a protreptic ἐλεγχτικός which itself consists of three subunits: 1.16–2.11; 2.12–3.20, and 3.21–4.25.⁴⁸ He believes that Paul moves from arguing with an unconverted Gentile in Romans 1.16–2.11 to an unconverted Jewish interlocutor in the following two subunits. In the next major textual unit, 5.1–8.39, Paul focuses on the life of the insider, the Christian who has been justified. From the perspective of the protreptic genre, this section serves the positive function of ἐνδεικτικός.⁴⁹ Aune's remark concerning the "striking structural and phenomenological similarity between the anthropological dualism" of popular Greek tradition and that of Paul is interesting.⁵⁰ He thinks that Paul's view of the dilemma of the Christian who serves the law of God with his mind but the law of sin with his flesh (Rom. 7.25) is similar to the situation of Greeks "to whom a philosopher would direct his Λόγος Προτρεπτικός, offering freedom from the material bondage of wealth and reputation."⁵¹ With reference to Romans 9–11, Aune fails to uncover a protreptic function and falls back to a familiar position that it is a "kind of excursus or digression."⁵² His blindspot with respect to the audience, and thus purpose of Romans, prevents him from seeing the integral role these chapters play in Paul's protreptic attempt to convince his hearers to approve both his message and mission. Aune thinks that despite this "digression," Paul returns in Romans 12.1–15.13 to provide a protreptic appeal that is a "fitting conclusion."⁵³ According to Aune, Paul appeals in 12.1–15.13 to his readers to devote themselves fully to God; the section explains the practical implications for living of Paul's abstract formulations in 5.1–8.39.⁵⁴ Having dismissed the significance of Romans 14–15 for determining the audience of Paul's letter, Aune naturally overlooks the emphasis in these two chapters on avoiding the negative models

---

⁴⁷ Donfried, *Debate* (1991), p. LX.
⁴⁸ Aune, p. 114.
⁴⁹ Ibid., p. 116.
⁵⁰ Ibid., p. 117.
⁵¹ Ibid., p. 117.
⁵² Ibid., p. 118.
⁵³ Ibid., p. 119.
⁵⁴ Ibid., p. 119.

of communal conflict and on the exaltation of Christ as the positive model providing the possibility for unity among differing Christians.

In summary, Aune thinks that three of the main textual units, Romans 1.16–4.25, 5.1–8.39, and 12.1–15.13, were originally discrete Protreptics in their original settings;[55] Paul linked them together to form a "relatively coherent Λόγος Προτρεπτικός in the present context of Romans." He believes Romans 9–11 to be a digression and also points to its uncharacteristically copious use of Old Testament quotations as another indicator that this section is of a different kind from the rest of the letter.[56] Aune has made a major contribution towards understanding the genre of Romans; unfortunately his hasty decisions with respect to the audience and purpose of Romans, and particularly his misreading of Romans 9–11, has precluded him from appreciating the extent of Paul's success in achieving a Christian appropriation and transformation of the protreptic genre.

Second-century apologetic literature and Protreptic

Over the past fifty years a consensus of scholarship has been emerging concerning the protreptic character of most of the so-called apologies of second-century Christianity. When Christian writers of the second century looked for models for conversion literature, they did not turn to the religious cults, which offered only myths and rituals, but rather to the philosophical schools that presented worldviews by means of long-developed persuasive literary genres. As already mentioned, the most famous ancient example of the genre, Aristotle's *Protrepticus*, exhorts the King Themison to pursue the path of philosophy, while presuming a generally hostile attitude towards such endeavor. Thus in the course of setting out a comprehensive view of philosophy and praising its virtues, Aristotle defends it against a number of objections to the recommended pursuit. Isocrates, in his Protreptic *Nicocles on the Cyprians*, has the King exhort his subjects to abide by the highest standards of private and civic ethics while gratefully serving the Kingdom and obeying

[55] Ibid., p. 120.
[56] This is a questionable argument even with respect to other parts of Romans, as Romans 4 also has a very high rate of quotations and allusions – see below. It should also be noted that other protreptic works, e.g. Iamblichus' *De Vita Pythagorae*, rely mightily on an earlier authoritative text, Aristotle's. Augustine's protreptic *Contra Academicos* is said to have relied heavily on Cicero's *Hortensius* which in turn borrowed extensively, again from Aristotle.

his rule. Before pressing his demands, Nicocles recognizes the need to show that the Cyprian monarchy is superior to other forms of governance such as aristocracy and democracy. He also thinks it necessary to prove that he is the legitimate heir to the throne and that his own personal ethical conduct is exemplary. In these earliest protreptic works, the promotion of a specific worldview and its attendant lifestyle in a competitive situation in which other views and practices are widely seen as more satisfying, reasonable, and beneficial points to the characteristic purpose and provenance of the genre that was so appealing to second-century Christian apologists.

The characteristics of ancient Christian apologetic writings

The determination of the genre of a writing has import for its overall interpretation and may predispose an interpreter to concentrate on particular elements in the work and to ignore other possibly more weighty and extensive textual evidence. Thus, in assuming that Justin's *First Apology* is an "apology" with respect to genre, the interpreter may naturally emphasize its defensive, political features while recognition of it as a Protreptic will afford appreciation of the work as primarily one of exhortation and positive advocacy of a distinctive worldview. The following inventory of prominent motifs is not intended to be exhaustive, but rather to identify the motifs and argumentative strategies that characterize and distinguish second-century Greek–Christian apologetic literature. A given apologetic writing will not necessarily – indeed almost certainly will not – have all the features enumerated, and will have many other characteristics not listed here which it will share with other Christian and Graeco-Roman literature of the period. It may be said, nevertheless, that the presence of several of the noted features in a given writing would identify it as second-century Christian apologetic literature. Further, the particular motifs listed would be more or less readily employed depending on whether the primary dialogue partner or audience intended were Jewish and/or Graeco-Roman. Put in other words, the following list represents the repertoire from which ancient Christian apologists would draw in making their particular appeals.

(1) The articulation of a proposed relation between the apologist's religious position and an older and often revered religious and intellectual tradition: this relationship is often expressed as one of

continuity with, as well as superiority to, the older tradition, sometimes including an argument for historical priority. Thus Moses and
the Greek philosophers are not merely described as sharing a single
source of inspiration but the latter are said to have plagiarized from
the Hebrew prophet (see e.g. Justin, *Apol.* 1.59.1–6, 1.60.1–10).[57]
However implausible this dependency theory appears to others, it
reveals the apologist's hegemonic propensity to see all truths as
possessions of his own community. So Justin confidently avers that:
"It is not, then, that we hold the same opinions as others, but that all
speak in imitation of ours" (*Apol.* 1.60.10). In his discussion of the
mythic analogues to Christ – Asclepius, Bacchus, Hercules, and
Perseus – Justin less generously attributes the inspiration to
demonic spirits who foreknew the divine plan and led the poets to
fabricate their mythologies (*Apol.* 1.23.3).[58] Justin affirms that the
Hebrew Prophets predate all other authors and thus effectively
delimits their significance in an age when antiquity was a central
criterion of validity.

(2) Critiques of other religious, intellectual, and cultural traditions: the ambivalence of the apologist towards the past is evident in
the often strident polemic against other traditions, exposing both
internal criticisms (for example, logical inconsistencies and insufficient illumination on a topic) and external criticism (for instance
alleged moral turpitude of the adherents of other traditions) which
countervail the claims for continuity (see (1) above):[59] "On some
points we teach the same things as the poets and philosophers whom
you honor, and on other points are fuller and more divine in our
teaching, and we alone afford proof" (*Apol.* 1.20). Athenagoras
castigates Homer for contradictory theological assertions as the
poet, at one point, attributes a temporal beginning to the gods
(*Supp.* 18.2–4) but does not realize that then they logically cannot be
divine (*Supp.* 19.1). Athenagoras notes that his reasoning is sup-
ported by the Greek philosophers: "On this point there is no
disagreement between myself and the philosophers" (*Supp.* 19.1).

---

[57] Aristobulus may have invented the apologetic topos that Greek philosophers
plagiarized Moses (*Praep. Evang.* 13.12.1). The assertion of agreement with an
ancient or classical source rarely satisfies the apologist and there is the tendency to
argue for priority. See Arthur J. Droge, *Homer or Moses: Early Christian Interpretations of the History of Culture*, Hermeneutiche Unter suchungen zur Theologie 26
(Tübingen, Mohr-Siebeck, 1989).
[58] In *Dial.* 69, Justin combines the charges of demonic inspiration and plagiarism
and accuses the devil of imitating scripture.
[59] See Appendix.

Athenagoras, however, considers the morally repugnant conduct ascribed to the gods the more compelling reason to reject Greek mythology (*Supp.* 21.3).

(3) A positive appeal to standards of rationality in both substance and mode of argumentation: both reason and common sense or experience are allowed a legitimate, even if limited role, while by contrast, in apocalyptic these accesses are foreclosed by the exclusive valuation of revelation. Athenagoras boasts that Christians "can establish with compelling proofs and arguments (ἀληθείας σημείοις καὶ λόγοις) the correctness of what we think and believe – that God is one" (*Supp.* 7.1). In *Supp.* 8.1–4, the apologist does demonstrate some skill in dialectical reasoning but this is prefaced by the claim that Christians possess divine assurances in revelation for their beliefs: "We, however, have prophets as witnesses of what we think and believe. They have spoken out by a divinely inspired Spirit about God and the things of God" (*Supp.* 7.2).[60] Justin insists that Christians worship God in accord with reason (μετὰ λόγου – *Apol.* 1.13.3) and also that the power of reasoning is given by God (δι' ὧν αὐτὸς ἐδωρήσατο) to human beings so that faith may be arrived at by persuasion (*Apol.* 1.10.4). Most significant is the very attempt of the Greek–Christian apologists to present Christianity as a philosophy. Towards this end, Aristides opens his apology by introducing himself as the typical philosopher contemplating the "creation and its Mover" (*Arist.* 1.1–3). While Justin more audaciously argues that Christianity is the divine philosophy,[61] recovering the one primordial philosophy that the Greek schools have distorted and falsified.[62]

(4) The appeal to common scriptural authority in order to substantiate the apologist's claims, even though those claims usually diverge from received interpretations of quoted material: the apologist frequently affirms his point of view by reference to testimonial

---

[60] Following the translation of William R. Schoedel, *Athenagoras: Legatio and De Resurrectione* (Oxford, Clarendon, 1972).

[61] Cf. *Dial.* 2.1: φιλοσοφία κατεπέμφθη εἰς ἀνθρώπους.

[62] For a careful exposition of the logic of Justin's argumentation on this topic, see J. C. M. van Winden, *An Early Christian Philosopher: Justin Martyr's Dialogue with Trypho Chapters One to Nine*, Philosophia Patrum 1 (Leiden: Brill, 1971), pp. 42–8. Cf. also the more unreserved judgment of Nils Hyldahl, *Philosophie und Christentum: Eine Interpretation der Einleitung zum Dialog Justins*, Acta theologica Danica 9 (1966).

figures.[63] From the classical side, Socrates became a favorite of early Christian apologists, no doubt in part because of the similarity of the circumstances of his death (that is, capital punishment) to that of Jesus, as well as the charge of atheism leveled against both Socrates and early Christians. From the biblical quarter, Abraham was seized upon in both Jewish and Christian apologetic literature and later in Islamic apologetics as well. Justin presents Joshua, who in the place of Moses leads the people into the Promised Land (*Dial.* 13), as well as Noah who represents a new beginning for humanity after the deluge (*Dial.* 38), as types of Christ. Typological exegesis of Scripture and the spiritualizing interpretation of ritual commandments, as well as the use of Scripture as prophetic proof-texts, are the ready tools of the apologist. For this last use of Scripture, Justin's *First Apology* and the *Dialogue with Trypho* provide copious examples (see Appendix III. a. and *Dial.* 36–43, 50–66).

(5) The appropriation of history dialectically by the apologist, in contrast to the apocalypticist, who simply negates it:[64] from the Christian apologetic perspective, although the past can never be fully approved, it may be given its highest estimation when seen as *Preparatio Evangelica*. The apologists' ambivalence is most evident with respect to the nation of Israel and the Hebrew Bible/Septuagint.[65] The Scripture is affirmed to have been given by God to the founding Fathers of the Jewish nation, but all traditional Jewish lines of interpretation are negated as distortions of the truth. Determined by the leitmotif of promise and fulfillment, the Christian apologists read the Hebrew Bible/Septuagint primarily as prophecies whose accuracy is testified to by the "historical records" of the New Testament.[66] More than one third of Justin's *First Apology* and

[63] See Th. Wehofer, *Die Apologie Justins des Philosoher und Märtyrers in literarhistorischer Beziehung zum erstenmal untersucht*, Roemische Quartalschrift, Suppl. 6 (1897), pp. 90–106.

[64] For a penetrating analysis of Josephus' ambivalence toward history, see Drodge, *Homer or Moses*, pp. 36–44.

[65] The view towards the Roman empire and the classical sources, especially the Greek philosophers, as already mentioned, is also often designedly equivocal. J. C. M. van Winden has reservations concerning Justin's endorsement of a preparatory function for Greek philosophy with respect to Christian faith. While seeing it as a possible construal, he observes that another idea predominates, namely "that Greek philosophical systems deviated from the true philosophy." See *An Early Christian Philosopher: Justin Martyr's Dialogue With Trypho Chapters One to Nine*, Philosophia Patrum 1(Leiden, Brill, 1971), p. 121.

[66] See Oskar Skarsaune, *The Proof from Prophecy: A Study in Justin Martyr's Proof-Text Tradition:Text-Type, Provenance, Theological Profile, NovTSup*, 56 (Leiden, Brill, 1987) pp. 11–12, 140.

a sizeable portion of his *Dialogue with Trypho* are occupied with precisely such use of the Septuagint as proof-texts of the fulfillment of messianic expectations by Christ.[67]

(6) The affirmation of monotheism as the central criterion by which the boundaries of community are defined: exclusion and inclusion are promoted respectively by polemics against polytheism "censoring out" its adherents and appeals to shared monotheistic tenets "censoring in" believers. Aristides in his *Apologia*[68] excludes from salvation on the grounds of their polytheism: the Barbarians/ Chaldeans (*Arist.* 3–7), the Greeks (8–11), and the Egyptians (12); the probative force of this warrant for the apologist is underscored by Aristides' difficulties with Jewish practices when he is led to contend that worshippers only seem to glorify the One God but are in fact venerating angels (*Arist.* 14.3–4). Philo of Alexandria employs the "One God" topos to advocate the inclusion of prose-lytes as equal members of the Jewish community.[69]

(7) The call of Christians to a higher standard of private and public morality. Justin contrasts his image of a corrupt Roman society where infanticide, incest, and the pimping of family members abound (*Apol.* 1.27.1–5) to that of Christian chastity: "we do not marry except in order to bring up children, or else renouncing marriage, we live in perfect continence" (*Apol.* 1.29.1). Unlike the classical context, the problem is not one of moral relativ-ism but rather living up to the principles that one espouses. The apologists argue, to be sure, that Christ is a higher expression of Logos, Truth, or Principle – indeed may equate Logos and Christ –

---

[67] Trypho, Justin's Jewish dialogue partner, is so impressed by the apologist's enthusiasm for the Hebrew Prophets that he inquires of Justin if it is acceptable for one who comes to believe Jesus is the Christ also to obey the Law of Moses. The apologist responds somewhat haltingly: "In my opinion, Trypho, such an one will be saved, if he does not strive in every way to persuade other men,I mean those Gentiles who have been circumcised from error by Christ, to observe the same things as himself, telling them that they will not be saved unless they do so" (*Dial.* 47.1). Trypho replies that Justin is expressing only his own opinion – suggesting others consider Jewish Christians not to be saved, which Justin in fact confirms to be the case (*Dial.* 47.2). Justin remarks further that there are some who have renounced their belief in Christ and returned to the "legal dispensation." To them Justin grants no escape from damnation short of their repentance before death (*Dial.* 47.4). See below discussion on Paul's view of Jewish Chistians in his own time.

[68] See J. Rendel Harris, *Texts and Studies, no. 1: The Apology of Aristides* (Cambridge, University Press, 1891).

[69] See below section on "One God," especially on Philo, and also Anthony J. Guerra, "The One God Topos in Spec. Leg. 1.52" in David J. Lull (ed.), *Society of Biblical Literature 1990 Seminar Papers*, pp. 148–57.

and that Christians live in a manner completely consonant with his absolute standard of morality. Christians constitute the community whose higher moral standard if embraced by the whole population would remedy the social ills and restore the moral well being of society.

(8)   The apologist's invitation to his audience to consider and then embrace the truth which he presents: Aristides closes his apology with precisely such an invitation and thus underscores the significance of this motif in the apologetic tradition:

> Let all those then approach thereunto who do not know God, and let them receive the incorruptible words, those which are so always and from eternity: let them, therefore, anticipate the dread judgment which is to come by Jesus the Messiah upon the whole race of men.   (*Arist.* 17.8)

Similarly, Justin closes his *Dialogue* sounding the same call to conversion:

> But now, since I expect with God's will and aid to set sail, I exhort you to give all diligence in this very great struggle for your own salvation, and to be earnest in setting a higher value on the Christ of the almighty God than on your own teachers.   (*Dial.* 142.2)

Further the apologist encourages his audience to amend their behavior and instructs them as to how they should live.[70] In attempting to educate his imperial audience, Justin refers repeatedly to the ideals of "piety and philosophy" in his apology (*Apol.* 1.1.1;1.2.1;1.2.2;1.3.2;1.12.5) and although these ideals are ones of which he knows they in principle approve, Justin seeks not only to influence imperial judical policy but also to make them devotees of a higher piety and philosophy.[71]

(9)   The use of political apologetic: the apologist, who represents a minority and often suspect if not overtly persecuted community, affirms the political status quo, the governing authorities of the civil society.[72] Expressions of loyalty and dutiful intentions to fulfill the subjects' obligations and religious sanction for the right of rulership are commonplaces. Justin claims that excepting "emperor worship," Christians gladly serve the emperor and pray for him

---

[70] Justin *Apol.* 1.2.1–3, 1.3.2–5, 1.4.6, 1.8.1–2; Athenagoras *Supp.* 1.3.

[71] Cf. H. Hermann Holfelder, "Εὐσέβεια καὶ φιλοσοφία"; *ZNW*, 68 (1977), 48–66.

[72] See Athenagoras, *Supp.* 37, and also Appendix.

(*Apol.* 1.17.3). Moving beyond the ambiguous formulation of Matthew 22.21: "Render to Caesar the things that are Caesar's," he also specifies that Christians promptly pay the annual and occasional tax assessments (φόρους, εἰσφοράς – *Apol.* 1.17.1). Athenagoras' expression of respect for the emperor may be less disingenuous than that of Justin;[73] the former concludes his apology by declaring that Christians "pray for your reign – that the succession to the kingdom may proceed from father to son, as is most just and that your reign may grow and increase as all men become subject to you" (*Supp.* 3.7.1).[74] Although this is one of the more well-known features of ancient apologetic literature, it should be observed that it does not occupy a significant portion of such texts.

(10) An understanding of the apologetic theologian as a representative of his people, a guide for the community, and an ambassador on its behalf toward the wider society:[75] Philo tells us that he was in fact a member (and perhaps even head) of a delegation to the Roman emperor on behalf of the Jews of Alexandria (*Leg. Gaium* 178–9, 181–6). Likewise, in the light of William Schoedel's observation that the language of petition frames and subordinates that of apology in the opening and closing sections of Athenagoras' *Legatio*, the use of the word "embassy" in the title of his address to the emperor is suggestive of the author's self-understanding. At the opening of the *First Apology*, Justin states that he makes his "address and petition (ἔντευξιν) on behalf of (ὑπέρ) those of all nations who are unjustly hated and wantonly abused myself being one of them." A final point of clarification is necessary. The debate as to whether the apologist is addressing outsiders or insiders is not a genuine issue. The apologist has a dual intent: to confirm the believer's confidence in the truth and to convert the non-believer to it. Moreover, this dual intent is based on the existential and social situation of the apologist who is deeply rooted in the "outsider" traditions and now must reconcile in himself, as well as for the "insiders" and "outsiders," the old and new ways of being. The

[73] Justin ends the same paragraph with more than a bit of braggadacio as he notes that Christians are not so worried anyway as they know that the "punishment of eternal fire" is reserved for their earthly persecutors (*Apol.* 1.17.4).

[74] See also *Supp.* 2.3: "we are the most pious and righteous of all men in matters that concern both the divine and your (i.e. the addressee, Marcus Aurelius) kingdom."

[75] See William R. Schoedel, "Apologetic Literature and Ambassadorial Activities," *HTR*, 82:1 (1989), 55–78.

ambassadorial role is common to Jewish and Christian apologists (see Philo, *Leg. Gaium*; Justin, *Apol.* 1.1.1; Athenagoras, *Supp.* 1.3.).

(11)   The affirmation of Roman authority and preferences in the attempt to secure fair treatment or at the least survival of the minority community represented by the apologist: Athenagoras applauds the fact that various national customs and laws are protected within the Roman Empire:

> the various Races and Peoples of mankind perform whatever sacrifices and mysteries they wish ... all these both you and the laws permit, since you regard it as impious and irreligious to have no belief at all in a god and think it necessary for all men to venerate as gods those whom they wish, that through fear of the divine they may refrain from evil.   (*Supp.* 1.1–2)

This recognition as well as approval of differences of views, practices, and so on may be seen as an expediency by which the apologist argues for acceptance or equal treatment for his oppressed minority community. Thus, the motive of Athenagoras' liberality is made apparent in the subsequent paragraph as he points out that Christians have not received the same consideration as all others and are, indeed, worthy to be so considered (*Supp.* 1.3).[76] Philo's use of the motif exhibits the same function when his delegation is ridiculed before Gaius for dietary restrictions, as they respond: "Different people have different customs and the use of some things is forbidden to us as others are to our opponents" (*Leg. Gaium* 362).

(12)   A response to moral and/or theological accusations levied against the apologist's position:[77] the accusations to which the early Christian apologists responded ranged from charges of infanticide and promiscuity to atheism (see Appendix, p. 180). Athenagoras answers to three common charges made against Christians in the Roman empire namely, cannibalism, incest, as well as atheism.[78]

---

[76] Note that the plea for justice characteristically turns to the demand to be considered on individual merits and not to be condemned merely by association (*Supp.* 2.1). Justin emphasizes this point by calling for condign punishment of any Christian who is, in fact, guilty of crimes (*Apol.* 1.7.1–4). The analogy with some who call themselves philosophers and who act otherwise may suggest that Justin is thinking of heretical Christians, particularly libertines.

[77] At the same time, it should be noted that this response is most often made in the context of a positive proclamation of the message which employs analogical or typological argument.

[78] Athenagoras, *Supp.* 3.1: "Three things are alleged against us: atheism, Thyestean feasts, Oedipodean intercourse."

With the exception perhaps of Athenagoras' work, however, such material is not predominant either quantitively or structurally in second-century apologetic writings.

It should be noted that the first eight features of second-century Christian apologetic literature identified above are indicative of the protreptic genre whereas the last four features are arguably more suggestive of the apology genre as previously defined. Yet as has already been demonstrated in the classical protreptic writings, the response to objections is common to the genre.

The second-century Christian apologies constitute a subset or a specific historical development of the protreptic genre. Alastair Fowler refers to such a subset as a "kind" or "historical genre" which defines a group of literary writings in a delimited period, having closer family resemblances than do members of the entire genre.[79] As already suggested, the "historical genre" or "kind" of second-century Christian Protreptics holds the greatest explanatory power and the closest parallels to the content, function and structure of Paul's communication to Rome. A determination that Romans is a protreptic writing will not only have important implications for the interpretation of Romans but also points to the latter as the origin of the "historical genre" evidenced in second-century Christian apologetic writings. The Protreptic would be another genre that Paul is responsible for first appropriating for Christian use. It is an achievement that had a definitive impact on the Christian apologetic movement, most notably in Justin's *Dialogue with Trypho* and his *First Apology*. Paul's letter to the Romans is at the beginning of a trajectory of Christian writings, most especially those of the second-century Greek Christian apologetic writers who widely employ the protreptic genre. One might wonder how the apostle could have gained knowledge of the Protreptic? Since the Λόγος Προτρεπτικός was the preferred form of advertisement by recruitment officials of the ancient schools of philosophy and rhetoric, it is entirely possible, if not probable that Paul and other inquisitive Christians would have been exposed to protreptic writings and/or speeches. Although, it is plausible that Paul was exposed to the Protreptic, it can be no more proved than the widely embraced hypothesis of the apostle's exposure to Stoic and other proponents of the sort of popular ethical/philosophical wisdom

---

[79] Alastair Fowler, *Kinds of Literature: An Introduction to the Theory of Genres and Modes* (Cambridge, Harvard, 1982), p. 56.

evidenced in his writings. The point of this work is not to argue for Paul's historical encounter with the Protreptic but rather to explore the implications of reading Romans in terms of structure, content, and purpose as a protreptic writing.

PAUL'S PURPOSE AND AUDIENCES IN ROMANS

A minimal education in rhetoric (which Paul likely possessed)[80] as well as common sense would indicate that the openings and closings of writings are especially significant for establishing the aims of one's communication. Accordingly, in the remainder of this chapter, Romans 1.1–18 together with 15.14–29 will be examined in order to discern Paul's purpose in this communication. Romans 14.1–15.13, the concluding section of the body of the letter, will also be treated and the relevance of this section in determining the Jewish or Gentile composition of the Roman community will be discussed.[81] I use the term "Jewish Christians" in this work as a category designating Christians who abide by some or all of the ritual commandments of Judaism. The designations "Jewish Christians" and "Gentile Christians" should be used to denote differing religious orientations rather than ethnic identities – after all, Paul is ethnically Jewish while being our foremost representative in the early church of Gentile Christianity![82] As Romans 16 is not directly relevant to the religious composition of the Roman community but is relevant to the "Roman Factor," the social and political nuances of the text, it will be treated below in chapter 6.

Romans 1.1–7: two lines of defense: apostolic authority and the gospel of God

The superscription of Romans, running through six lines of the

[80] See the reserved opinion of Günther Bornkamm, *Paul*, trans. D. M. G. Stalker (New York, Harper & Row, 1971), pp. 9–10.

[81] In *The Reasons for Romans*, A. J. M. Wedderburn has offered a perceptive review of recent scholarly opinion with respect to the purpose and audience of Romans, obviating the need for such a summary here. Instead, dissenting views on the interpetation of particular passages in Romans will be treated *inter alia* in the course of our discussion.

[82] See the discussion in Gerd Luedemann, *Opposition to Paul in Jewish Christianity*, trans. M. Eugene Boring (Philadelphia, Fortress, 1989), pp. 28–30.

Nestle–Aland text, is by far the longest in Paul's letters. It is often assumed that this expansiveness is necessitated by Paul's need to introduce himself to a community in which he is relatively unknown.[83] It is more likely, however, that the members of the Roman community at least think they "know" a good deal about Paul and his gospel, and that Paul is eager to correct what he perceives to be their misunderstandings. As to Paul's awareness of Roman Christians' perspectives on various matters, given that Paul's specific knowledge of the political and economic scene in Rome can be demonstrated (see chapter 6 on Rom. 13.1–7), it is, *a fortiori*, to be surmised that Paul knows the theological and ethical proclivities of Christians in Rome (see chapter 6 on Rom. 16). Paul's concerns are indicated by the carefully formulated self-references specifying his office and mission which constitute the superscription. Contrast this with the superscription of the unambiguously cordial communication to the newly founded community of Thessaloniki, where Paul dispenses with all titles and simply gives his own name and that of two fellow workers (cf. 1 Thess. 1.1). In Galatians 1.1, Paul uses the title "apostle" which he then awkwardly defines with the double negative "not from men nor through man" and then positively "but through Jesus Christ and God the Father." The expansion in Galatians is significant and reflects the polemical situation which Paul confronts.[84] He exhibits hesitancy throughout Romans 1 in the assertion of his authority; as in Galatians, this manner of expression in Romans reflects his perception of the probable lack of receptivity to his assertion of authority. In Romans 1.1 Paul also claims to be an apostle and underscores the element of divine election in this role by the immediately preceding and following modifiers: κλητός and ἀφωρισμένος.[85] As Käsemann rightly observes, Paul's self-understanding as an apostle was not uncontested because he did not fit the traditional criterion of appointment by the historical Jesus.[86] This handicap would, of course, be far more pronounced in gaining the respectful attention of a community that he had not founded. Paul's effort to underscore his divinely authorized mission is further

---

[83] See e.g. Cranfield, *Romans*, p. 47.

[84] A common view among exegetes of Galatians; see e.g. Koester, *History and Literature*, p. 119, but note the reservation of Hans Dieter Betz, *Galatians: A Commentary on Paul's Letter to the Churches in Galatia*, Hermeneia (Philadelphia, Fortress, 1979), p. 39.

[85] Käsemann defines the latter as indicating "the election which precedes a concrete commission," *Romans*, p. 6.

[86] Käsemann, *Romans*, p. 6.

evidenced by his initial self-designation in Romans 1.1 as δοῦλος (slave), which is the honorific title of an Old Testament man of God, expressing election as well as submission to the will of God.[87] When one asks the question to whom this language would communicate, it becomes clear that only those familar with Jewish usage would understand Paul's intent. Indeed, as has been widely acknowledged by exegetes, the term "slave" would be an offensively startling one to Gentiles. One should not rule out the real possibility, however, that Paul anticipated both reactions.

In addition to his apostolic status, Paul's concern moves to the central responsibility of his apostleship, namely the preaching of the gospel. His initial characterization of the gospel as θεοῦ (of God) recalls the Galatian definition of the "apostle" mentioned above and likewise indicates the presence of opposition to his version of the gospel. Accordingly, Paul immediately proceeds to an apologetic description of the gospel in Romans 1.2: "which he promised beforehand through his prophets in the holy scriptures."[88] Paul here presages the extraordinary recourse to Scripture which he will make in Romans (see chapters 3 and 5 on Romans 4 and 9–11). The prefix in προεπηγγείλατο intensifies the sense of priority already present in the verb ἐπαγγέλλομαι (promise).[89] The theme of continuity between the gospel and Scripture (that is, the Old Testament) is the chief onus of the apologetic enterprise of early Christianity[90] and, as previously mentioned, is a primary feature of Christian apologetic writings that identifies them with the protreptic genre.

Paul explains the content of the gospel in 1.3 in a similarly apologetic fashion. Jesus is described as born "from *the seed of David.*" It should be noted that only in Romans does Paul adopt this Jewish–Christian apologetic designation of Jesus. The function of the designation is to affirm the equation between Jesus pro-

---

[87] Ibid., p. 5. It is interesting to note that the only other superscription where Paul uses the word δοῦλος is in a correspondence in which his opponents preach circumcision and obedience to the law (cf. Phil 1.1, 3.3, 5–6; also see chapter 6).

[88] The use of "Holy" (ἁγίαις) to modify "Scriptures" occurs only here in the New Testament and reflects a common Hellenistic Jewish usage: Philo, *Fuga* 4; *Spec. Leg.* 1.214; *Heres* 106, 159.

[89] Cranfield, *Romans*, p. 55 n.3. On the predictive function of Scripture, see chapter 5.

[90] See Barnabas Lindars, *New Testament Apologetic* (London, SCM, 1961). The earliest Christian apologists were, of course, primarily interested in demonstrating the gospel's continuity with the Scriptures of Judaism as well as their superior understanding of them.

claimed as Christ and the messianic hopes of traditional Judaism.[91] The adoptionist christology of 1.4: "appointed (ὁρισθέντος) son of God in power according to the Spirit of holiness by his resurrection from the dead," serves the same end.[92] The Davidic christology unique to Romans together with the adoptionist tendency evident in 1.4 and the use of the "One God" topos in 3.30 (see chapter 2) suggest that Paul was concerned not to leave himself vulnerable to the charge of compromising monotheist convictions. Remarking on his apparent reluctance to refer to Jesus as "Lord" in Romans, Leander Keck states that Paul "sensed that the absolute use of κύριος for 'Jesus' might imply that he blurs the distinction between 'Jesus' and God; he would then have diminished his own usage lest he be accused of compromising monotheism."[93] The question arises: to whom would the extraordinary cluster of concerns evident in Romans 1.2–4, namely, the continuity between gospel and Scripture, the Davidic Messiahship of Jesus Christ, and the adoptionist formula of 1.4, be directed? The answer is undoubtedly Jewish Christians in Rome. Indeed, the question would appear merely rhetorical were it not for the history of scholarship on Romans. An alternative hypothesis that Paul is rehearsing in Romans his speech to be given in Jerusalem upon delivery of the collection is itself testimony to the fact that these and numerous other topics and formulations in Romans demand Jewish Christians to be in view.[94] Note that Jews of ethnic descent who have been thoroughly Hellenized and reject the binding authority of ritual laws such as circumcision are viewed as apostates even by Philo of Alexandria. Paul would be aware that there would be neither reason for, nor effect from, assuring such Hellenized Jewish Christians that he is respectful of the traditions of the Fathers. This point would be

[91] See the still important work of Oscar Cullmann, *The Christology of the New Testament* rev. edn, trans. Shirley C. Guthrie and Charles A. M. Hall (Philadelphia, Westminster, 1959), especially pp. 111–33. Paul seems to express a less ambiguous appropriation of this tradition than is the case with the gospel traditions; cf. Mark 14.61–2. and par.; Mark 15.2–5. and par.; and Mark 8.27–30. and par.

[92] Käsemann understands Rom. 1.3b–4 as a pre-Pauline formula and makes the observation that it is Paul's decision to show "he shared the same basis of faith as the Christians in Rome." See Käsemann, *Romans*, p. 3.

[93] See Leander E. Keck, "Jesus in Romans," *JBL*, 108 (1989), 446–7. A further factor in Paul's reservation may be the political apologetic with respect to Rome. Dunn dismisses the view that Christians at this time were concerned with the possible problematic implications of claims regarding Jesus Christ for Jewish monotheism; see Dunn, *Romans*, p. 25.

[94] For a critique of this alternative hypothesis see my "The Purpose and Audience of Romans," *RB*, 2 (1990), 219–37.

relevant only to "Jewish Christians" in the sense defined above –
doubtless including a good number of ethnic Gentiles, especially
God-fearers and proselytes.

In returning to his apostleship in Romans 1.5, Paul seeks further
to define the apostolic task. In 1.5a he affirms that his apostleship is
"received" through Jesus Christ; the insistence on the divine origin
of his commissioned task expresses his refusal to allow even an
implicit accusation of self-assertiveness in this regard – once again
reminiscent of Galatians 1.1. The purpose and scope of the given
task is characterized in Romans 1.5b: "for the obedience of faith
among all the Gentiles." Romans 1.5–6 has been frequently
adduced as evidence that the composition of the Roman church
which Paul addresses is exclusively or at the least predominantly
Gentile,[95] but Cranfield is surely correct in differing with this
opinion and holding that the expression ἐν οἷς ἐστε καὶ ὑμεῖς refers
to the "geographical situation in the midst of the Gentile world."[96]
Cranfield suggests that if Paul intended to say that the Church is
made up mostly of Gentiles he would have used instead ἐξ ὧν (cf.
e.g. Rom. 9.6). More cautiously one may prefer to say that Romans
1.6 does not preclude alternative construals and cannot constitute
proof of the composition of the community. The restraint of the
standard translations (RSV, KJ) is to be commended with respect to
ἐν πᾶσιν τοῖς ἔθνεσιν (1.5, among all the nations).[97]

In Romans 1.7, Paul for the first time identifies the community
that he addresses as "in Rome." The ancient world's predilection
for antiquity, and especially the specifically Jewish form of this
predilection, may explain in large part Paul's extraordinary efforts
to demonstrate the continuity between the gospel and the traditions
of the forefathers. Arguably this predilection is further enhanced by
the Roman ethos, characterized by a pronounced reverence for
tradition and conceivably impacting all Roman Christians.[98] Paul is
here directly responding to fundamental concerns of *Roman Jewish*
Christians as well as Roman Gentile Christians.[99]

---

[95] See e.g. Käsemann, *Romans*, p. 15; Dunn, *Romans*, pp. 18–19.
[96] Cranfield, *Romans*, p. 68.
[97] See *BAG*, s.v. ἔθνος.
[98] Note that later Roman criticism of Christianity would emphasize that Christianity was an apostasy from Judaism which, however distasteful to Roman sensibilities, was at least an ancient religious tradition. See e.g. Celsus in the late second
century.
[99] Käsemann's view that Roman Christians shared the renown of the imperial city
and that this fact influenced the "style" of Paul's introduction should be amended to
include as well the "content." See Käsemann, *Romans*, p. 3.

Paul toward Rome: correlations between
Romans 1.8–15 and 15.14–29

It has been argued cogently that the Pauline thanksgiving should be given special attention in determining the author's intentions in a given communication.[100] It may be suggested further that when items in the introductory part of the letter are repeated in the concluding section of the same letter, it is even more likely that a central concern of Paul has been identified.[101] Thus, concerns that Paul voices in both the thanksgiving and the concluding section of the body of the letter to the Romans merit special attention.

Paul's missionary intentions in coming to the West are explicitly and carefully stated in the opening and closing of the letter. In Romans 1.13b, he expresses his aim to win converts in Rome; the "some" (τινὰ) which modifies "harvest" (καρπὸν) reassures that he has no designs to displace missionaries already operating in the imperial city. There are, to be sure, plenty of places in Rome where Gentiles have not heard the gospel. Paul underscores the assurance of non-interference in Romans 15 by enunciating his missionary principle and practice of preaching the gospel "not where Christ has already been named, lest I build on another man's foundation" (15.20). At the end of the letter he specifies that the main locus of his mission activity will be Spain (15.24, 28). Paul appears to be quite aware that his authority as the apostle to the Gentiles is not necessarily acknowledged in the capital city; thus the careful declarations followed by rapid qualifications in 1.13b and 15.20 are appropriate. He is even more pensive when it comes to his role in Rome *vis à vis* those already converted. Paul's assertion of his apostolic authority is noticeably circumspect in both the opening and the closing of the letter to the Romans (see above discussion of Rom. 1.1). The usual Pauline confidence expressed in the affirmation at 1.11 of his intention to fortify the community with his communication and presence is immediately nuanced in 1.12 with the stress on mutuality of benefit: "that is, that we may be mutually encouraged by each other's faith, both yours and mine." Paul exhibits in 15.14–15 this same sensitivity to possible resentment towards such assertiveness. As, in 1.8, acknowledgment is made of the faith of the Roman

---

[100] Paul Schubert, *Form and Function of the Pauline Thanksgiving* (Berlin, Topelman, 1939).

[101] For a list of such parallels in Romans, see Paul Minear, *The Obedience of Faith: The Purpose of Paul in the Epistle to the Romans* (London, SCM, 1971), p. 37.

Christians, so in 15.14 they are described as "full of goodness, filled with all knowledge, and able to instruct one another."[102] The compliment is, of course, somewhat undermined by the fact that he has thought it necessary to write "boldly" about fundamental issues of faith as he admits in the next verse (15.15). Paul's attempt to characterize the instruction as a "reminder" is not convincing, as if this were the case an outline would have sufficed and the extensive exposition of themes found in Romans would have been unnecessary. To summarize, Paul expresses at the beginning of the letter the intention "to strengthen their faith" (cf. 1.11,15) and at the end of the letter he acknowledges that he has in fact been instructing his addressees unabashedly in matters of faith (15.15). In both instances, however, he is diffident about the likely response to his assertions of authority (cf. 1.12 and 15.14).

In Romans 15.15–16 Paul states that he has written to the Roman community because of the "grace given me by God to be a minister of Christ Jesus to the Gentiles ... so that the offering of the Gentiles may be acceptable." Again, it simply reads too much into the statement to conclude from 15.15–16 that the audience which Paul addresses is comprised mainly if not exclusively of Gentile Christians. He speaks to both Jewish and Gentile Christians in Rome because their mutual respect for one another is critical in his view for his "offering" to be acceptable to God. Paul's special mission is to the Gentiles, but he is willing to risk his life to maintain unity with the Jerusalem church, as is apparent in his intention to deliver the collection there before visiting Rome (15.30–2). Likewise Paul is compelled to communicate to both the Jewish and Gentile Christians at Rome in order to promote the mutual respect that should in his view characterize the Christian community and be the foremost sign of God's work in Christ. He needs the help of Gentile Christians and at least the absence of hostility and opposition from Jewish Christians in Rome (opposition which has often impeded his efforts in the East) in order to execute his responsibilities in the West. Paul has both ends in mind in this communication to Rome.

Another topic which appears most prominently in the thanksgiving and then at the closing of the letter is the delay in Paul's visiting Rome. Indeed, the oath at 1.9 suggests that the sincerity of

---

[102] Käsemann refers to Romans 1.8 as "*captatio benevolentiae*"; see *Romans*, p. 17. Several exegetes have suggested that Paul here is simply acknowledging that Christians elsewhere point with pride to the fact there is a Christian community in the imperial city; see e.g. Cranfield, *Romans*, p. 75.

his expressed desire to visit is questioned by some in Rome.[103] Such doubt would further account for the second and third iterations respectively at 1.11–12 and 1.13a that Paul really has desired to meet the addressees previously. The latter verse specifies that the failure to do so was involuntary ("have been prevented"). Again in 15.21–2, Paul explains that he "many times" has been frustrated in his intention to visit Rome because of the onus of mission work in the East (15.19). In 15.23 he once again stresses that he has "longed for many years" to visit them. The topic is another indicator that his authority – even his veracity – is not taken for granted in the Roman community.

Paul does not mention the collection which he is shortly to bring to Jerusalem in the introduction but only in the closing (15.25–6, 30–1). This fact alone suggests that one should beware of too readily discerning here a primary concern of the apostle. Moreover both of these later references are best understood as explanations of the primary statement of his unrealized previous intentions of visiting Rome. In the first instance, Paul has just mentioned that he has finished his work in the East and now at long last will soon be able to come to Rome (15.23), but not immediately as he must first deliver the collection to Jerusalem. The brief description of the motivation of the contributors to the collection in 15.27 is appropriate because it exemplifies the main theme of Paul's communication to the Roman Christians, namely the exhortation for mutual respect between Jewish and Gentile Christians in Rome (see below on Rom. 14.1–15.13). In the second mention of the collection in 15.30–1, Paul requests the Roman Christians to pray both that he be protected from harm in Jerusalem and that the collection be acceptable to its intended beneficiaries. The *hina* clause in 15.32, however, makes it clear that the purpose of the request is to allow Paul finally to fulfill his desire to visit the Roman community. If it is the case that he actually feared for his life in visiting Jerusalem, then the link between a "successful" trip to Jerusalem and the plans to come to the West is a vital one. None of this should be seen as providing any justification for the speculation that Paul is so preoccupied with his imminent trip to Jerusalem that he rehearses the arguments to be made before his audience there in the letter to the Romans. This unfortunately widely circulated assumption is without textual support and ignores the seriousness of the apostle in attempting to

---

[103] So Dunn, *Romans*, p. 34.

fulfill his perceived mission. From Paul's perspective the entire "Western world" awaits his missionary efforts and he is now writing to the community that can provide the needed support for these anticipated labors; it should be considered highly unlikely that Paul would allow his fears concerning the upcoming visit to Jerusalem to dominate his purpose in writing to Rome.[104] One should not, however, confuse his stated intention of undertaking missionary activity in Spain with the purpose of the letter to the Romans. A successful communication, to be sure, could be expected to make more likely Roman cooperation in such work. However, Paul must first confront two problems with respect to the Roman community, namely their suspicion and perhaps outright rejection of his office and mission, and the related criticism of the gospel which he preaches, and the content of his teaching. Only after attending to these two issues by presenting himself and his teaching as acceptable and worthy of respect can Paul be sanguine about receiving the requisite help when he finally arrives in Rome.

Romans 1.16–17: "To the Jew first and also to the Gentiles"

Richard Hays has rightly directed attention to the Old Testament passages informing Paul's language and thought in 1.16.[105] The central text underlying Romans 1.16a is Psalm 119.46: "I will also speak of thy testimonies before Kings, and shall not be put to shame."[106] Likewise both the thought and language of Romans 1.16b–17a are to be found in Isaiah 51.4–5:

> Hear me, hear my people
> And Kings, give ear to me.
> For the law will go forth from me,
> And my judgment will go forth as a light to the Gentiles.
> My righteousness (δικαιοσύνη) draws near quickly,
> And my salvation (τὸ σωτήριον) will go forth as a light,
> And in my arm will Gentiles hope.

---

[104] See e.g. Jacob Jervell, "The Letter to Jerusalem" in Karl P. Donfried (ed.), *The Romans Debate* (Minneapolis, Augsburg, 1977), pp. 61–75. See also note 1, above.

[105] See Richard B. Hays, *Echoes of Scripture in the Letters of Paul* (New Haven, Yale, 1989), pp. 36–41.

[106] Hays is astute in pointing to passages which echo "subliminally in Paul's diction" (*Echoes*, p. 37) but he often overlooks the most direct allusions as with Psalm 119.46 (which is listed in the margin of the Nestle text).

Thus the two primary scriptural passages which are reflected in Romans 1.16–17 are addressing "kings." This would not have been lost on either Paul or his addressees. As will be shown, Paul is acutely sensitive to what we have called the "Roman factor" (see chapter 6). Even in this verse where explicit address is to all people, indicated by the phrase: "Jew and Greek," he is mindful of the fact that he is communicating with Christians residing in the imperial city. The implicit assertion of divine authority over temporal power in this verse, will be seen to be an important undercurrent of Paul's communication in Romans.

Paul's description of the gospel as δύναμις θεοῦ εἰς σωτηρίαν ("the power of God for salvation") employs language that would be familiar to a Hellenized audience both Gentile and Jewish. The words δύναμις and σωτηρία occur frequently in Hellenistic religions and magical papyri.[107] The emphasis upon the availability of this "power of God for salvation" *to all – both Jews and Greeks –* is characteristic of Paul's own thought (cf. below on 3.29–30). Whereas the Bible (Hebrew and LXX) distinctively transforms the terms for power by stressing God's effective shaping of history rather than nature as in most of the surrounding cultures,[108] one should not exaggerate this tendency in Paul. For his use of δύναμις in 4.20–1 evidences that he affirms God's power as capable of transforming nature in the most miraculous sense – "bringing life out of death."[109] Paul does nuance this venerable apologetic topos of miraculous power both here and in Romans 4 by emphasizing the necessary human response of believing/trusting – παντὶ τῷ πιστεύοντι (1.16; cf. also 4.17–20).[110] For Paul the righteousness of God has been revealed (1.17) and this is the reason that now all those believing receive the "power of God for salvation."

[107] See Grundmann, δύναμις᾽, *TDNT*, 2 (1964), esp. 286–90 and s.v. σωτηρία, *BAGD*.

[108] Grundmann, *TDNT*, 2, 291–9. Note that the use of δύναμις is relatively infrequent in the LXX, ἰσχύς being much preferred.

[109] Paul's affirmation there is, of course, only preparation for the gospel proclamation of Christ's death and resurrection in Romans 4.24 (see below on Romans 4). A demythologizing of Paul at this point may be comforting to modern sensibilities but does not advance our historical understanding of the gospel that Paul preached.

[110] Cranfield points to the influence of the Old Testament tradition of the divine word (Gen. 1.3, 6 etc.) on Paul's thinking about the gospel as effective power (Cranfield, *Romans*, p. 88); cf. also Ulrich Wilckens, *Der Brief an die Römer*, *EKKNT*, 6 (Zurich, Benziger, 1978) exkursus, "Evangelium," vol. 1, 74–5. In apologetic literature, the supernatural or miraculous expression of power does not contradict natural or rational standards but is rather the exceptional manifestation of the real power of the God who has created *ex nihilo*. See Justin, Athenagoras, et. al.

The most significant sign of the manifestation of this power of God for the apostle is the new historical situation presently possible between Jew and Greek (or Gentile; 3.28). Paul's formulation in 1.16: Ἰουδαίῳ τε πρῶτον καὶ Ἕλληνι (to the Jew first and also to the Greek) expresses the apostle's central concern in this communication to Rome, that is, to present his understanding of the gospel so as to win the approval not only of Gentile Christians but also of Jewish Christians. Repeatedly throughout Romans, Paul will acknowledge the special significance of the Jewish heritage (as e.g. 3.2; 7.12; 9.4–5). The question of priority with respect to Jews and Gentiles in the plan of salvation will be addressed in an extended fashion in Romans 9–11.[111] Paul is at great pains from the beginning to the end of Romans to present himself and the gospel that he preaches as respectful and solicitous towards the Jews and their heritage while at the same time refusing to compromise his conviction that God will welcome both Jews and Gentiles fully on the basis of their faith.

The question of the extent to which Paul was successful in this effort is not answerable on the historical evidence; what we can learn from the apostle's expressed sensitivity to Jews and their heritage in Romans concerns Paul's image of the composition of the addressed community. As already suggested above, the context and mode of his argumentation in the opening and closing (and throughout Romans, as will be shown in subsequent chapters) makes the most sense if we assume that Paul is addressing a Roman Christian community which is composed of a significant number of Jewish Christians.

Romans 14.1–15.13: the audiences of Romans

It has been argued here that Paul is addressing an audience which includes a significant number of Jewish Christians as well as Gentile Christians in the letter to the Romans. This passage (14.1–15.13), which concludes the body of his letter, permits a more specific characterization of the two elements comprising the Roman community. Put simply, perhaps the two most crucial questions to be answered regarding Romans 14.1–15.13 are: (1) who are the "strong" and "weak"? and (2) what does Paul wish them to do? Several commentators have concluded that the "strong" and the

---

[111] Pace Wilckens, *Römer*, vol. 1, p. 86. See below chapter 5.

"weak" represent respectively Gentile Christians and Jewish Christians.[112] More precisely, the latter group are those Christians who observe the Mosaic Law, which may include some Gentiles, and the former are those who do not, which could indeed include Jews in the pattern of Paul himself.[113] From the information to be found in Romans 14–15 it can be known that: the "weak" do not eat meat (14.2); observe ceremonial days (14.5); and also abstain from drinking wine (14.21). This group is also said to "judge" or "condemn" the "strong" (14.3b, 4a, 10a). On the other hand, the "strong" are admonished not to "despise" the "weak" (μὴ ἐξουθενείτω; 14.3, 10b).

Käsemann has contended that the "weak" represent a Jewish group under syncretistic influence,[114] but Watson and Wedderburn demonstrate that such behavior was widespead among Jewish groups in the diaspora.[115] Presumably the extreme dietary restrictions on the part of the "weak" were followed to avoid precisely such an "influence." Wedderburn thinks it likely that the observance or non-observance of "days" in 14.5 concerns Jewish holy days.[116] He acknowledges the obvious difficulty for this view posed by the practice of abstaining from meat (14.2) and wine (14.21) as normally Jews ate certain kinds of meat if properly slaughtered and drank wine at least on special occasions. Following Watson's lead, however, he points to Daniel 1.12,16 where Jewish youths abstain from the King's rich food and wine and eat only vegetables and drink water. Similarly, Philo of Alexandria explains that a group of pious Jews, the Therapeutae, living near Alexandria also abstain from meat and wine.[117] In the *Testament of Isaac*, the patriarch is depicted as a life long abstainer from meat and wine (4.5) and even fruit (4.6). Wedderburn finds especially relevant an account in Josephus (*Life*, p. 141) which concerns Jews in Rome around the time Paul writes the letter to the Romans. Josephus reports that certain priests, "not forgetting their pious practices," ate only figs and nuts. The evidence seems to point to a pattern of pious Jews in pagan circumstances avoiding meat and wine. Wedderburn concludes that if such ascetic groups existed in Diaspora Judaism, then

---

[112] For a survey of opinions on the matter cf.; Cranfield, *Romans*, pp. 694–5.
[113] Watson, *Paul*, pp. 94–5.
[114] Käsemann, *Romans*, p. 368.
[115] Cf. Watson, *Paul*, pp. 95–6.
[116] Wedderburn, p. 33.
[117] Philo, *Contemplative Life*, pp. 73–4.

it is likely that Christians, who were still associated with Judaism, followed similar practices.[118] The "strong" share none of the scruples of the "weak." It is, of course, the case that the terminology of "weak" and "strong" must come from the latter and not the former group. Paul identifies himself with the "strong," as is clear from 15.1: "We the strong." Paul's fundamental position seems to be that though the "strong" are doctrinally correct in asserting that Christ has liberated believers from all requirements of the ritual law, they should not exercise this freedom in view of the "weak" who may be harmed by being influenced to act contrary to their consciences (14.13–23). This is the view already expressed by Paul in 1 Corinthians 8.7–13 and there is no compelling reason to believe that he is being disingenuous when he repeats it in Romans 14.[119]

Thus serious concessions are demanded by Paul of Gentile Christians in order to promote peaceful relations between Jewish and Gentile Christians.[120] That Paul continues to acknowledge the legitimacy and honorable status of Jewish Christianity is attested by the collection which he has raised during the period of his missionary efforts in the East (2 Cor. 8–9; 1 Cor. 16.1–3) and is presently contemplating delivering to the Law-abiding Christian community in Jerusalem (15.25). Few would seriously contend that Paul intends to persuade Jewish Christians in Jerusalem to desist from obeying the Law and there is also no evidence to suggest that he wishes to do so in Rome. He firmly believes that one of the most significant signs of the new age which Christ has inaugurated is that both Jews and Gentiles now praise the same God (cf. 10.12, also Gal. 3.28). Moreover, antagonism between the two groups may lead to the same obstacles to Paul's ministry in the West as it has in the East. As 1 Thessalonians 2.16 and 2 Corinthians 11.26 indicate, this would include primarily Jews (including Jewish Christians) attempting to hinder his preaching to Gentiles.[121] Further, Paul is aware that such conflict between the two dominant Christian groups in the capital city of the Empire could elicit a severe civil response and perhaps even a repetition of the expulsion of 49 CE, leaving the apostle without a base from which to carry on his mission in Spain. Thus,

[118] Wedderburn, p. 34.

[119] E. P. Sanders on the basis of Galatians 2 concludes that in a situation wherein Gentile and Jewish Christians ate meals together, Paul would require the latter to forsake the dietary laws (*Paul*, pp. 177–8) but this can only be maintained by denying the plain meaning of both 1 Corinthians 8 and Romans 14.

[120] Contra Watson, *Paul*, p. 96.

[121] On this issue cf. E. P. Sanders, *Paul*, pp. 181–92.

his central plea in this section is unambiguous and genuine: "accept one another" (14.1, 3; 15.1). Both the length and detail of this section as well as its position as the last section of the body of the letter, standing right before the closing material, suggest Paul is thinking seriously and specifically of the situation in Rome.[122]

Romans 14. 1–12: issues dividing the Roman community

Romans 14.1 makes clear that Paul is addressing the "strong" but by v.3 (if not already by v. 2) Paul provides advice for the "weak" also. The prohibition against "quarreling about opinions" (14.1) suggests that this was in fact taking place among Christians in Rome. If, as argued in chapter 6 below, it is the case that Paul knows the socio-political scene in Rome, then it is hard to imagine that he is not at least as well informed about issues specific to the Christian community there. The "strong" who felt free to eat meat despised the religious scruples of the "weak" who, in turn, judged the former (14.3a–b). The rationale of 14.3c: "for God has received him" (that is, the Gentile Christian) expresses a central theological axiom for Paul (see below on 15.9–13) which undergirds his apostolate and serves well here his purpose to gain support for his mission to the Gentiles.[123] With respect to the second isssue causing conflict between the two groups, namely holy days (14.5ab), Paul again relativizes the difference by appealing to the subjective criterion of motivation ("fully convinced in his/her own mind," 14.5c). To be sure the final criterion, for Paul, is theological, for both groups "give thanks to the Lord" (14.6) and live and die "for the Lord" (14.7–8). The confessional statement of 14.9 makes clear that Christ's Lordship is not created by the willful obedience of his subjects, but by his own sacrificial life and death. In 14.10–12, Paul will again appeal to the eschatological judgment scene in order to support his plea for attitude and behavior modification on the part of the two groups. The "strong" and "weak" should cease despising and judging one another, as everyone will render his or her own account before God in the end time (14.12). Apocalyptic is once again subordinated to social and paranetic interests.

---

[122] Pace Käsemann, *Romans*, p. 366.
[123] The αὐτόν of Romans 14.3c must refer to the "eater" of 14.3b – Pace Cranfield, *Romans*, p. 702.

Romans 14.13–23: admonitions to the "strong"

Romans 14.13a may apply to both groups, but from vv.13b–23 the address is specifically to the "strong."[124] But note that Paul both realizes and expects that when he specifically addresses one group, the other group would also listen – perhaps even more attentively than when directly addressed, so as to check his integrity (see below, chapter 5 on this topic). In 14.14a, Paul expresses his theological agreement with the "strong" that "in the Lord Jesus that nothing is unclean in itself" but this is preceded (v.13b) and followed (vv.15–22) by admonitions against acting out this conviction when harm to the weak "brother" may result. Wedderburn observes that the fact that many commentators have seen in 14.14a an echo or deliberate quotation of Mark 7.14–23 where the issue is the ritual sanction of the Jewish law also suggests that the obstacle to "acceptance" for the two groups derives from a disagreement over the validity of the law. Paul affirms the theological convictions which he shares with the "strong" while at the same time seeking to minimize the hostility which the "weak" may feel towards him as a consequence of their contrary opinions. He firmly believes that the fact of Jews and Gentiles worshipping together the same God is the great sign of the Christ event (3.29–30; 10.12–13; 15.7–9). Mutual acceptance of Jews and Gentiles is a distinctive and most significant characteristic of the Christian community by which it imitates Christ's own acceptance of both peoples (15.7).

Paul's strategy seems to be one of stating uncompromisingly his view of the truth and then counselling restraint of actions that are theoretically sanctioned by him, when such actions would cause grief to the "weak" (v.15) or lead outsiders to discredit the Christian movement (v.16). That the scruples of the "weak" concerned matters of ritual purity is further attested by the use of the words κοινός[125] (common) and καθαρός (clean).[126] Paul does not share the religious concern to which these terms point, but he is not willing to see Jewish Christians at loggerheads with Gentile Christians over this matter or even worse to see the former influenced so as to act in violation of their own consciences (vv.22–3). The spiritual well-being of the "brother" must be put above the exercise of freedom deriving from the robust faith of the "strong." The

---

[124] Käsemann, *Romans*, p. 374.
[125] Cf. *BAGD*, s.v. κοινός.
[126] *BAGD*, s.v. καθαρός.

polemical definition of the "kingdom of God" serves to support Paul's request for a restriction on the exercise of such freedom in the interests of unity: "For the kingdom of God is not food and drink but righteousness and peace and joy in the Holy Spirit" (14.17). It is not surprising that, among the three characteristics, "peace" (εἰρήνη) is repeated in 14.19. Peace is a good to which one would expect that those exposed to imperial propaganda should be especially responsive. Excluding standard greetings, the word "peace" occurs seven times in Romans as compared to six times in all other extant writings of Paul. It is a main theme of Paul's communication throughout Romans that Christ has made peace possible at the highest level between God and humankind as well as on the horizontal plane between those most distanced from each other, represented for Paul by the phrase: Jews and Gentiles.

Romans 15.1–6: Christ, God, and Scripture in support of Paul's plea

Romans 15.1–3 summarizes Paul's exhortation to the "strong."[127] Romans 15.1–2 continues the general "peace exhortation" of Romans 14.[128] In 15.1 Paul clearly identifies himself with the "strong." Romans 15.3 provides support for 15.1–2 by appealing to the example of Christ's sacrifice.[129] Though sometimes referred to as a digression on Scripture,[130] Romans 15.4 is consonant in context as it represents another instance of Paul's apologetic use of Scripture as foretelling the gospel (see chapter 5). Scripture, by telling in advance (προεγράφη) the passion of Christ, provides hope to Christians.[131] The repetition of "steadfastness and encouragement" attributed to God in 15.5 is meant to underscore the fact that God is the source of Scripture, which Paul has just characterized as offering these same two virtues in 15.4. The prayer wish of verses 5–6 requests that God grant especially to the "strong" the mind to behave in the same manner as that of Christ, namely as ready "to bear the reproaches of humankind against God"

---

[127] See above note 93. In 15.1, Paul substitutes οἱ δυνατοί for the expression "the strong" of Romans 14. Cranfield, *Romans*, pp. 729–30.

[128] Käsemann, *Romans*, 380.

[129] Romans 15.3b is an exact quotation of the LXX Psalm 68.10. The σε in the Psalms and Romans refers to God and thus Paul has Christ addressing God directly.

[130] So Barrett, *Romans*, p. 269.

[131] Barrett, p. 270; Leenhardt, p. 362; Käsemann, p. 382.

(15.3).[132] The hoped-for outcome is expressed in 15.6: Jews and Gentiles praising God "with one mind." Given Paul's subordination of conduct to attitude throughout Romans 14, it is not likely that he means to insist that all Christians worship in the same place at the same time.[133] For Paul, to glorify God is one of the most significant acts of which human beings are capable. Paul considers the event of both Jews' and Gentiles' worshipping the same God with the same mind to be a truly momentous sign of the work of God in Christ.[134]

Romans 15.7–13: the fulfillment of Scripture

The fundamental motif of mutual acceptance from 14.1–15.6 is repeated in 15.7a and the primary reason for this command is given, namely that "Christ has welcomed you" (v.7b). The prepositional phrase "for the glory of God" at the end of 15.7 is a thoughtful expression that looks backwards and forwards to Paul's stated conviction that Gentile Christians now worship the same God with the same mind as Jews. We have arrived at the concluding part of the main body of Paul's letter to the Romans and are not surprised to encounter the expression of a central culminating concern. The two chief purposes of Christ's earthly mission are given: Christ has both confirmed the promises given to the Fathers (v.8b) and opened the way for Gentiles "to glorify God for His mercy."[135] The first stated reason for Christ's ministry (Christ's confirmation of the promises to the fathers) Paul assumes is uncontested; however he adduces four biblical quotations in support of the second – inclusion of Gentiles in the believing community. The texts are drawn from all three main divisions of the Scripture: Law, Prophets, and Writings. The keyword ἔθνη (Gentiles) is common to all four quotations. The first quotation is carefully chosen and there can be little doubt that Paul expected some of his audience to know that Psalm

---

[132] The τὸ αὐτό refers backwards to Romans 15.3 as is made clear from κατὰ Χριστὸν Ἰησοῦν.

[133] Watson's reading constrains Romans 14–15 to support his hypothesis of the uniting of the two groups under Paul's hegemony, but this demands a tortured interpretation of several passages including 15.6. See Watson, *Paul*, pp. 96–7.

[134] On Paul's understanding of "glorifying God'" see the sadly neglected work of G. H. Boobyer, "Thanksgiving and the Glory of God in Paul" (Diss., Leipzig, 1929).

[135] See *BAGD*, s.v. βεβαιόω. The meaning here is explicitly "prove the promises reliable." Barrett is correct to note that the word "circumcision" in Romans 15.8 is a collective term meaning the Jews. See Barrett, *Romans*, p. 271.

17.50 (18.49) is introduced as spoken by David.[136] The first part of the final quotation (Rom. 15.12) refers to the promise of the appearance of the messianic Son of David ("root of Jesse"). Likewise, καὶ ὁ ἀνιστάμενος ἄρχειν ἐθνῶν (who rises to rule the Gentiles) points to the Son of David.[137] Paul's appeal to David, here as well as earlier in Romans (cf. 1.3; 4.6), is purposeful; David was the first to acknowledge the Gentiles' praise of God and the mention of the Son of David presages the time when the nations praise God.[138] At this critical point near the end of his communication Paul once again seeks to prove that the inclusion of the Gentiles was foretold by Scripture.[139] His concern to defend his mission to the Gentiles before Jewish Christians and to win their support, as well as that of Gentile Christians in Rome, for the furtherance of his mission in the West is evident. Ironically, it is E. Käsemann who has offered the most insightful comment on this section of Romans: "The Old Testament foreshadows this message. The recipients of the epistle must recognize this agreement with Scripture. An apology could hardly have a more magnificent conclusion."[140]

External evidence for Jewish Christians in Rome

Wedderburn has examined the external evidence for the existence of Jewish Christians in Rome. A late fourth-century commentary on Romans, whose author has been given the name "Ambrosiaster," relates that the "Jews who had believed [in Christ] passed on to the Romans the tradition that they ought to profess Christ but keep the law ... they nevertheless accepted faith in Christ, although according to a Jewish rite." More circumstantial evidence for the presence of Jewish Christians in Rome is to be found with the Letter to the Hebrews and the *First Letter of Clement*. The former was sent to the church in Rome (13.24) which appears to be susceptible to the attractions of Judaism and compels the apologetic attempt to demonstrate the superiority of Christian beliefs over Judaism. The

---

[136] "A psalm of David the servant of the Lord, who addressed the words of this song on the day the Lord delivered him from the hand of all his enemies, and from the hand of Saul."

[137] Cranfield, *Romans*, p. 747. See below on Romans 3.29–30; and 4.

[138] Amos 9.11; Acts 15.16–18; cf. Lohse, *TDNT*, VIII, p. 483.

[139] Barrett, *Romans*, p. 272.

[140] Käsemann, *Romans*, p. 387. The irony, of course, lies in the fact that Käsemann has throughout his commentary consistently tried to foreclose the reading of Romans as apologetic theology.

First Letter of Clement, wherein the Jewish cult is described without criticism, was written from Rome in the nineties CE. A few years later it is interesting to note Ignatius of Antioch chose to address the Roman Church as "to those who are united in flesh and spirit in every one of [God's] commandments." The plausibility of the hypothesis that early Christianity in Rome was of the Judaizing sort is enhanced by the famous passage from Suetonius' "Life of Claudius" which refers to an imperial decree in 49 CE expelling Jews and Christians for disturbances provoked by preaching Christ (see more on this passage in chapter 5). The decree would only be enforced until the death of Claudius and thus presumably Jews and Jewish Christians returned to Rome during the reign of Nero. While Wedderburn argues strenuously and for the most part convincingly for the presence of Judaizing Christians in Rome, he is quick to point out that they are quite different from those of Galatia as there is no mention of circumcision but ritual concerns present in Romans, as mentioned, could be taken very seriously indeed by Jews as well as by Jewish Christians.[141]

Conclusion

Though the merits of Wedderburn's efforts are considerable, there are two problematic conclusions that need to be questioned. Wedderburn is misled by John L. White's opinion that "it will not greatly advance our understanding of Romans to place it within this or that category of epistolary type." The view expressed ignores a significant characteristic of ancient world culture, namely a marked concern to find the most appropriate literary forms to achieve the purpose of a communication. The literary genre of a work may be the most important indicator for discerning the intentionality of an author and in overlooking this question for Romans, one of the few objective criteria for determining the purpose of Paul's writing is left unexamined. A second error, in my view, is his conclusion that the audience of Romans is predominantly Gentile.[142] More important, and also more susceptible to resolution, is the question as to which group Paul seems most intent on influencing in this communication. Ironically, Wedderburn's own analysis seems better to support the proposal here advanced that Paul is most concerned to persuade

---

[141] See Wedderburn, *Reasons*, pp. 51–9
[142] Wedderburn, pp. 5, 20.

Jewish Christians, for he rightly perceives that Paul in Romans 1–8 as well as much of 9–11 is engaged in defense of his gospel against Jewish criticisms.[143] He notes that the criticism of Jews would be indistinguishable from that of Judaizing Christians and that because the letter is addressed to Christians, it is reasonable to assume that Paul believes his audience to be in part composed of Judaizing Christians. One of the strengths of Wedderburn's work is his recognition of the multiple purposes or reasons in Paul's writing to Rome; this strength also becomes the author's Achilles' heel as he sometimes avoids the task of prioritizing the "reasons" or, as in the instance under consideration, does so incorrectly.

Most important to Paul is the encouragement of mutual respect between the Jewish and Gentile factions in the Roman community. A right understanding of the gospel should produce greater respect between Jewish and Gentile Christians, not enhance conflict. Paul is concerned also with lessening the likelihood of the kind of direct opposition to his projected missionary labors which he had frequently encountered in the East and which was certainly one of the primary impediments to his work there. In Romans, he is committed to promoting harmonious relations between Jewish and Gentile Christians in the imperial city. At the same time, he presses for a vertical submission of all Roman Christians to the gospel of God. Francis Watson's view that Paul in Romans seeks to separate Jewish Christians from the synagogue and then to have them join the Law-free Gentile Christian community is not to be affirmed.[144] In Romans 14–15, Paul repeatedly advocates mutual respect between Gentile and Jewish Christians despite their differences – not capitulation of one group to the views of the other! He firmly believes that if the Roman Christians – Jewish and Gentile – truly understand the gospel that he preaches then they will, indeed, assist him in his efforts in the West. As in the earlier chapters of Romans (see below), Paul continues to have two aims in mind: (1) to teach his Law-free gospel to Gentiles while controverting Jewish Christians' objections to it and hopefully winning support from both groups for his planned Western mission; and (2) to lessen the antagonism between the two groups so as to avoid civil disturbances that led to such dramatic consequences in 49 CE, and to help the community manifest more fully the fruits of God's work, the reconciliation

[143] Wedderburn, pp. 93, 139

[144] See Francis Watson, *Paul, Judaism and the Gentiles: A Sociological Approach*, SNTSMS, 56 (Cambridge, University Press, 1986).

between Jew and Gentile, accomplished through Christ. Paul is vitally concerned to present his gospel in a manner which will promote mutual acceptance between the two components of the Roman Christian community and is willing to allow both theological and cultic differences within the community. He does not require uniformity of either theology or practice within the community of Jesus believers.

Pioneering a path to be traversed several times by second-century Christian apologists, Paul writes a Protreptic presenting his gospel with the intention of persuading Jewish Christians as well as Gentile Christians in Rome that his planned efforts in the West are worthy of support. Just as with the later apologetic writings, Romans offers positive arguments for the author's worldview while secondarily defending it against objections and asserting the inferiority of competitive, alternative views. In the next two chapters, Romans 1.18–3.31 and Romans 4 will be discussed respectively, and it will be demonstrated that this interpretive perspective advanced with respect to the openings and closings of Romans is also applicable to these sections of Paul's letter.

2

APOLOGETIC MOTIFS IN ROMANS 1.18–3.31

Many commentators on Romans have considered Romans 1.18–3.20 to be a digression.[1] Perhaps this is a reasonable construal if the audience of Romans is understood to be composed entirely of Gentile Christians. But if, instead, Paul is addressing Jewish as well as Gentile Christians with the primary intention of promoting harmony between these two groups of Christians, then this section of Romans is both appropriate and even essential for accomplishing his purpose in Romans. Paul declares that the distinctions between Jews and Gentiles are irrelevant from the most important perspective, that of God; both Jews and Gentiles are without merit before God. The negative task of destroying the false bases of pride that divide Jews and Gentiles is propaedeutic to fostering the new community of Jewish and Gentile Christians. Thus in this section of Romans, Paul makes frequent use of σύγκρισις which, as already pointed out, is characteristic of the Protreptic.[2] In addition to this generic feature, the material content of Romans 1.18–3.31 can be seen in large part to be expressive of the motifs characteristic of the apologetic[3] literature surveyed in chapter 1 and indicative of this literature's Protreptic thrust as evidenced especially by Paul's concern to demonstrate his gospel's continuity with Scripture.

---

[1] See Aune, "Logos Protreptikos", 28–9.

[2] See chapter 1; Aune, "Logos Protreptikos", 34. σύγκρισις – comparison of good and bad people or things to demonstrate the superiority of the one and the inferiority of the other. As will be made clear, Paul alters the purpose as he seeks to demonstrate that both Jews and Gentiles are inferior to Jewish and Gentile Christianity and thus the latter two groups should embrace each other as true equals.

[3] See Barnabas Lindars, *New Testament Apologetic* (London, SCM, 1961). A central characteristic of NT (and later Christian) apologetics is the concern to demonstrate the gospel's continuity with the Scriptures.

Günther Bornkamm on Romans 1.18–3.31

The case that the apologetic tradition is a significant contributor to Romans 1.18–3.20 was first cogently argued by Günther Bornkamm. Günther Bornkamm in his article "Die Offenbarung des Zornes Gottes (Rom. 1–3)",[4] recognized the substantive parallels between Paul's expression of natural theology in Romans 1.19–32 and Stoic terminology and most particularly Hellenistic Jewish apologetic thought (especially the Wisdom of Solomon and Philo).[5] He identified the shared essential propositions between Paul and the parallel literature as follows:

(a) The ingenious construction of the world gives cause for human viewers to ask about their Creator and to infer his divine greatness from the glory of his work. Though invisible to the senses, the deity is seen in his works by the "mind" (cf. Rom.1.19 ff).

(b) This knowledge of the Creator does not only represent a theoretical confirmation of the existence of a prime cause but is at the same time a comprehension (cf. 1.21, "knowing God" – 1.32, "knowing God's decree") of the Law.

(c) Therefore the honoring of God and an obedient life belong to the right knowledge of the Creator (cf. 1.21 ff, 28).

(d) The closing of oneself to the true knowledge of God leads to the abomination of idolatry and a brutal life (cf. 1.23 ff).[6]

At the same time, Bornkamm is careful to point out that in Paul one fails to find the common Hellenistic worldview wherein the deity is the life principle (Logos) of the world.[7] This fully immanent theology (pantheism) allows for "the from below to above epistemology" inherent in natural theology and according to which the fullness of the Godhead is knowable. The Stoic concept of the omnipresent Logos which functions as the "mind" of all things is

---

[4] *Das Ende des Gesetzes* (München, Kaiser, 1953); ET, "The Revelation of God's Wrath, Romans 1–3," in *Early Christian Experience*, trans. P. L. Hammer (New York, Harper & Row, 1969).

[5] *Das Ende des Gesetzes*, 13 (ET, 50). A case for direct dependency of Romans on the Wisdom of Solomon has been argued by E. Grafe, "Das Verhältnis der paulinischen Schriften zur Sapienta Salomonis," in *Festschrift C. V. Weizsäcker* (1892), 251–86. Following Otto Michel in *Paulus und seine Bibel*, BFCTh (2/18,1929; reprint 1972), 14–18, Käsemann, correctly in my view, rejects this contention and appeals instead to the use of a common tradition (*Commentary on Romans*, p. 35).

[6] *Early Christian Experience*, p. 50 (*Das Ende des Gesetzes*, pp. 13–14).

[7] Chrysippus, see J. von Arnim, *Stoicorum Veterum Fragmenta*, 2.1076.

operative here and allows for the further commonplace Hellenistic idea that duty is the "common law" itself and the law is "the king of all divine and human things."[8] Bornkamm cautions against seeing the Hellenistic concept of the world as only "a system of abstract principles" and the deity as only the "principle of reason."[9] Awe, praise, and above all ecstatic union with the deity are by no means foreclosed possibilities in this Hellenistic worldview as seen, for example, in the Hermetic literature.

Bornkamm says that critical to an understanding of Romans 1.19 is an underlying presupposition of all the propositions of Hellenistic theology stated above. This presupposition is epitomized in the Stoic concept that the human person realizes her/himself in the knowledge of God and of the Law.[10] The law of nature is seen as also the law of humanity, and the entire created order reflects the divine image, which is "One."[11] It is this philosophical understanding of the Law which influenced the apologetic argumentation of the Hellenistic Jewish writings that attempt to demonstrate the agreement of the Mosaic Law with the law of reason (Aristeas, 4 Macc., Sibyll, Philo) and "led to the resulting theory of the dependence of Greek philosophy on Moses' giving of the law that extends into early Christian apologetics."[12] The unity of the knowledge of God, the world, and humanity is grounded in a conception of the Law which equates the divine Law with the innate laws of natural and historical development. As Bornkamm says of Philo, "in him the Stoic 'to live comfortably with nature' finds its 'goal' in the fellowship with God."[13] The prerequisite for right moral living is true knowledge of God as creator and sustainer:

> He that has begun by learning these things with his understanding rather than in his hearing and has stamped on his soul impressions of truths so marvelous and priceless, both that God is and is from eternity, will lead a life of bliss and

---

[8] *Stoic Vet. Frgm.*, 3.314.

[9] *Early Christian Experience*, p. 51 (*Das Ende des Gesetzes*, p. 15).

[10] Bornkamm (*Early Christian Experience*, pp. 51–2, *Das Ende des Gesetzes*, p. 16) refers here to Cicero's statement "whoever will not obey the law flees from himself and denies human nature" (*de republ.* III.33) and also to Dion of Prusa (XII.28), "they do not linger away from and outside of the divine ... but come into existence in it, even more grow together with it and adhere to it in every way."

[11] Cf. Cleanthes' *Hymn to Zeus*, l.4.

[12] *Early Christian Experience*, p. 52 (*Das Ende des Gesetzes*, p. 16).

[13] *Early Christian Experience*, p. 52 (*Das Ende des Gesetzes*, p. 17).

blessedness, because he has a character moulded by the truths that piety and holiness enforce.[14]

The conclusion that idolatry and immoral living are the results of an irrational and deficient conception of God becomes a popular theme of Jewish apologetics. Bornkamm mentions only summarily the parallels between Wisdom of Solomon 12 and 13 and the Pauline ideas about the knowledge of God from his works, the resulting responsibility of the Gentiles, the foolishness of their idolatry, and idolatry per se as a punishment of God.[15]

After all this, Bornkamm concludes that it would be wrong to call Romans 1.18–3.20 an "apologetic excursus."[16] Paul speaks the language of Hellenistic and Jewish missionary apologetic sermons but has a very different aim.[17] This other literature has as its goal the instilling of knowledge of God from examination of the world whose operative principles are instructive for right human conduct. Paul turns this idea on its head by asserting that the knowledge of God is a reality under which the world is judged. As Bornkamm says, "not the 'ignorance of God' but the knowledge of God is the sign of the ungodly world. They have the truth of God, albeit as those who 'suppress the truth by wickedness'" (Rom.1.18, also 1.19, 20, 21, 28). Bornkamm states that the question of the knowledge of God does not occur to Paul further. Paul does not engage in speculations concerning the degrees and manner to which the levels of creation reflect the qualities of God as, for example, Wisdom 13.3–5. Bornkamm notes that Romans 1.19b: "for God has shown it to them," is not superfluous for Paul, as it might very well be considered from the Greek worldview, because the apostle seeks to underscore God's willful activity. Likewise, Paul does not understand human failure *vis à vis* the revelation of God to consist in ignorance of God but rather in the refusal to give thanks and praise to God (1.21). For Paul, it is the apparent contradiction of "knowing God" and yet having "thoughts made foolish" and a darkened heart which explain the real conditions of human existence. Knowledge about God does not necessarily result in the

---

[14] *de opif. mundi*, p. 172.

[15] *Early Christian Experience*, p. 53 (*Das Ende des Gesetzes*, p. 18).

[16] *Early Christian Experience*, p. 54 (*Das Ende des Gesetzes*, p. 19).

[17] Note that A. J. Malherbe thinks that Bornkamm has overstated the differences between Paul and his philosophical sources. Malherbe, "The Apologetic Theology of the Preaching of Peter," *Restoration Quarterly*, 13 (1970), 213. Nevertheless, whatever the precise degree, the significance of the differences cannot be denied.

proper personal relationship between God and the human person. Whereas in Philo the praise of God is "the last attainable step" to which the human can raise her/himself, and thus this moment is fulfilled in the moment of ecstasy (*Leg. All.* 1.82), for Paul it is nothing more nor less than the acceptance of human existence as determined by the Creator.[18]

Bornkamm concludes that Romans 1.18–3.20 is not an apologetic discussion because the intention of the apostle is not to infer God's being from the world, but to uncover the being of the world from God's revelation. Further, its purpose, he concludes, is not to prove the revelation of God before the judgment of the world, but to unveil the judgment of God over the world revealed in the law.[19] Although this observation is certainly correct as it stands, a cardinal issue for me is precisely the other kinds of questions about God. And there are several, which Paul does address throughout Romans. I do not agree with Bornkamm when he says that what concerns Paul in Romans 1.18–3.20 "has nothing to do with the disclosure of the divine being but with the uncovering of human existence."[20]

In turning to Romans 2, Bornkamm asserts that Paul presents to the Jews[21] the same sharp declaration of punishment (or reward) commensurate with their deeds (2.6–11) as he had in his address to the Gentiles.[22] Romans 1.18–3.20 is seen as a large unit in which it is affirmed that both Gentile and Jewish self-understanding and understanding of God has provided no excuse in light of their just condemnation: "Romans 1.18–3.20 is the penetrating accusation that 'all are under sin'(3.9, cf. 10–18)."[23]

Bornkamm has shown that Paul has employed specific apologetic traditions in Romans 1–3, albeit the apostle has given them a radically new orientation. He does not, however, identify the "life situation" which prompts Paul's use and transformation of apologetic traditions. If, as argued in chapter 1 above, Paul is concerned to foster harmony between Jewish and Gentile Christians in Rome, then a primary intention of traditional Jewish apologetics, namely to demonstrate the superiority of Judaism over all other religions, is

[18] *Early Christian Experience*, p. 57 (*Das Ende des Getzes*, pp. 22–3).
[19] *Early Christian Experience*, p. 59 (*Das Ende des Getzes*, p. 26).
[20] *Early Christian Experience*, p. 56 (*Das Ende des Getzes*, p. 21.)
[21] Bornkamm understands 1.18–32 as directed to the Gentiles and 2.1–29 as directed to the Jews (p. 26).
[22] *Early Christian Experience*, pp. 59–60 (*Das Ende des Getzes*, p. 27).
[23] *Early Christian Experience*, p. 61 (*Das Ende des Getzes*, p. 30).

of course rejected, but the apologetics of a "new religion" which asserts its superiority over both Jewish and Gentile piety is given birth.[24] At the same time, Paul seeks to promote equality among Christians having Jewish and Gentile religious and ethnic origins. Bornkamm could have fruitfully extended his comparison between apologetic literature and Romans to include Romans 3.21–4.25. Once the significance of the "One God" topos of Romans 3.30 for the construal of 1.18–3.29 is recognized then, indeed, the application of Bornkamm's comparison to the remainder of Romans 3 is irresistible.

There is no question that Paul differs from Jewish apologetic (and, for that matter, from all other non-Christian Jewish literature) in proclaiming the gospel of Christ crucified and that this proclamation, in turn, necessitated apologetic argumentation against the same Jewish Hellenistic missionary apologetic traditions which the apostle knew so well. This patent fact of Pauline theology, however, raises the possibility that Pauline apologetics stands at the decisive crossroad of the Jewish apologetic tradition and what was to become the Greek Christian apologetic tradition.[25]

Apologetic motifs in Romans 1.18–32

Several important apologetic themes in both Hellenistic Jewish and Christian literature are to be found in Romans – often transformed, to be sure. The dominant apologetic tendency to reinterpret mythological and particularistic religious traditions so that they become more inclusive as well as more theologically and personally meaningful, and thus consistent with the purpose of Protreptic, can be discerned.[26] In the following exegetical discussion of Romans 1.1–3 specific motifs will be noted, which evince such apologetic reinterpretation. These include the eschatological judgment scene, human cognition of God, circumcision, and the trustworthiness of God. Further, the apologetic critique of other peoples and religions

[24]In my view, Bornkamm tends, on the one hand, to exaggerate the "particularist" emphases of Jewish apologetic and, on the other hand, to overestimate the "universalism" of Paul.

[25] See J. Geffcken, *Zwei Griechische Apologeten* (Leipzig/Berlin, Teubner, 1907). Further, it is interesting to observe that the Greek apologists were fond of creating diatribal encounter with representative Jews. The most notable instance is Justin's *Dialogue with the Jew Trypho*.

[26] See chapter 1.

is not directed to asserting the superiority of one people or religion over others but to promoting harmony between two different Christian groups in Rome. In this regard, Paul is distanced not only from first-century Jewish apologetics, but also from second-century Christian apologetic traditions.

In Romans 1.18–32, Paul draws substantially from apologetic traditions. Three apologetic motifs are to be found in 1.18–32: (1) natural revelation and knowledge of God (1.19–21); (2) the critique of idolatry (1.21–5); and (3) immorality as the disordering of nature (1.25–32).

Romans 1.19–21: natural revelation

διότι τὸ γνωστὸν τοῦ θεοῦ φανερόν ἐστιν ἐν αὐτοῖς· ὁ θεὸς γὰρ αὐτοῖς ἐφανέρωσεν. τὰ γὰρ ἀόρατα αὐτοῦ ἀπὸ κτίσεως κόσμου τοῖς ποιήμασιν νοούμενα καθορᾶται, ἥ τε ἀΐδιος αὐτοῦ δύναμις καὶ θειότης, εἰς τὸ εἶναι αὐτοὺς ἀναπολογήτους, διότι γνόντες τὸν θεὸν οὐκ ὡς θεὸν ἐδόξασαν ἢ ηὐχαρίστησαν, ἀλλ᾽ ἐματαιώθησαν ἐν τοῖς διαλογισμοῖς αὐτῶν καὶ ἐσκοτίσθη ἡ ἀσύνετος αὐτῶν καρδία.

Hellenistic Jewish apologetics had decisively related monotheism to natural theology (*LetAris* 132; Wis.13.1–9).[27] The argument of Hellenistic Jewish apologetics is that at least a partial knowledge of the invisible God can be had by Gentiles through the visible works of creation. Paul employs this motif in Romans 1.19–21a and even escalates the concession by not distinguishing between degrees of knowledge, for his intent is to charge all humanity as sinners.

The interplay of apocalyptic (1.18) and apologetic (1.19–21) elements is immediately apparent. Paul does not elaborate the details of the final judgment as is common in apocalyptic literature, but rather immediately moves to an explanation of why humankind is "without excuse" and deserving of God's wrath. This explanation is given in 1.19–21 (note διότι); the human suppression of truth[28] warrants the wrath of God for it is done despite the fact that that which is knowable of God (τὸ γνωστὸν τοῦ θεοῦ) is manifest to

---

[27] See Hans Conzelmann, *Heiden–Juden–Christen*, BHTh, 62 (Tübingen, Mohr/Siebeck, 1981), pp. 125–6.
[28] ἀλήθεια is best understood as meaning "that which is" or simply put "reality," i.e. God). See Bultmann, *TDNT* 1 (1964), 243.

them.[29] Thus appeals to the mitigating circumstances of ignorance are denied to humankind.[30] This manifestation of God is made possible through God's act of creation (ἀπὸ κτίσεως κόσμου) and is realized by rational perception (νοούμενα καθορᾶται). It renders humanity *qua* humanity without defence (1.20c, ἀναπολογήτους). Paul is using the language of traditional apologetics not to prove the existence of God, but rather to charge humanity with refusing to praise and thank a God whom they know (1.21a).

E. Norden, who did not fail to note the points of similarity between Romans 1.18–20 and the Areopagus speech attributed to Paul in Acts,[31] has observed the very different conclusion of the two texts.[32] Strikingly, the description of the Gentiles' relation to God is diametrically opposite. In Acts 17.23b the Athenians are described as worshipping an unknown God whereas in Romans Paul states that those knowing God nonetheless refuse to worship God (Rom.1.19–21). In other words Paul has accepted wholeheartedly the assumption of natural theology that God's existence can be known and thus has turned it around to use it as the grounds for condemning idol worship.

The question of whether Paul's discourse in 1.18–31 is to be categorized properly as one of "natural theology" has been much debated in the history of interpretation of this passage. Obviously a definition of the term "natural theology" is a prerequisite for the adjudication of the issue. The term has often been used to identify the position which affirms that God is knowable by human reason.[33] The existence of God can be proved from reflecting upon the world, and this may mean, as it does for the Stoics, that God is fundamentally an entity of the same kind as the world. Natural theology

[29] In 1.19b Paul stresses that this disclosure of God is self-disclosure (ὁ θεὸς γὰρ αὐτοῖς ἐφανέρωσεν) and thereby introduces his theological emphasis into the discourse of natural theology which appears in Romans 1.19a-21.

[30] Note the similarity and dissimilarity with Wis. 13.1–9 where the concession of the possibility of knowing God through the investigation of knowledge becomes the grounds of accusation when it is not realized: Yet again, not even they are to be excused; for if they had the power to know so much that they could investigate the world, how did they fail to find sooner the Lord of these things? (13.8–9). Paul grants the knowledge but condemns the failure to respond appropriately in light of this knowledge (Rom.1.21).

[31] Most especially the doctrine that the unseen God is known from God's visible works of creation. See Eduard Norden, *Agnostos Theos* (Darmstadt, Wissenschaftliche Buchgesellschaft, 1956), p. 28. Cf. Acts 17. 24.

[32] Norden, *Agnostos Theos*, p. 128.

[33] See R. Bultmann "The Problem of 'Natural theology'" in *Faith and Understanding* (London, SCM, 1969), 1.313.

can be distinguished from natural revelation, which presumes that God is made manifest in nature and history. Thus the view of natural revelation is to be contrasted with the perspective which contends that God is manifested only in Christ.[34] Bultmann says that despite the apparent conflict between the advocates of these two views, they both hold a common presupposition, namely that there is a "pre-understanding of God" which makes it possible for them to judge that "God" is manifested in Christ or in nature or history. Bultmann implies that it is possible to reconcile these two positions and sees Paul as doing so. Thus Bultmann grants that Paul articulated a "natural revelation" of God in Romans 1.19–20,[35] but also maintains that the purpose of the revelation of God in nature and history for Paul is that it "constantly refers us to the revelation of the forgiving grace of God in Christ."[36] In this sense it is proper to speak of Paul as espousing natural theology or, if the distinction above is granted, "natural revelation."[37] He may be close to the Wisdom of Solomon wherein three paths to the knowledge of God are proposed: (1) humans receive directly the spirit of Wisdom (Wisdom 7.7; cf. the function of the Holy Spirit in Paul); (2) God can be known through historical events (Wisdom 10–12); and (3) God can be known through the revelation of nature (Wisdom 13).

A further point of continuity between Romans 1.19–20 and apologetic theology should be noted in that Paul expresses this knowledge in the terms of negative theology: τὰ ἀόρατα αὐτοῦ (1.20, his invisible nature); ἀΐδιος (1.20, eternal); ἄφθαρτος θεός (1.23, immortal God).[38] D. W. Palmer has demonstrated how uniformly the second-century Greek Christian apologists used negative theology in opposition to pagan concepts of the gods.[39] One other, often concomitant, characteristic of defining God in negative terms is the avowal that God can only be grasped by the intellectual faculty and not by the senses: ἕνα τὸν ἀγένητον καὶ ἀΐδιον καὶ ἀόρατον καὶ ἀπαθῆ καὶ ἀκατάληπτον καὶ ἀχώρητον, νῷ μόνον καὶ λόγῳ καταλαμβανόμενον (Athenag.: *Suppl.* 10.1). Likewise, Paul in

[34] Bultmann, "The Question of Natural Revelation" in *Essays* (New York, Macmillan, 1955), p. 90.

[35] Bultmann, "Natural Revelation," p. 114.

[36] Ibid., p. 118.

[37] Gaertner, *The Areopagus Speech and Natural Revelation*, trans. Carolyn Hannay King (Uppsala, Almquist & Wiksells, 1955), p. 139.

[38] Cf.Wis. 12.1;18.4; – Wis. 7.26.

[39] D. W. Palmer, "Atheism, Apologetic, and Negative Theology in the Greek Apologists of the Second Century," *VC*, 37 (1983), 252.

Romans 1.20 emphasizes that God's attributes are mentally perceived, νοούμενα. Palmer, who argues correctly that the main
source of the Apologists' negative theology is the contemporary
Middle Platonism, grants that Hellenistic Judaism plays a significant role in mediating this tradition.[40]

Romans 1.23: the critique of idolatry

The evidence of I Thessalonians 1.9 shows that Paul confronted the
problem of idolatry in his missionary efforts and that it was by no
means a merely theoretical concern.[41] Likewise, 1 Corinthians 8.4–7
testifies that the continued attraction of some members of the
Christian community towards pledging allegiance to other gods
demands Paul's attention. The formal critique of idolatry in
Romans 1.23 is ensconced in the section 1.18–27 which abounds
with polemical language against false worship: ἀσέβεια (impiety),
ἀδικία (wickedness), μάταιος (foolish), and ψεῦδος (false).[42] As
Paul believes that human beings, by virtue of their created and
dependent status, realize their own existence in relation to the
transcendent, he considers the failure to worship God to lead them
to an inversion of values such that they exchange "the glory of the
incorruptible God" for images of mortal persons and animals
(1.23).

Geffcken has stated that between the Greek philosophers and the

---

[40] Cf. Palmer, "Atheism," 251, 234. On the role of Philo here, see Erwin R.
Goodenough, *The Theology of Justin Martyr* (Jena, 1923; Amsterdam, Philo Press,
1968), pp. 127–32.

[41] 1 Corinthians 5.10 confirms the prevalence of idol worship in the world with
which Paul interacts. The trend towards monotheism which had taken hold from the
time of Plato was restricted primarily to the cultured classes and by no means
displaced polytheistic beliefs and worship among the masses. Moreover, it should be
remarked that in the early imperial age there was widespread revival in traditional
polytheistic forms of religion. See Adolf Harnack, *The Expansion of Christianity in
the First Three Centuries*, trans. James Moffatt (Freeport, Books For Libraries,1972),
1. 365. For an excellent summary of the shifts in religious thinking and practice
among the Greeks in this as well as earlier periods see Martin P. Nilsson, *A History of
Greek Religion*, trans. F. J. Fielden, 2nd edn (Oxford, Clarendon, 1952), esp. pp.
263–304.

[42] See Gaertner, *Areopagus Speech*, p. 75. In the apologetic critique of idolatry of
Wisdom 13 μάταιοι describes those who by nature are ignorant of God (13.1) and
account cosmic phenomena as gods (13.2). The word ψεῦδος (Romans 1.25) is often
used in the *LXX* to denote idols (cf. Jonah 2.9, Jer. 16.9, Is. 44.20). The terms ἀσέβεια
(from σέβομαι) and ἀδικία are used as a hendiadys and the relation to God is
determinative for the meaning of both terms. See Foerster, "Σέβομαι", *TDNT*,
7 (1971), 187–90.

second-century Christian apologists stand Paul and Philo.[43] It should be noted that whereas Geffcken made this comment specifically referring to the discourse of "natural theology" in Romans 1.20, the critiques of idolatry to be found in such second-century literature also have their most direct parallel in Romans (1.23) as the following form critical analysis demonstrates.

One finds that the critique of Egyptian religion, which had successfully infiltrated the Greco-Roman world, is rendered in the form of a list of various animals which are connected by the repetitive use of καί (and):

Romans 1.23	Justin I.24.1	Athenagoras I.1–2	Theophilus I.10
¹καὶ ἤλλαξαν τὴν δόξαν τοῦ ἀφθάρτου θεοῦ ἐν ὁμοιώματι εἰκόνος φθαρτοῦ ἀνθρώπου	¹ἄλλων ἀλλαχοῦ ²καὶ δένδρα ¹σεβομένων	¹οἱ δὲ αἰγύπτιοι	¹τί μοι λοιπὸν καταλέγειν τὸ πλῆθος ὧν σέβονται ζώων αἰγύπτιοι
²καὶ πετεινῶν καὶ τετραπόδων καὶ ἑρπετῶν	²καὶ ποταμοὺς καὶ μῦς καὶ αἰλούρους καὶ κροκοδείλους καὶ τῶν ἀλόγων ζώων τὰ πολλά	²καὶ αἰλούρους καὶ κροκοδείλους καὶ ὄφεις καὶ ἄσπιδας καὶ κύνας ¹θεοὺς νομίζουσιν	²ἑρπετῶν τε καὶ κτηνῶν καὶ σηρίων καὶ πετεινῶν καὶ ἐνύδρων νηκτῶν ἔτι δὲ καὶ ποδόνιπτρα καὶ ἤχους αἰσχύνης

Athenagoras introduces his list by identifying the Egyptians as worshippers of animals (cf. Wisdom 11) and then names five species of animals each of which is preceded by the repetitive καί used to underscore the concept of the multiplicity of objects that are considered to be divine. Theophilus expresses this concept of multiplicity explicitly in τὸ πλῆθος ζώων (the multitude of animals) and thus is not dependent on polysyndeton to make the point; he alone of the four examples takes the liberty of beginning his list without καί but ἑρπετῶν τε (and reptiles). Justin uses the most general subject "others in other places" to introduce a mixed list which includes trees, rivers and then three kinds of animals; he concludes with the technical term for all animals (ἄλογον ζῷον).[44] Justin emphasizes the concept of plurality by closing his list with the words τὰ πολλά, and καί is used six times preceding each member of the

---

[43] Geffcken, *Apologeten*, p. 34.
[44] Cf. Wisdom 11.15 ἀλόγων ζώων. The Stoics distinguished sharply between non-rational animals and humans (*Arnim* 2.725–6).

list. In Romans 1.23 Paul also employs the repetitive καί preceding
each of the three genera of animals mentioned. He appears,
however, in verse 23 to have elided together a critique of idols
εἰκόνος φθαρτοῦ ἀνθρώπου (the image of a mortal human being)[45]
with the traditional critique of animal worship. In any case, Paul
introduces this with language very close to Psalm 105.20 (καὶ ἠλλά-
ξαντο τὴν δόξαν αὐτῶν ἐν ὁμοιώματι), but the provenance of
Psalm 105.19 f, which is restricted to criticism of the golden calf, is
too narrow for Paul's purposes. We have here a dramatic instance of
how Paul joins together Old Testament and Hellenistic traditions in
accord with his intention to wield the sword of criticism in all
directions.

In Romans 1, Paul provides the negative counterpart to the
affirmation of the One God in the critique of polytheism. As has
been stated (see excursus), the apologetic affirmation of the One
God was commonly accompanied by a critique of pagan religion.[46]
In the two other uses of the "One God" topos in Paul's letters, the
context explicitly makes reference to multiple deities. In 1 Corinthians 8.4 the One God is contrasted to the idols (1 Cor. 8.4a) and
"those called gods" (1 Cor. 8.5). In Galatians a comparable contrast
is to be found between the many "angels" (Gal. 3.19) and the One
God (Gal. 3.20). In the critique of the many gods and idolatry in
Romans 1, Paul emphasizes the social implications of the failure to
worship the One God and of the recourse to surrogate gods: the
degradation of human life and relationships. This is indeed consonant with the special emphasis on the human and social implications of the "One God" topos in Romans 3.29–30. Only the One
God who acts in Christ can restore the proper God–human and
social relations which have been destroyed in Adam.[47]

Romans 1.25–6: immorality as the disordering of nature

The linkage between idol worship and immorality is firmly established in Jewish Hellenistic apologetics (cf. e.g. Wis. 14.12–31).

[45] Most commentators, following Jervell, seem to understand ὁμοίωμα εἰκόνος as
pleonastic, and both terms mean image as with 1.26f. κατ᾽ εἰκόνα καὶ κατ᾽ ὁμοίωσιν.
Cf. Jacob Jervell, *Imago dei: Gen 1:26f. in Spatjudentum, in der Gnosis und in der
paulinschen Briefen* (Göttingen, Vandenhoeck & Ruprecht, 1960), pp. 319–22.
[46] Schrenk in "Der Römerbrief als Missionsdokument", 47, 64, pointed to the
monotheistic doxology which ends Romans 11 (cf. 11.33–6) as significant for understanding both 1.18 ff and 3.29–30.
[47] In Romans 5, the implications for the Many of the One Adam and the One
Christ are explicitly contrasted.

Philo avers that "atheism is the cause of all iniquities" (*Decal.* 91).[48] In Romans 1, Paul understands homoeroticism as an exchange of proper natural relations which results from the exchange of the true God for idols:[49]

> 1.25a οἵτινες μετήλλαξαν τὴν ἀλήθειαν τοῦ θεοῦ ἐν τῷ ψεύδει καὶ ἐσεβάσθησαν καὶ ἐλάτρευσαν τῇ κτίσει παρὰ τὸν κτίσαντα 1.26b αἵ τε γὰρ θήλειαι αὐτῶν μετήλλαξαν (2)τὴν φυσικὴν χρῆσιν εἰς τὴν παρὰ φύσιν

Paul explicitly parallels the exchange of God for idols with the exchange of proper sex relations.[50] His creation theology entails an understanding of a natural order which is rational. The Stoic view of nature, which was so readily utilized in Jewish apologetics, is operative here and both the adverbial παρὰ φύσιν and the adjectival φυσικὴ χρῆσις (Rom. 1.26–7) express the idea that homoeroticism is a violation of nature.[51] The repetition of the clause "God handed them over" (1.24, 26, 28b) after each of the three assertions of idolatry underscores Paul's startling view that immorality is to be construed as punishment for idolatry. He describes divine and human activity in a consistently relational mode which has its starting point in the divine act of creation and allows for the human response of gratitude or ingratitude, which in turn provokes the punishment of immorality. This is not the Stoic view which would identify all reality including God as instances of a single principle but a relational "ontology" which understands existence as fundamentally interdependent.

In accord with this rationalistic understanding of ethics is Paul's use of the root word γιγνώσκω (to know) in Romans 1.[52] The expression "ἐπίγνωσις ἀληθείας" in the Pastoral epistles (1 Tim. 2.4; 4.3; 2 Tim. 2.25; 3.7; Titus 1.1) is used in contrast to the "ἐπίγνωσις μύθων" of the opponents and distinguishes Christian knowledge of truth as including right living, in agreement with

[48] See Conzelmann, *Heiden,* p. 178.

[49] See Bernadette Brooten, "Paul's Views on the Nature of Women and Female Homoeroticism," in Clarissa Atkinson, *Immaculate and Powerful,* pp. 63, 71–81.

[50] Note the use of ἀλλάσσω in Romans 1.23 also referring to the transfer from worship of the incorruptible God to that of images and animals.

[51] See Helmut Koester, "φύσις," *TDNT,* 9 (1974), p. 273.

[52] See Martin Dibelius, "ἐπίγνωσις ἀληθείας," in *Botschaft und Geschichte* (Tübingen,Mohr/Siebeck, 1956), pp. 1–13. Dibelius points to parallels between Epict. and Paul.

Stoicism. In Romans 1.28, the refusal τὸν θεὸν ἔχειν ἐν ἐπιγνώσει (did not acknowledge God) leads ποιεῖν τὰ μὴ καθήκοντα (to do things not proper) which in turn introduces the long list of vices of 1.29–31.

Finally, as to the catalogue of vices in 1.29–31, its provenance is generally conceded to be that of Hellenistic philosophy.[53] The entire list refers back to the αὐτούς of 1.28 and is directly introduced by the ethico-philosophical term τὰ μὴ καθήκοντα (improper conduct).[54] The Stoics frequently employed such catalogues of vices (cf. *Diog. L.* 7.110–114; Cicero,*Tusc.* 4.5–10.24); the examples from Jewish Hellenistic literature (Wis. 14.23–30; 4 Macc. 1.20–27; Philo[55]) also evince Stoic influence. It should be noted that the emphasis on vices and virtues in Jewish apologetic literature, especially Philo, reinforced the reinterpretation of the Law that consciously underplayed the cultic aspect of the Law and stressed its ethical import. The catalogues of vices and virtues assisted in the apologetic task of rendering the Law comprehensible and relevant to both Jews and Gentiles of the Hellenistic world.

In employing the motifs and genre of Jewish apologetics in Romans 1 (as well as Romans 2–4), Paul modifies traditions which at times may be irrelevant to or incompatible with his own theological intentions. In so doing he may come dangerously close to contradicting his theological interests as he expresses them elsewhere. There is no question that the insight that one not only uses language and traditions, but is used by them, applies also to Paul.

Apologetic motifs in Romans 2

In Romans 2, Paul employs three apologetic motifs with characteristic modifications: (1) the attribution to the Gentiles of an innate or natural understanding of the Law (2.12–15); (2) the stereotyping critique of other religions/nations (2.17–24) ; and (3) the spiritualizing reinterpretation of the meaning of circumcision (2.25–9).

---

[53] Lietzmann, pp. 35–6 and appendix; Barrett, p. 40; Käsemann hesitating but finally admitting as to the material center, "In the present passage it probably lies closer to popular philosophy," p. 50. Similar lists are to be found in Paul at 13.13; 1 Cor. 5.10–11; 2 Cor 12.20–1; Gal. 5.19–21.

[54] The debate over this term is restricted to whether it is a technical term of Stoicism – Barrett; Cranfield, or derives from the sphere of popular philosophy – Käsemann.

[55] For the plethora of citations from Philo cf. Lietzmann, p. 36.

Romans 2.12–15: innate knowledge of the Law

In addition to its granting a partial knowledge of God to the Gentiles,[56] Jewish apologetics also allowed to the Gentiles a partial knowledge of the Law. Paul utilizes this tradition in his attempt to demonstrate that both Gentiles and Jews are equally culpable before God in Romans 2.12–15. The preceding section (2.1–11) speaks of the judgment of God. Legal terminology abounds here (κρίνω, 2.1, 3; τὸ κρῖμα, 2.2; δικαιοκρισία, 2.6). The emphasis in 2.1–11 is not on the details of the final judgment, as is typical in apocalyptic literature, but rather on issues of the grounds and equity of the judgment. The specific jurisprudential concerns discussed in 2.1–11 indicate the influence of the dominant standards of the Roman legal system and are also reflected in Jewish apologetic presentations of the Mosaic legislation.[57] Paul insists that judgment is executed on the basis of objective or demonstrable wrongdoing (note that the phrase τὰ τοιαῦτα πράσσοντες occurs here in three consecutive verses – 1.32; 2.2,3).[58] The expression κατὰ ἀλήθειαν in 2.2 means in accordance with objective facts.[59] Secondly, Paul's concern to demonstrate that the principle of *talio* (2.5–6) applies equally to Gentiles and Jews[60] (2.9–11) is in accord with the universalizing tendency of Imperial jurisprudence.[61]

---

[56] See above on Romans 1.

[57] See e.g Josephus *Ap.* 2.151–221. It should be noted that the presentation of the Law with emphasis on rewards and punishments is an apologetic development. See Gutbrod, "νόμος", *TDNT*, 4 (1967), 1049.

[58] We know that Roman jurisprudence reflected on the issue of whether mere identification as a member of a group (Christian) was sufficient grounds for conviction. That there was need of evidence of criminal behavior connected with the name is made clear in Pliny's letter to Trajan. Trajan responds that anonymous accusations should not be admitted. Further, Hadrian – Eusebius *Hist. Eccl.* 4.9.1–3 instructed that only accusations against Christians be considered that could be brought in a public trial and, most pertinent to the concern here, that Christians should be punished only when they had done something illegal: εἴ τις οὖν κατηγορεῖ καὶ δείκνυσίν τι παρὰ τοὺς νόμους πράσσοντας, οὗτος ὅριζε κατὰ τὴν δύναμιν τοῦ ἁμαρτήματος.

[59] Bultmann, "ἀλήθεια", *TDNT*, 1(1964), 243.

[60] Jouette Bassler, "Divine Impartiality in Paul's Letter to the Romans,", *NovT* 26 (1984), 43–58.

[61] Gaius defines the *jus gentium* as that part of the law which applied to both "ourselves" and foreigners (Gai. 4.37). Gaius states that civil law – *jus civile* is extended to foreigners by the "fiction" that the foreigner is a citizen (cf. also discussion below, Rom. 2.25–9). Citizenship had been formally extended to the whole of Italy before the end of the Republic and with the Principate began the policy of extending it gradually also to the provinces ; H. F. Jolowicz, *Historical Introduction to the Study of Roman Law* (Cambridge, University Press, 1952), p. 356. The concern

As K. Grobel has observed, the phrase: Ἰουδαίου τε πρῶτον καὶ Ἕλληνος disrupts the chiastic pattern of the traditional formula in 2.7–10 and thus reveals Paul's special theological concerns.[62] The repetition of this phrase Ἰουδαίου τε πρῶτον καὶ Ἕλληνος at the end of verses 9 and 10 underscores both the universality and equality of God's judgment. The denial that there is προσωποληµ-ψία (partiality) before God reiterates the central concept of this section, namely that God is impartial and judges all persons without regard to such natural circumstances as national and ethnic origins.[63]

In accord with this universalizing tendency,[64] Paul employs two interrelated Jewish apologetic concepts of the Law. Thus in 2.14, he states that the Gentiles, who not having the revealed Law, do by nature the Law[65] and further, that in so doing the Law they: ἑαυτοῖς εἰσιν νόµος (they themselves are Law).[66] Perhaps, the central contribution of Philo's thought is to have united the revealed and natural law by stressing the implications that the One God is

of Augustus to be viewed as the benefactor to all peoples within his empire is testified to by the *Res Gestae*, 3. 16.

[62] "A chiastic Retribution Formula in Romans 2," *Zeit und Geschichte: Dankesgabe an Rudolf Bultmann zum 80 Geburtstag*, ed. E Dinkler (Tübingen, J. C. B. Mohr, 1964) pp. 255–61. vv. 7–10 abba but this phrase appears in both vv. 9 and 10.

[63] Note that Luke puts into the mouth of Peter at Acts 10.34b–35 this universalist assertion that God shows no partiality [οὐκ ἔστιν προσωπολήµπτης ὁ θεός] but accepts those in every nation [ἐν παντὶ ἔθνει] fearing God and doing righteousness [ἐργαζόµενος δικαιοσύνην]. Thus we find the typical Lukan conversion of Pauline terminology and meaning while yet maintaining substantial parallelism on both levels. See also Philo, *Praem. Poen.*, 152.

[64] See chapter 3 for more on the apologetic claim of universality.

[65] The key exegetical issue in 2.14 turns on whether one takes φύσις with that which precedes (ἔχοντα) or follows (ποιῶσιν) it. In the former case the sense would be "by birth" and Cranfield (*Romans* 1.155–6) who prefers this option concludes that the reference is to Gentile Christians. Cranfield can point to the use of φύσις in Galatians 2.15 in support of this reading but he also admits that Paul's use of this word elsewhere is not decisive in this matter – p. 157 n. 2. Furthermore, it is highly questionable whether Gentile Christians would be ignorant of the OT. On the construal of this word in Romans 2.14, Käsemann contradicts himself in the space of one page (cf. *Romans*, p. 63), φύσις should be understood as referring forward in light of the immediate context of 14b and 15 and as such it circumscribes the provenance of νόµος. As Koester puts it, "The close relation between φύσις and νόµος points specifically to the context of Hellenistic–Jewish apologetic in which, as in Philo, there could be performance of the law of Moses by nature and the identity of the moral law with the revealed law of the Old Testament could be maintained" (φύσις, *TDNT*, 9,274).

[66] Plato distinguished between the divine law (usually identified with the law of the polis) and the natural law (φύσις). At the death of Socrates, Plato posits a transition of the norm and law from state institutions to the psyche of Socrates. See Kleinknecht, "νόµος," *TDNT*, 4 (1967), 1031.

both the giver of the Law and the Creator of nature. In Philo, Hellenistic apologetic theology also moves to affirm the concept of νόμος ἐμψυχός:

> "this man (i.e. Abraham) did the divine law and the divine commands." He did them, not taught by written words, but unwritten nature (ἀγράφῳ τῇ φύσει) gave him the zeal to follow where wholesome and untainted impulse led him. And when they have God's promises before them what should men do but trust in them most firmly? Such was the life of the first, the founder of the nation, one who obeyed the law, some will say, but rather, as our discourse has shown, himself a law (νόμος αὐτὸς ὤν) and an unwritten statute.[67]

In continuity with this interiorization of the Law is the use of the thoroughly Greek concept of conscience in Romans 2.15.[68] Paul achieves here a radical reinterpretation of the mythological judgment scene as he emphasizes the anthropological dimensions of conscience, and as he depicts the scene each individual is now made his or her own prosecutor or advocate (2.15). God still is judge for God determines the individual conscience, but the judgment is simply the moment of exposing the individual's own self-judgment. In Jewish apocalyptic literature one simply does not find this anthropological dimension in the depiction of the final judgment scenes. In Paul a new synthesis is achieved wherein on the one hand the Hellenistic philosophical concepts of conscience and self-judgment and on the other the eschatological role of God the Judge are integrated within the same context. The theocentric characterization of the judgment scene is maintained as all stand παρὰ θεῷ (2.13) and yet the judgment rendered is in agreement with or mirrors the self-judgment of the individual on trial. This mode of reinterpretation, which is so characteristic of Hellenistic Jewish apologetic, is also evident in Paul's discussion of circumcision at the end of Romans 2.

Romans 2.17–24 : Paul and the critique of other religions/nations

A characteristic feature of Jewish Hellenistic as well as Christian apologetic literature is the sweeping ethnological assertions about

---

[67] See *Vit. Mos.* 1.162; *Abr.* 276.
[68] C. A. Pierce has shown that its derivation for Paul is not Stoicism but popular philosophy. *Conscience in the N.T.* (Chicago, Allenson, 1955), pp. 13–20. Margaret

peoples and religions.[69] Most common in apologetic literature is the negative assessment of the character of a given ethnic group. Thus Philo without hesitation remarks that "jealousy is part of the Egyptian nature" (*Flacc.* 29) or at the local level: "The Alexandrians are adept at flattery and imposture and hypocrisy" (*Leg. Gai.* 164). Josephus depicts the Greeks as "conceited about their history" (*Ap.*1.15) and as "our jealous enemies" (*Ap.* 1.72). Josephus includes among the "evil habits" of the Egyptians the tendency to "chronic sedition" (*Ap.* 2.69–70). The stupidity (*Ap.*2.86.) and misanthropy (*Ap.* 2.66) of Egyptian animal worship is also declared by Josephus. Particularly relevant to Romans 2.17–24 is the accusation levied against several ethnic groups by Josephus that nations/ peoples violate their own laws (he mentions here the Λακεδαιμό-νιοι, Ἠλεῖοι, θηβαῖοι, Ἕλλενες; cf. *Ap.* 2.273–6).[70] To be sure, Josephus is responding to the equally slanderous ethnic and religious accusations against Jews by Greeks and Egyptians, and Philo was attempting to halt the political injustice against Alexandrian Jews which was instigated by an anti-Jewish faction in that city, but the fact is that ethnic/religious polemics were engaged in by all parties.[71] Christian apologists followed this tradition of one-upmanship as is readily seen in the earliest extant apology. Aristides, in fact, used ethnological classifications to structure his work and after mentioning the five races of humankind – Chaldeans, Greeks, Egyptians, as well as Jews and Christians, he proceeds to describe in serial fashion the religious beliefs and practices of each

Thrall has suggested that Paul readily adopted the concept of conscience with respect to the Gentiles on the basis of a perceived functional equivalency with the Law for Jews, i.e. as proving all people are guilty (3.19; 2 Cor. 3.9). See Margaret E. Thrall, "The Pauline Use of συνείδησις," *NTS*, 14 (1967–8),118–25.

[69]Note that in apologetic literature an ethnic group is often identified as holding without exception particular religious beliefs and practices. A prime example of this tendency is the Apology of Aristides. The relevance of this apologetic motif throughout Romans 1–4 and particularly 1.18–32 is apparent. Further, note that Käsemann builds his case for apocalyptic influence in Romans 2.17–29 on the tendency to take the exception as representative of the community (*Romans*, p. 69) – a tendency which, I demonstrate here, is characteristic of apologetic literature. Morover, Käsemann's acknowledgment that there are strong Stoic influences in Romans 2.17–29 militates against his own thesis.

[70] Of course, this critique is central to the positive propaganda aim of Josephus in this work – to uphold the superiority of the Mosaic legislation over all other available legal systems.

[71] For further information on anti-semitic literature and attitudes in the ancient world see John Gager, *The Origins of Anti-Semitism* (New York/Oxford, Oxford University, 1985).

people. All except the Christian are declared to have gone astray (πλάνῶμαι) to varying degrees. The Greeks are more in error than the Chaldeans as the former have greater knowledge but nevertheless commit the double folly of making their gods in the image of immoral human beings and then imitating these same gods (9.8–9). The Egyptians are depicted as the most evil and ignorant of all peoples (12.1).[72] Both these accusations are inextricably bound to the propaganda against animal worship with which the Egyptians are identified (12.1). Aristides lauds Jews both for their monotheistic belief (14.2) and their humanitarian practices towards the needy (14.3). The Jews are critiqued, however, for their observance of ritual laws which manifest an allegiance, in Aristides' view, to one other than God (14.4). Finally, Aristides presents the Christians as "nearer to the truth and to exact knowledge than the rest of the peoples" (15.3) and their benevolence extends even to enemies (15.5).

Romans 2.17–24 speaks to the Jew who is described as knowing the Law, but not abiding by it.[73] Paul apostrophizes the typical Jew as is indicated by the first explicit reference in 2.17 (σὺ Ἰουδαῖος).[74] It is important to note that he does not begin in 2.17–20 by rendering a negative evaluation of Judaism but rather simply describes the self-understanding of the Jewish missionary.[75] In this regard the often quoted parallel of Matthew 15.14: τυφλοί εἰσιν ὁδηγοί should not be, as is now commonplace, seen as similar to Romans 2.19: ὁδηγὸν εἶναι τυφλῶν, but rather as contrasted to the

[72] This estimation follows that of the Jewish apologetic tradition – Wisdom of Solomon, Josephus.
[73] It should be remarked at the outset that Romans 2.17–24 does not constitute a new section but rather continues the exemplification of the principle of impartiality which Paul asserts characterizes God's judgment (cf. 2.11–13). Romans 2.14–15 has just dealt with the Gentiles who are without the revelation of the Law but who fulfill its moral requirements.
[74] The influence of the diatribe is most discernible here; Bultmann, *Stil*, p. 70. See also Cranfield, *Romans*, vol. 1, pp. 137–8.
[75] Missionary terms abound in Romans 2.18–21: κατηχούμενος (2.18); ὁδηγός (2.19); παιδευτής (2.20); διδάσκαλος (2.20); διδάσκω (2.21); κηρύσσω (2.21). On the relation between this passage and Jewish missionary literature Hans Lietzmann (105) has said: "19f machen den Eindruck, als zitiere Pls die Worte einer judischen für Proselyten berechneten Schrift." cf. also Bornkamm, "Paulinische Anakoluthe im Romerbrief" in *Das Ende des Gesetzes*, p. 77. It is, in my view, not unlikely that Paul hopes that Jewish Christians in his audience will also be brought to self-reflection by the criticism in 2.17–24.

latter.[76] Paul does reproach missionary Judaism on the grounds of hypocrisy (2.21–2) as they do the very things which they admonish others to resist. The anacoluthic style of Romans 2.17–24 reinforces the substantive issue of the discrepancy between word and deed that Paul now most directly expresses in 2.21–2.[77] In 2.23 he summarizes the argument of 2.17–22: ὃς ἐν νόμῳ καυχᾶσαι, διὰ τῆς παραβάσεως τοῦ νόμου, and concludes this section by linking this charge of hypocrisy with the accusation of blasphemy : τὸν θεὸν ἀτιμάζεις. Paul, then, quotes Isaiah 52.5 to confirm the point (cf. Rom. 2.24). Note that the quotation of Scripture is so appropriate to the context that Paul simply adds it directly to the previous verse adding only γάρ and reserves the quotation formula καθὼς γέγραπται until the very end of the verse. Jews especially dishonour God, for by their hypocrisy in teaching the Law which they themselves do not fulfill, they cause the Gentiles to blaspheme the Giver of the Law, that is, God.

Romans 2.25–9: the spiritualizing reinterpretation of circumcision

Jewish apologetics reinterpreted circumcision so as to render it meaningful to Hellenized Jews and Gentiles. Philo's decision to begin his treatise *De Specialibus Legibus* with a defense of circumcision is one indicator of the significance which he invested in this task. Philo asserts that there are practical/rational benefits from circumcision that enhance human life. The rationales for circumcision that he provides are intricately bound up with the wider apologetic reinterpretation of Judaism that underplays the offensive (to Hellenized Jews as well as Gentiles), literalistic version of Judaism. Philo disclaims any uniqueness for Jewish circumcision and avers that it is practiced by "many other nations, particularly by the Egyptians" (*Spec. Leg.* 1.2). He lists four reasons which the ancients gave for its adoption (*Spec. Leg.* 1.3): (1) the preventative medical rationale that it prevents anthrax as "those who retain the foreskin are more susceptible" (*Spec. Leg.* 1.4); (2) the hygienic

---

[76] The expression φῶς τῶν ἐν σκότει in 2.19 should be compared with Wisdom chaps 17–18 wherein light is used of both Israel and the Torah while darkness is associated with the Egyptians (see esp. 18.3–4).

[77] "Der Stil des ganzen Abschnittes 2.17–24 entspricht so genau der Sache, um die es Paulus geht. Die Diskrepanz von Anspruch und Leistung spiegelt sich in der Inkongruenz der ganzen Satzkonstruktion." Bornkamm, "Paulinische Anakoluthe," 78; cf. also 76.

argument that it "promotes the cleanliness of the whole body" (*Spec. Leg.* 1.5); (3) the sacralizing of the reproductive process (*Spec. Leg.* 16); and (4) the argument which Philo describes as the most cogent: that circumcision increases fertility and "therefore the circumcized nations appear to be the most prolific and populace" (*Spec. Leg.* 1. 7). More important to Philo than the pragmatic rationales is the ethical/spiritual interpretation of circumcision. Philo suggests that circumcision symbolizes "the excision of excessive and superfluous pleasure," and also the banishing "from the soul of the grievous malady of conceit" (*Spec. Leg.* 1.8–10). This ethical/spiritual interpretation of circumcision was also championed by some Jews (the "philosophical spiritualists") who were willing to forgo the practice of circumcision as well as observance of all other ritual laws.[78] Philo differs with these radical interpreters of circumcision except in the case of proselytes: ὅτι προσήλυτός ἐστιν, οὐκ ὁ περιτμηθεὶς τὴν ἀκροβυστίαν ἀλλ᾽ ὁ τὰς ἡδονὰς καὶ τὰς ἐπιθυμίας καὶ τὰ ἄλλα πάθη τῆς ψυχῆς.[79] In this last context Philo blurs the distinctions between the literal meanings of περιτομή (circumcision) and ἀκροβυστία (uncircumcision) in his effort to allow that the proselyte need only "circumcise his desires not his uncircumcision".

In accord with Jewish apologetics, Paul asserts in Romans 2.25–9 that the status of being physically circumcised has no decisive spiritual import and that the true meaning of circumcision is ethical/spiritual. Just as mere knowledge or possession (or even less the preaching to others) of the Law does not exempt the Jew from the decisive requirement of "doing the law" (2.17–24) neither will circumcision allow the circumvention of this norm.[80] If the Gentile

---

[78] See Philo, *Migr. Abr.* 92: "It is true that receiving circumcision does indeed portray the excision of pleasure and all passions, and the putting away of the impious conceit, under which the mind supposed that it was capable of begetting by its own power: but let us not on this account repeal the law laid down for circumcising." On the relationship between Philo and Galatians 5, see Peder Borgen, *Paul Preaches Circumcision and Pleases Men*, Relieff 8 (Dragvoll, University of Trondheim, 1983), pp. 15–57.

[79] *Quaest.* in Exodus 2.2, Philo continues: "For in Egypt the Hebrew nation was not circumcised but being mistreated with all kinds of mistreatment by the inhabitants in their hatred of strangers, it lived with them in self-restraint and endurance, not by necessity but rather of its own free choice, because it took refuge in God the Savior, Who sent his beneficient power and delivered from their hopeless situation those who made supplication."

[80] See Galatians 5.11–24 where Paul denies that he teaches circumcision (11) and immediately proceeds to explain the meaning of the Law in terms of the golden rule (14) and then provides a vice list (19–21).

practices the Law[81] then his status will be estimated as equal in value to that of the circumcised (2.26).[82] Paul is effectively undermining the language which tribalizes ethnic and religious groups and establishes special privileges. At the same time, it should be noted that he does not indulge in a wishful thinking that would ignore the real ethnic and religious divisions which define the human condition. Indeed, Paul in Romans 9–11 and also 14–15 expresses the deepest concern over the relation between Jews and Christians and the intra-Christian problem between Jews and Gentiles. He encourages not simply tolerance but love of the other (cf. Rom.15.1–2). Moreover, although Paul distinguishes between macro and micro levels of discourse, at both levels he exempts neither any individual nor any social or religious group from criticism (cf. Rom. 11 where Paul indicts the arrogance of Gentile Christians).

To be sure, this is the intended effect of the repeated rhetorical equating of the seeming opposites as ἡ περιτομή σου ἀκροβυστία γέγονεν (2.25) and ἡ ἀκροβυστία αὐτοῦ εἰς περιτομὴν λογισθήσεται (2.26). In 2.27 Paul strikes a very hard blow against any presumption of superiority on the basis of religious or ethnic affiliation, for here the Gentile who fulfills the Law becomes the standard of judgment against the circumcised who transgresses the Law. Paul questions the very presupposition by which one is called a Jew or Gentile as well as the segregating terminology of circumcision and uncircumcision.[83] The unexamined and seemingly self-evidently true human conventions of social and religious distinctions (cf. 2.28–9: ἐν τῷ φανερῷ ... ἐν τῷ κρυπτῷ)[84] are questioned at the most fundamental level as he asserts that God recognizes none of these human distinctions.[85] The contrast between appearance and reality which Paul draws here has its closest parallels in Stoicism.[86] Epicte-

[81] For the use of the word φυλάσσω with this meaning see Diognetus 1.

[82] The expression λογίζομαι carries the meaning of estimating one thing (the subject of the verb) as equivalent in value to a second (the object of the preposition); cf. Bauer, p. 476.

[83] In Romans 3.29–30, Paul unmistakably uses the terms περιτομή and ἀκροβυστία as synonyms for Jews and Gentiles respectively. See also Galatians 2.7–8.

[84] See A. Fridrichsen, "Der wahre Jude und sein Lob, Rom. 2.28f," *Symbolae Arctoae* 1 (1927), 39–49. See also Nils A. Dahl, *Studies in Paul*, p. 190.

[85] Paul never uses the term "Christian" but if he had he undoubtedly would have been equally intent on opposing its tribalizing effects. In the entire New Testament the word Χριστιανός is found only three times – twice in Acts (11.26, 26.28) and once in I Pe. 4.16.

[86] See parallels with Epictetus *Discourses* 2.19.19 ff; 3.7.17 which inquire about the essence of the true Stoic.

tus asked the question of the true Stoic and distinguished between the appearance, which depends on the evaluation of spectators and the essential value of the individual which is determined by the degree to which one is in harmony with God and the all.[87] The true Jew may be a Gentile without demonstrable signs either γράμμα[88] (written law) or περιτομή, but who has a radically transformed orientation of heart and mind such that she/he is satisfied with ἔπαινος οὐκ ἐξ ἀνθρώπων ἀλλ᾽ ἐκ τοῦ θεοῦ (2.29).[89]

In conclusion, Romans 2 exhibits several points of similarity with critiques of other religions/races by Jewish apologetics and especially its spiritualizing interpretations of the Law and circumcision. Paul's theological emphasis, however, is directed against precisely the assertion of superiority that normally crowns apologetic argumentation. Likewise, in utilizing the apologetic reinterpretation of circumcision, Paul ˙obviously does not intend to make it more acceptable or meaningful to his contemporaries but rather intends to put forth a very different standard of salvation, namely, the act of God in Christ. In this last concern, Paul is required to pursue the line of the earliest Christian apologetics[90] in an attempt to demonstrate the continuity between the gospel and Scripture in Romans 3 and 4.

Apologetic motifs in Romans 3

In addition to the "One God" topos, three apologetic modes of argumentation dominate in Romans 3: (1) the answering of three specific objections[91] to Paul's gospel (3.1–8): (a) that the denial of presumed special privileges to the Jews makes God untrustworthy and untruthful (vv. 1–4), (b) that God is made an unjust Judge (vv. 5–6), and (c) that Paul preaches libertinism (vv. 7–9); (2) the use of Scripture to prove a point of theology (3.9–21,31); and (3) the use of the Hellenisitic Jewish martyrological tradition (3.24–6).

Although the common understanding of the primary purpose of apologetic literature as that of defending the beliefs and practices of

[87] Fridrichsen, pp. 44–5.
[88] See Schrenk, *TDNT*, 1 (1964), 765.
[89] The Stoic fought the desire for the ἔπαινος of onlookers; Fridrichsen, pp. 46–9.
[90] See chapter 1 on this motif.
[91] Note that the number of objections to be found in Romans 3.1–8 is much disputed: Käsemann counts only two objections (*Romans*, p. 78); Bornkamm three ("Theologie als 'Teufelkunst'" in *Geschichte und Glaube* 2.143–4); and Stowers six (*Diatribe*, p. 120).

a given community against objections which arise from various quarters has already been questioned in this study, it should not be denied that a strong secondary characteristic of apologetic writings is to counter criticism and accusations from hostile and/or misinformed sources. Philo and Josephus engaged in the task of refuting perceived erroneous views with respect to Jewish beliefs which were propagated by Gentiles. Likewise, Christian apologists responded to political, cultural, as well as ethical/theological objections which were directed against their communities. A pronounced characteristic of Christian apologetics of the first two centuries is its attention to objections from Judaism wherein the Scripture became the common ground of appeal. New Testament authors as well as second-century Christian apologists appealed to the Scripture to confirm the gospel.

While the scholarship on apologetic literature often gives high profile to the response to objections, it has also tended to overlook the prominent role of Scripture in these writings. This inappropriate distribution of interest is abetted by the generic misconception that the primary purpose of such works is to defend against accusations and halt state persecution. This defensive aspect of apologetic literature is subordinate to its central aim to convince the outsider of the truth of the message which is proclaimed and/or to strengthen the beliefs of the insider.[92] Only in this light does the performance of a Justin, who engaged in Scripture exegesis for 134 chapters in his *Dialogue with Trypho* (as contrasted to the eight chapters devoted to philosophy) and even more strikingly engaged in the same exegetical labors for thirteen consecutive chapters in his first Apology ostensibly addressed to the Roman emperor, become comprehensible. The use of Scripture is characteristic of Christian apologetic traditions both in the New Testament and in the non-canonical literature.[93] Paul in Romans has quoted Scripture a roughly equal number of times to that of all his other letters combined.

[92] For an interesting discussion of the question of whether apologetic literature is directed to the outsider or to the members of the community from which the literature emerges, see V. Tcherikover, "Jewish Apologetic Literature Reconsidered," in *Symbolae R. Taubenschlag Dedicatae*, 3 (1957).

[93] See Lindars, *Apologetic*, also Halvor Moxnes, *Theology In Conflict*, NovTSup 53 (Leiden, Brill, 1980), pp. 57–77.

Romans 3.1–4: God is not untrustworthy

Following inexorably upon the denial of special privileges and protection to Jews before God's judgment in Romans 2, the objection arises to Paul's preaching that it implies that God's word and even God are untrustworthy and untrue (3.1–4).[94] Accordingly, Paul underscores God's fidelity; God's act of giving τὰ λόγια to the Jews is expressed by the verb πιστεύω (3.2) in order to communicate the sense that the action is per se an expression of God's loyalty to his people.[95] There are three plausible meanings in this context for the word τὰ λόγια (τοῦ θεοῦ) : (1) promises and in particular God's promises to Abraham (cf. 9.6,9);[96] (2) Scripture and some would include here also the gospel;[97] and (3) oracles of God.[98] With all three options, it is clear that the apologetic concern in this passage is with the correspondence between the revealed words of God and the preaching of Paul. This motif is programmatic for much of Justin Martyr's writings and marks its protreptic character. In Romans 3.3 God's loyalty is contrasted with the disloyalty of humankind: τὴν πίστιν τοῦ θεοῦ ... ἡ ἀπιστία αὐτῶν.[99] The logic of the objection against Paul is that by his assertion of the Jews' disloyalty a corres-

[94] See Richard Hays, "Psalms 143 and the Logic of Romans 3," *JBL*, 99 (1980), 109.

[95] In Galatians 2.7 and 1 Thessalonians 2.4 the object of the verb πιστεύω is τὸ εὐαγγέλιον.

[96] S. K. Williams has suggested that Paul is referring specifically to the promises to Abraham when he uses the expression τὰ λόγια τοῦ θεοῦ in 3.2. In Romans 9.6 and 9 the term ὁ λόγος refers to God's promise to Israel: ἐπαγγελίας γὰρ ὁ λόγος οὗτος. See Williams, "The 'Righteousness of God' in Romans," *JBL*, 99 (1980), 266–8. Yet Paul does not use the word ἐπαγγελία here which elsewhere he has shown little reluctance to do when he wishes to refer to the Abrahamic promise, as for example in Romans 4.13 and 20.

[97] τὰ λόγια τοῦ θεοῦ in Hellenistic Judaism means "God's revelation in Scripture." See J. W. Doeve, "Some Notes with Reference to τὰ λόγια τοῦ θεοῦ in Romans 3:2," in *Studia Paulina*, pp. 111–23. Kuss (p. 100), Barth and Cranfield (p. 179) believe that the expression τὰ λόγια τοῦ θεοῦ should be taken in its widest sense to include the gospel. This seems to me less likely; Paul's referent here, however, is the Scripture inclusive of the Prophets and Writings as well as Pentateuch and thus of the promise to Abraham. Indeed, the immediate context in Romans 3 collocates numerous scriptural passages from all three sections, although most frequently from the Psalms.

[98] Plutarch uses the word τὰ λόγια to refer to words from the *Sibylline Oracles* in *Fab. Max.* 4.4: καὶ λέγεται συνδραμεῖν ἔνια τῶν ἀποκειμένων ἐν αὐταῖς λογίων πρὸς τὰς τύχας καὶ τὰς πράξεις εκείνας. Note the interest in the correspondence between word and event.

[99] In Romans 11.20 the noun ἀπιστία is ascribed to the Jews and given as the reason for God's temporary exclusion of Israel (τῇ ἀπιστίᾳ ἐξεκλάσθησαν).

ponding disloyalty on God's side is implied. The presupposition is
that the Jews' behavior directly reflects back upon their God as
already expressed in 2.23–4. Paul's response in 3.4, however, is quite
opposite to that in Romans 2, because the issue now is the
trustworthiness of God's words, the very credibility of God and not
merely the Gentiles' attitude towards God. Romans 3.4b is an exact
quotation of the LXX Psalm 50.6b except for the use of the future
indicative in place of the subjunctive. In Psalm 50.5–6a David
recognizes and confesses his sinfulness against God and this surprisingly in order that God's judgment may be acknowledged as just.
Should not there be a perfect correspondence between God's words
and reality? Paul's answer is unequivocal: God's words are indeed
determinative of reality, but it is important to understand that God
has proclaimed precisely that all humanity is sinful (cf. esp. Rom.
3.9–19; 3.5–6).

The question of whether this and any of the other objections to
Paul's gospel are known or imagined by Paul to emanate from the
historical community to which the letter is addressed is of course
impossible to answer. The further question of whether these objections are distilled from past real encounters with opponents (Bornkamm) or are engendered by virtue of the author's dialectical mode
of thinking or by the diatribal literary style which is evident in this
letter (Stowers) cannot be decided on the evidence. It should be
noted that these three just mentioned options are by no means
intrinsically exclusive of each other and, in my opinion, all may be
operative factors. The key point is that I am not positing historical
opponents here, but rather affirming that Paul is aware of the
potential objections which may occur to his contemporary audience
and which the members of the Roman Christian community may
themselves raise and/or be confronted with in their interaction with
outsiders. I think also that it is highly unlikely that later Christian
apologists are at every turn answering to immediate historical
opponents.

Romans 3.5–6: God is not unjust

Thus the objection naturally arises in Romans 3.5 – is not God
unfair to vent wrath on a humanity whose iniquity is both ordained
by the word of God and serves to sustain God's righteousness?[100]

[100] The objection in Romans 3.5 is introduced by εἰ δέ (as is the third objection in
3.7) and its response (3.6) by μὴ γένοιτο and concluded with a rhetorical question.
See Stowers, *Diatribe*, p. 120.

Paul distances himself immediately from the assertion in 3.5 which he considers to be impious as indicated by his use of the expression κατὰ ἄνθρωπον λέγω. The strong denial to the objection of 3.5 elliptically argues the case that the principle of a moral universe necessitates the affirmation of a universal righteous judge, God (3.6).

Romans 3.7–9: "We are blasphemed"

Romans 3.7 shows that the objection of 3.5 is not entirely overcome as it now puts this objection in other words by asking: τί ἔτι κἀγὼ ἁμαρτωλὸς κρίνομαι(7b) if human falsehood, the human condition, serves the divine purpose of verifying God's words. This objection carries particular weight in light of the presupposition of predestination[101] to which Paul adheres, namely that God's words determine reality and thus God's assertion that humanity is sinful allows no possibility of resisting sin. The objection that Paul teaches "the doing of evil in order that good may come" (3.8) is a corollary to the argument that human falsehood contributes to the glory of God (3.7a).

The use of βλασφημούμεθα in 3.8 is noteworthy at both the formal and substantive levels. The first-person plural passive form of the verb is commonly employed to express the objection of opponents in apologetic literature as in Justin's statement of the repeated accusation of atheism against Christians: ἔνθεν δὲ καὶ ἄθεοι κεκλήμεθα (*Ap.* 1.6.1; cf. Athenag. *Suppl.* 4.2). At the substantive level, Halvor Moxnes has pointed out that the word βλασφημέω continues to bear its usual meaning of slander against God although the slander is directed specifically against Paul's preaching.[102] At 2.23–4 Paul has explicitly stated that the Jews

---

[101] See Serek hayyahad (Rule of the Community, Manual of Discipline), 3–4 where the doctrine of the two spirits of truth and falsehood who rule over individuals and determine their status as children of light or children of darkness respectively is articulated. The angel of darkness also leads righteous people astray until the end time appointed by God : "For God has established the two spirits in equal measure until the determined end time, and the Renewal, and He *knows* the reward of their deeds from all eternity" (4). Paul dispenses with all such intermediaries in his concept of predestination. In Romans 8.29 Paul uses the terms προγιγνώσκω and προορίζω together in the positive sense with reference to those whom God justifies. In Romans 5.18–19 (cf.1 Cor. 15.21–2) Paul has made clear also that all people were made sinners in Adam and thus the determination of the human situation is predicated on an historical event in Paul's view.

[102] Moxnes, *Theology*, p. 60.

"blaspheme" God, by disobeying the Law which is given by God. Here in 3.8, he asserts that by slandering his gospel which is also given by God, his opponents, likewise, are blasphemers.

The preponderant opinion of scholarship is that 3.8 is a digression which is only picked up again in Romans 6 and that there is no further word from Paul on this issue in Romans 3.[103] I understand Romans 3.9 as providing a curt repartee to the accusation of 3.8.[104] If it is allowed that Romans 3.9 is possibly a response to the immediately preceding objection that Paul is preaching moral libertinism, then it would be perfectly natural for Paul to say, as I would prefer to translate 3.9a: "What then? Do we defend ourselves?[105] Not at all!"[106] Both the brevity and peremptory character of this response are apposite. Paul later, in Romans 6, will directly confront in this letter the charge of 3.8, but he immediately renders it moot as he has already charged that all humankind is under the power of sin, rendering the accusation of encouraging others to do evil as absurd, rather like prodding a grazing cow to eat grass. Paul's defense against the accusation rests in the assertion that the accusers fail to understand the human condition.[107]

---

[103] Even Käsemann, who wishes to argue against this consensus view, relates Romans 3.9 to 3.1, not to the preceding verse 8; *Romans*, p. 85.

[104] The decisive issue is the determination of the sense of the verb προέχω. Both Barrett and Cranfield lay out neatly the grammatical and textual options for this verse. Three options for the meaning of the verb have some plausibility: (1) the proper middle sense which may be rendered in English – "we excuse or protect ourselves"; (2) a middle with an active force ("excel", "be first") and (3) a passive sense which would be translated as "excelled by" or "worse off than." Cranfield rejects option three on the grounds that this meaning of the verb is unsuitable to the context. He prefers the second even though he grants that there are no other examples of the verb being used in the middle voice with this meaning. He rejects option one and argues that the verb would require a direct object and if it were taken as such then οὐδέν and not the given οὐ πάντως would be the appropriate repartee. Cranfield, however, is surely mistaken, for the normal middle reflexive sense of this verb is entirely apposite when one considers the strongly attested lexical meaning "not at all" rather than "not altogether" for οὐ πάντως. This, incidentally, is how the Vulgate understood the text, translating οὐ πάντως by the adverb *nequaquam*. Barrett, pp. 66–9 and Cranfield, I, pp. 187–91.

[105] For the use of προέχω with precisely the same sense as suggested here, see Soph., *Ant.* 80 and Thuc. 1.140.

[106] RSV translation reads: "What then? Are we Jews any better off? No, not at all" (Rom. 3.9a).

[107] That the accusation against Paul may have been provoked by flagrantly immoral behavior in the Pauline communities cannot be dismissed in the light of the evidence of 1 Corinthians 5.

Romans 3.9b-20: the apologetic use of Scripture

One of the distinguishing marks of missionary apologetics is the use of a circumscribed body of scriptural quotations which has repetitive character in order to affirm a specific contention.[108] Romans 3.9b (Ἰουδαίους τε καὶ Ἕλληνας πάντας ὑφ' ἁμαρτίαν εἶναι) states the thesis which the catena of scriptural quotations in 3.10–18 sustains.[109] The negative sentences (οὐκ ἔστιν occurs six times in Rom. 3.10–18) deny that there are any exceptions to human sinfulness. The most significant parallel to Romans 3.10–18 is to be found in Justin's *The Dialogue with Trypho*, 27.9–12 where the following material is found in common:

πάντες γὰρ ἐξέκλιναν
πάντες ἄρα ἠχρειώθησαν

οὐκ ἔστιν ὁ συνίων
οὐκ ἔστιν ἕως ἑνός

ταῖς γλώσσαις αὐτῶν ἐδολιοῦσαν
τάφος ἀνεῳγμένος ὁ λάρυγξ αὐτῶν
ἰὸς ἀσπίδων ὑπὸ τὰ χείλη αὐτῶν
σύντριμμα καὶ ταλαιπωρία ἐν ταῖς ὁδοῖς αὐτῶν
καὶ ὁδὸν εἰρήνης οὐκ ἔγνωσαν

Justin uses a briefer, independent version of the catena of scriptural quotations which are to be found in Romans 3.[110] For Justin the context is also that of accusing Jews and, along with the common material of Romans 3.10–18, he adds Psalm 105.37, Isaiah 1.23; 3.16.[111] This material was used extensively in apologetic circles.

In 3.19–21, Paul defines two functions of νόμος as Scripture.[112]

---

[108] See Robert Hodgson, "The Testimony Hypothesis," *JBL*, 98 (1979), 369 n. 43.

[109] Romans 3.9 also summarizes the arguments of Romans 1.18–2.29; cf. Bultmann, *Theology*, 1.263.

[110] See Leander A. Keck, "The Function of Romans 3.10–18 – Observations and Suggestions" in *God's Christ and His People: Studies in Honor of Nils Alstrup Dahl* (Oslo, Universitetsforlaget, 1977), p. 150.

[111] Keck observes that the material similar to Romans 3 is marked off from other quotations by Βοά which indicates that Justin knew the former material as an independent piece, "Rom. 3.10–18," p. 150.

[112] There are at least two other senses in which Paul uses the word νόμος in Romans 3, namely, as the rules that regulate daily religious life as in the expression ἔργα νόμου (3.20, 27, 28) which are, of course, derived from the Scripture (note the play on words in 3.21 where Law as Scripture (see also Mt. 5.17, 7.12, 22.40) is clearly distinguished from Law in the sense just indicated) and also as a general principle or norm (νόμος πίστεως 2.27). For the range of lexical possibilities, see Bauer, pp. 542–3.

First, he appeals to the Law to demonstrate the universal condition of sinfulness (3.19).[113] This is indeed the import of this long assemblage of scriptural passages which he has presented in 3.10–18. For Paul, Scripture testifies to both the sinfulness of humanity and the righteousness of God. In 3.20 Paul concludes that through the Law there comes the knowledge (ἐπίγνωσις[114]) of sin. Thus, he here inverts the Jewish apologetic presentation of the Law as providing wisdom and the knowledge of goodness. Second, Paul affirms a positive function of Law (Scripture) as testifying (μαρτύρομαι) to the gospel which he preaches (3.21). It is this latter use of the Law which is the trademark of early Christian apologetics.

Romans 3.24–6: Paul and Jewish martyrological tradition

The closest parallel to the concept and terminology of Romans 3.24–6 is to be found in the Maccabean martyrological tradition.[115] The concept of expiation of sin by the blood of the martyr is to be found in 4 Maccabees 17.21a–22b: ὥσπερ ἀντίψυχον γεγονότας τῆς τοῦ ἔθνους ἁμαρτίας. καὶ διὰ τοῦ αἵματος τῶν εὐσεβῶν ἐικείνων καὶ τοῦ ἱλαστηρίου τοῦ θανάτου αὐτῶν.[116] The collocation of αἷμα, ἱλαστήριον, and ἁμαρτία bears striking similarity to Romans 3.25. Most especially the unusual use of τὸ ἱλαστήριον which is shared by the two texts is to be noted. In 2 Maccabees, various forms of the word ἀπολύω (Rom. 3.24) are frequently employed as e.g. in 12.45b: "therefore he made atonement for the dead, that they might be delivered from their sin" (τῆς ἁμαρτίας ἀπολυθῆναι).[117] Here the parallels with the martyrological tradition of 4(2) Maccabees 7 are apparent. It is this quality of

---

[113] Paul's reasoning here is that if the Jew is silenced on this point then a fortiori all humankind should certainly acquiesce in their liability to judgment (3.19b).

[114] On this word see above.

[115] The frequent cited references to prophetic passages, e.g. Isaiah 53, are misplaced. See Sam K. Williams, *Jesus' Death as Saving Event*, HDR, 2 (Missoula, Scholars, 1976). Also see J. Cambier, *L'Evangile de dieu selon l'epître aux Romains*, StudNeot 3 (Bruges, Desclee De Brouwer, 1967), vol. 1, p. 111; and Barrett, *Romans*, p. 78.

[116] Nickelsburg suggests that 4 Maccabees be dated between 20 and 54 CE. On the apologetic character of the Maccabean literature, see Dieter Georgi, *Opponents*, and Conzelmann, *Heiden*, pp. 16–18.

[117] Käsemann agrees with Büchsel ("λύω", *TDNT*, 4 [1967], 353–5) that there is no sense of payment in Paul's use of the word ἀπολύτρωσις in Romans 3.24, but see Cranfield (*Romans*, vol. 1, pp. 206–8) for a more circumspect opinion on the matter. In the preponderance of its uses, the word carries definitively the meaning of payment and is often used in reference to the manumission of slaves.

trustworthiness under trial that provides the occasion for God to manifest righteousness. God is portrayed as both "Just and justifying on the basis of Jesus' loyalty" (contrary to the RSV "He justifies him who has faith in Jesus"). God is the actor and Jesus the one upon whom God acts. God puts forth Jesus as the ἱλαστήριον (3.25). There is considerable debate as to whether ἱλαστήριον means propitiation or the place of propitiation. In the LXX and in Philo the word refers to the lid of the ark of the convenant over which the blood of a sin offering is poured on the day of atonement (Ex. 25.16–22; Philo, Cher. 25; Fuga. 100; Mos. 2.95). In either case there can be little question that the appropriation of the term here serves to relate apologetically the crucifixion of Jesus to a traditional symbol of Jewish sacrifice and thus to attempt to provide an acceptable hermeneutic for understanding the cross which is central to the gospel that Paul preached.[118] The punishment suffered by Jesus is presented by Paul as further proof of God's righteousness and removes the objection that arises from "the passing over of previous sins" (3.25).[119] The fact that sinners have been unrequited in the past raises the question of the justice of the Divine Judge. The justice of God is proven for Paul by the cross (note the double use of ἔνδειξις in 3.25b and 26a). Paul has previously demonstrated that all are sinners (2.1–3.20), but God has not punished these sinners.

In the Maccabean literature the martyrological motifs serve the apologetic purpose of recommending the Law as the superior way to religious and moral self-realization (4 Macc 7.9–16, note the use of ἀποδείκνυμι)[120] but for Paul the christological event serves to give ἔνδειξις τῆς δικαιοσύνης (3.25–6) which is χωρὶς νόμου (3.21). There is no question, of course, that Romans 3.24–5 is a pre-Pauline christological formula,[121] but there were other formulae available to the apostle and thus the question becomes why Paul employed this particular tradition in Romans 3. This question is not fully answerable but what can be seen in the light of the foregoing analysis is that his decision to employ a tradition here that has considerable continuity with Jewish apologetic martyrological tradi-

---

[118] This apologetic move most probably preceded Paul but it is significant that Paul here repeats it.

[119] See Cranfield, pp. 211–12.

[120] See also the comparable use of the willingness to die motif in both Josephus *Ap.* 2. 232 and Philo *Leg. Gai.* 233.

[121] See Bultmann, *Theology*, vol. 1, p. 46.

tion is fully consonant with the use of apologetic material which has been discerned throughout Romans 1–3.

Romans 3.30: the "One God" topos in the context of Romans 1–3 and Jewish apologetic

Paul uses the "One God" formula in Romans 3.30 in an apologetic context to argue for the inclusion of the Gentiles. This affirmation of the One God is central to his argument from 1.18–3.31 as well as to its more immediate context, 3.21–31. While the history of interpretation of Romans 1.18–3.31 has focused sometimes exclusively on Paul's understanding of justification by faith and the righteousness of God, insufficient attention has been given in the history of interpretation of Romans to the significance of Paul's affirmation of monotheism at the end of Romans 3,[122] with several commentators leaving it entirely unmentioned.[123] Sanday and Headlam restrict their comments on 3.30 to a grammatical note on εἴπερ as emphasizing the fact of the condition. Hans Lietzmann confines himself to the observation that the two prepositions ἐκ and διά indicate only a stylistic variation without a difference in sense.[124]

Another group of interpreters suggest that Paul appeals to the One God in order to support his proclamation that there is only one way to salvation. For instance, C. H. Dodd thinks that he is asserting the superiority of Christianity over Judaism, praising the former as the only consistent monotheism. Dodd describes Paul as

---

[122] A useful summary of the debate in German scholarship over Paul's concept of God's righteousness is to be found in Manfred T. Brauch, "Perspectives of God's Righteousness in Recent German discussion" in E. P. Sanders, *Paul and Palestinian Judaism*. For an exception to this tendency to ignore Paul's monotheistic statement in Romans, see D. G. Schrenk, "Der Römerbrief als Missionsdokument, " *Aus Theologie und Geschichte der Reformierten Kirche, Festgabe für E. F. Karl Müler* (Erlangen, Neukirchen, 1933), pp. 39–72.

[123] As e.g. Franz J. Leenhardt, *L' Epître de saint Paul aux Romains*, CNT, 2.6, 2nd edn (Geneva, Labor et Fides, 1981) and Joseph Huby, *Saint Paul Epître aux Romains*, VS, 10 (Paris, Beauchesne et ses Fils, 1957).

[124] Hans Lietzmann, *An die Römer*, HNT, 8 (Tübingen, Mohr/Siebeck, 1928), p. 52. On this question, see the recent article by Stanley K. Stowers, "ΕΚ ΠΙΣΤΕΩΣ AND ΔΙΑ ΤΗΣ ΠΙΣΤΕΩΣ IN ROMANS 3:30, " *JBL*, 108/4 (1989), 665–74. Stowers contends that Paul employs the phrase διὰ τῆς πίστεως to refer to Jesus' atoning life and death for the redemption of the Gentiles and ἐκ πίστεως for the redemption of the Jews in 3.30 (elsewhere Stowers thinks Paul may use the latter phrase more loosely to refer also to the redemption of both Jews and Gentiles). It is peculiar, however, that Stowers insists without offering reasons that Paul writes to Gentile Churches about Gentile issues (pp. 673, 674) as his exegetical point as readily accommodates the view of a mixed audience of Jewish and Gentile Christians.

polemicizing against his Pharisaic past in which a tension exists between the affirmation of the unity and universality of God and the particularistic belief that Jews have a special status before God. Paul, according to Dodd, resolves this antinomy by his insistence that God must treat Jews and Gentiles on the same footing and thereby carries the principle of monotheism to its logical conclusion.[125] M. J. Lagrange thinks that Paul intends to deny to Judaism the right to say that God is the God of the whole world if at the same time it upholds justification by the Law. Lagrange sees 3.30 as completing the argument of 3.29 that God is the God of all and as such will justify the whole world by faith.[126]

The third and largest group of commentators point to the Shema or Deuteronomy 6.4 to explain Paul's reference to the One God in Romans 3.30. Otto Michel states that in 3.29 he raises a question which the synagogue answered differently. Yet Michel also thinks that Paul refers to the Shema in order to support the assertion that there is a unity in the events of salvation.[127] C. K. Barrett understands Paul in 3.30 to be saying that the Old Testament says that God is one and that he adduces Deuteronomy 6.4 as a case in point.[128] Both Barrett and C. E. B. Cranfield believe that the appeal to the One God is intended as a confirmation of the implied claim in Romans 3.29 that God is the God of the Gentiles.[129] Cranfield further thinks that Paul intends the relative clause in 3.30, which affirms that God will justify the Jews as well as Gentiles by faith, as a corollary to the confession that God is one.[130] Ulrich Wilckens suggests that Paul in 3.29 is continuing the discussion with his Jewish partner of Romans 3.3. Wilckens understands the view of the latter to be represented in the statement of *Exodus Rabbah* 29 (88d): "I am God over all that come into the world but I have joined by name only with you; I am not called the God of the idolaters, but the God of Israel." Wilckens says that Paul points to the confession of Deuteronomy 6.4 as the grounds for his assertion that it is the One

---

* [125] C. H. Dodd, *The Epistle of Paul to the Romans*, MNTC (London, Hodder and Stoughton, 1954), pp. 62–3. See also Anders Nygren, *Commentary on Romans*, trans. Carl C. Rasmussen (Philadelphia, Muhlenberg, 1949), p. 166.

[126] *Saint Paul Epitre Aux Romains* (Paris, J. Gabalda, 1916), pp. 79–80.

[127] Otto Michel, *Der Brief an die Römer*, Meyer K 4., 10th edn (Göttingen, Vandenhoeck & Ruprecht, 1955), p. 96.

[128] C. K. Barrett, *A Commentary on the Epistle to the Romans*, Black's New Testament Commentaries (London, Adam & Charles Black, 1957), p. 84.

[129] C. E. B. Cranfield, *The Epistle to the Romans*, ICC (Edinburgh, T. & T. Clark, 1980), p. 222.

[130] Cranfield, *Romans*, p. 222.

God of Israel who justifies all including the Gentiles.[131] H. Schlier suggests that in making reference to the Shema in 3.30, Paul intends to affirm an identity between the God who justifies all and God as Creator and Judge.[132] E. Käsemann disagrees with Wilckens that there is a continuation in 3.29 of Jewish objections from 3.1–3. Käsemann does think that Paul is attacking the dominant idea of God in rabbinic teaching and also refers to *Exod. Rab.* 29 (88d). He says that Paul links justification to the faithfulness of the Creator. Agreeing with Schlier, Käsemann thinks that Paul invokes the Shema in order to link Creation and salvation: "Sola Gratia has its basis in Solus Deus." The implication of the monotheistic confession is that God's activity must be allowed to extend to all creation.[133]

In my view, this near consensus among interpreters with respect to Romans 3.30 that Paul adduces a reference to the Shema or Deuteronomy 6.4 in opposition to the Jewish concept and in support of his own view of salvation is mistaken. Deuteronomy 6.4 does not provide the εἷς θεός formula which Paul uses here.[134] This formula is thoroughly Hellenistic as Eric Peterson has demonstrated, and, as I will show in the excursus, it is significant specifically to Hellenistic Jewish apologetic theology. This formula was exploited in Jewish apologetic literature not only in its "other religions" polemics, but also for its socio-political implications. Most relevant to Paul in Romans is Philo's use of the topos in order to draw the important theo-sociological conclusion that Gentiles *qua* Gentiles could not be excluded from the community. Philo forthrightly appeals to the One God to argue for equal dignity and rights for proselytes in the Jewish πολιτεία.[135] Paul and Philo shared in the Hellenistic Jewish apologetic traditions in which the "One God" topos figured prominently in Hellenistic Jewish apo-

---

[131] Ulrich Wilckens, *Der Brief an die Römer*, EKKNT, 6, 3 vols. (Zürich, Benziger, 1978), vol.1. p. 248.

[132] Heinrich Schlier, *Der Römerbrief*, HThKNT, 6 (Freiburg, Herder, 1977), pp. 117–18.

[133] Ernst Käsemann, *Commentary on Romans*, trans. Geoffrey W. Bromiley (Grand Rapids, Eerdmans, 1980), pp. 103–4.

[134] See excursus, where I argue that the Shema is relevant to the extent that it made for the more ready utilization of the "One God" topos by Jewish apologists who could plausibly contend for its compatibility with ancient Jewish tradition. The only use of εἷς with θεός in the LXX (Mal. 2.10), is in a context which has as its manifest concern the relationship between the people of Israel and other peoples.

[135] See Anthony J. Guerra, "The One God Topos In *Spec. Leg.* 1.52, " *SBL Seminar Papers* (1990).

logetics. Moreover, this suggestion concerning Romans 3.30 accords well with the wider hypothesis argued here that Romans 1–4 is indebted to Jewish apologetics.

Philo's primary efforts were not directed against polytheism, and the propagation of monotheism, for he was aware that since Plato the tendency in the Hellenistic world was towards a consensus theology which conceptualized God as one or at the least espoused henotheism.[136] Philo, like Paul, is concerned not with promoting monotheism as such but rather the worship of the One God. Philo's use of the εἷς ὁ θεός formula in his apologetic work *De Specialibus Legibus* 2.165. ascribes monotheism to both "Greeks and barbarians" (1.52 and 4.159) and links the topos to the issue of the status of the non-Jew. Outside *De Specialibus Legibus*, it should be noted that Philo employs the word εἷς with explicit reference to θεός in the following texts: *De Opificio Mundi*, 100, 171; *Legum Allegoriarum*, 2.1,3; 3.82,105; *Noah* 137; *De Virtutibus* 35.[137] In these instances the cardinal εἷς follows the noun (ὁ) θεός except in *De Virtutibus* 35, *Noah* 37, and *Legum Allegoriarum* 2.3. Philo's use of the "One God" topos in these several instances can be categorized according to function into three groups: (1) the monotheistic polemic against polytheism; (2) the philosophical/ontological significance of the oneness of God; and (3) the commonplace contrast between the One and the many.

In the first group, *De Opificio Mundi* 171 clearly belongs because here Philo contrasts Moses' teaching (ὅτι θεὸς εἷς ἐστι,) with polytheism (διὰ τοὺς εἰσηγητὰς τῆς πολυθέου δόξης). Likewise in *De Decalogo* 65, Philo explains the first commandment with frequent reference to the One (a word which, of course, is not to be found in Ex. 20):

> Let us, then, engrave deep in our hearts this as the first and most sacred of commandments, to acknowledge and honor one God ἕνα ... τιμᾶν θεόν) Who is above all, and let the idea that gods are many (δόξα δ᾽ ἡ πολύθεος) never even

[136] See Erwin R. Goodenough, *An Introduction to Philo Judaeus*, 2nd edn (Oxford, Basil Blackwell, 1962), pp. 80–2.

[137] T. Conley observes that Philo employs three types of "topoi" in his writings: (1) "commonplaces" to be found all over Hellenistic literature; (2) "philosophical, " generally traceable to a philosophical school; and (3) "dialectical, " related to lists of topoi collected by Aristotle in his *Topics*; "Philo's Use of Topoi" in David Winston & John Dillon (eds.), *Two Treatises of Philo of Alexandria*, Brown Judaic Studies 25 (Chicago, Scholars Press, 1983), pp. 171–8.

reach the ears of the man whose rule of life is to seek for truth in purity and guilelessness.

Philo's emphasis on ἀλήθεια here is repeated in *De Ebrietate* 45 where the many falsely called gods are contrasted to the true God and the ignorance of the One generates the illusion of the many who in reality (πρὸς ἀλήθειαν) do not exist. Here one comes to the border of the second category, namely, the philosophical/ontological use of the "One God" formula. In *Legum Allegoriarum* 2.1–3, Philo exegetes Genesis 2.18: "Why, O prophet, is it not good that the man should be alone? Because, he says, it is good that the Alone should be alone: but God, being One (εἷς ὢν ὁ θεός) is alone and unique, and like God there is nothing" (*Leg. All.* 2.1).

Philo proceeds beyond this apparently numerical explanation of the aloneness and oneness of God to affirm that God is a unity in the sense that his nature (φύσις) is simple whereas all created beings have a composite nature (2.2). He concludes this opening section of the second book of *Legum Allegoriarum* by affirming that "τέτακται οὖν ὁ θεὸς κατὰ τὸ ἓν καὶ τὴν μονάδα, μᾶλλον δὲ ἡ μονὰς κατὰ τὸν ἕνα θεόν"(2.3). Thus, he shows clearly that he understands the difference between monism and monotheism and decides unequivocally for the latter.[138] In *Legum Allegoriarum* 3.7–8, Philo sets his view of the one single cause of creation (ἑνὸς ὄντος αἰτίου τοῦ δρῶντος) against the two dominant philosophical options of his time, namely the Platonic understanding that combines God and matter as joint causes of the creation and Heraclitus' proposal that creation is an entirely immanent process. At the same time it should be acknowledged that Philo at points comes close to allowing some diversity within the Godhead in his frequent attribution of two powers to God (e.g. *Cher.* 27: τὸν ἕνα ὄντως ὄντα θεὸν δύο τὰς ἀνωτάτω εἶναι καὶ πρώτας δυνάμεις ἀγαθότητα καὶ ἐξουσίαν; also *Abr.* 122).[139] Yet Philo in these instances is normally quick to point out the difference between human ways of thinking and divine reality: "What could be more grievous or more capable of proving the total absence of nobility in the soul than this that its knowledge of the many, the secondary, the created, only leads to ignore the One, the Primal, the Uncreated and the Maker of all" (*Virt.* 213). In

[138] Frederick Copleston, *A History of Philosophy*, 8 vols. (Garden City, Image Books, 1962), 1.1.64.

[139] For further evidence see Alan F. Segal, *Two Powers In Heaven*, SJLA, 25 (Leiden, Brill, 1977), pp. 159–81.

the third category, Philo moves from the philosophical distinction between appearance and reality to the obvious real contrast between the many and the One. The simple antithetical pairing of the One and the many is found in *Legum Allegoriarum* 3.105: ὁ μὲν τῶν ἀγαθῶν εἷς-ἐπεὶ γὰρ ὁ θεὸς εἷς, καὶ ἀγαθῶν θησαυρὸς <εἷς>- πολλοὶ δὲ τῶν κακῶν, ὅτι καὶ ἁμαρτάνοντες ἄπειροι τὸ πλῆθος. In addition to this commonplace antithesis between the One and the many, Philo contrasts the One God and the Whole creation: ὡς εἷς ὄντος οὐ κυρίως βεβαία ἡ τῶν ὅλων κτῆσις (*Cher*. 109). It is clear that the valuation of the One is superior or at least equal to the many or whole:

> And that true servant and suppliant, even though in actual number he be but one, is in real value, what God's own choice makes him, the whole people, in worth equal to a complete nation. And, indeed, this is true to nature. In a ship the pilot is worth as much as all the crew, and in an army the general as much as all the soldiers, since if he fall, defeat results as certainly as it would if the whole force were annihilated. So, too, against the worth of a whole nation the wise man can hold his own, protected by the impregnable wall of godliness.[140]

In the use of the "One God" topos in *De Specialibus Legibus* 4, the immediate context finds Philo commenting on Deuteronomy 17.5, which directs against the appointment of a foreigner as a ruler over the Israelites (*Spec. Leg.* 4.157). Philo finds in Deuteronomy 17.16–17 (4.158) a negative reason for this exclusionary rule, namely that a foreign ruler would be likely to satisfy his greed by exploiting its native inhabitants. Having found in Scripture these cautious remarks concerning the foreigner, he next offers a positive reason for the biblical injunction to appoint to leadership only those native born, namely, that the solidarity which results from political and religious as well as ethnic bonding will protect the kinsmen from the temptation of such exploitation: "For he assumed with good reason that one who was their fellow-kinsman related to them by the tie which brings the highest kinship, the kinship of having one citizenship and the same law and One God who has taken all members of the nation for his portion, would never sin in the way just mentioned" (*Spec. Leg.* 4.159). Philo uses a triple formula of πολιτεία,

---

[140] Cf. Romans 5.

νόμος and θεός (where the first and the third term is modified by εἷς [μία] and the middle term by ὁ αὐτός) and thus affirms that the real basis of kinship is not ethnic identity, but the Law and the One God who is described in the relative clause (ᾧ πάντες οἱ ἀπὸ τοῦ ἔθνους προσκεκλήρωνται) as having designated all members of the nation. Philo's awareness of the "separating" implications of the "One God" topos is undoubtedly made clear in *De Specialibus Legibus* 3.29 where he admonishes:

> do not enter into the partnership of marriage with a member of a foreign land, lest some day conquered by the forces of opposing customs you surrender and stray unawares from the path that leads to piety and turn aside into a pathless wild. And though perhaps you yourself will hold your ground steadied from your earliest years by the admirable instructions instilled in you by your parents, with the holy laws always as their key-note, there is much to be feared for your sons and daughters. It may well be that they, enticed by spurious customs which they prefer to the genuine, are likely to unlearn the honour due to the One God (τὴν τοῦ ἑνὸς θεοῦ τιμήν), and that is the first and last stage of supreme misery.

In this digression in explanation of Exodus 34.16 and Deuteronomy 7.3, Philo approaches the use of the topos which is found in Malachi 2.10 (see excursus). He elsewhere charges the "Arabians" in ancient time of attempting to seduce them away from "honoring the One, the truly Existent, and to change their religion to impiety" (*Virt.* 34).[141] As is clear from the rest of the paragraph, Philo emphasizes the internal community building (over against the foreigner) function of the "One God" topos:

> You see how unlimited is the number of the Hebrews, but their number is not so dangerous and menacing a weapon as their unanimity and mutual attachment. And the highest and greatest source of this unanimity is their creed of a single God (ἡ περὶ τοῦ ἑνὸς θεοῦ δόξα), through which, as from a fountain, they feel a love for each other, uniting them in an indissoluble bond.   (*Virt.* 35)

[141] There are, to be sure, plenty of proselytizing foreign and indigenous religions in Alexandria in the 1 CE to allow a contemporaneous significance to these passages.

Thus the One God functions here in Philo to guarantee unity and harmony among believers as well as to distance the community from non-believers.

In accord with the highly flexible nature of the topos, Philo employs the "One God" formula in *De Specialibus Legibus* 1.52 to promote the acceptance and even privileged treatment of proselytes. Playing with the etymology of the word προσήλὕτος (προσελ-ηλύθέναι, "to have arrived"), he gives a positive valuation of proselytes in *De Specialibus Legibus* 1.51: καλεῖ προσηλύτους ἀπὸ τοῦ προσεληλυθέναι καινῇ καὶ φιλοθέῳ πολιτείᾳ.[142] In 1.52 Philo has Moses exhort that the proselytes be given not only due honors (τιμαῖς) but also "special friendship and more than usual goodwill" (φιλίᾳ καὶ εὐνοίᾳ περιττῇ). Such extraordinary regard for pros-elytes is justified because "they have left country, friends and relatives for virtue and holiness" (δι' ἀρετὴν καὶ ὁσιότητα).[143] The premise underlying all of the advice here with respect to the proselyte is that the Jew and proselyte are one as they worship One God: "εὐνοίας ἐνωτικῆς ἡ τοῦ ἑνὸς θεοῦ τιμή" (*Spec. Leg.* 1.52). The liberality of Philo is extended to foreigners in general in the following para-graph (53) as he advises proselytes against ridiculing their former religious beliefs and "blasphemy against those which others think to be gods."[144] Philo offers two rationales for restraint towards pagans, namely so as not to provoke their profaning "the real God," and second, that their ignorance is excusable, as they have been taught their beliefs ἐκ παίδων καὶ σύντροφον ἔχοντες, ἐξα-μαρτήσονται (*Spec. Leg.* 1.53). Subsequent in *De Specialibus*

---

[142] In an article entitled "Conversion, Circumcision and the Law, " *NTS*, 20, 328–9. Neil J. Mceleney concludes that circumcision was not always demanded if the convert otherwise practiced the Law. The insistence on fulfillment of this precept may be a reaction against a tendency that was already present in Judaism apart from Christianity. Philo is cited as a prime proponent of exempting proselytes from circumcision if they keep "the law and customs and worship the one God." Born-kamm had acknowledged that the liberal diaspora synagogue did not require circum-cision of converts to Judaism but rather encouraged observance of minimal ritual commandments and the confession of belief in One God; *Paul*, trans. D. M. Stalker (New York, Harper & Row, 1971), p. 10.

[143] Philo terms the proselyte an "incomer" (ἐπηλύτης) and immigrant who has turned his own kinsfolk into enemies "by honoring the One worthy of honor" (τὴν τοῦ ἑνὸς τιμίου τιμὴν) and rejecting the mythical and multitudinous sovereigns (μυθικῶν πλασμάτων καὶ πολυαρχίας). It is on behalf of such converts and not the rulers and despots of the world that, Philo says, God executes judgment (*Spec. Leg.* 4.178). On the implications of the affirmation that God is, in number, one, see Harry Austryn Wolfson, *From Philo to Spinoza* (New York, Behrman House, 1977), pp. 26–7.

[144] Cf. LXX Exod. 22.28.

Legibus 1, Philo employs the "One God" topos to propagandize on behalf of the temple:

> there should not be temples built either in many places or many in the same place for he judged that since God is one, there should be also only one temple (ἐπειδὴ εἷς ἐστιν ὁ θεός, καὶ ἱερὸν ἓν εἶναι μόνον). (*Spec. Leg.* 1.67)

He proceeds to explain that the existence of only one temple fosters bonds of unity among those from distant places:

> For one who is not going to sacrifice in a religious spirit would never bring himself to leave his country and friends and kinsfolk and sojourn in a strange land, but clearly it must be the stronger attraction of piety which leads him to endure separation from his most familiar and dearest friends who form as it were a single whole with himself. And we have proof of this in what actually happens. Countless multitudes from countless cities come, some over land, others over sea, from east and west and north and south at every feast ... Thus filled with comfortable hopes they devote the leisure, as is their bounden duty, to holiness and the honoring of God. Friendships are formed between those who hitherto knew not each other, and the sacrifices and libations are the occasion of their reciprocity of feeling and constitute the surest pledge that all are of one mind (ὁμόνοια). (*Spec. Leg.* 1.68–71)

For Philo, the One God justifies the One temple which leads in turn to ὁμόνοια among strangers and foreigners.

Thus in Philo we have come to the use of the "One God" topos in a context which encourages full inclusion of proselytes and also reasonable tolerance towards Gentiles.[145] Whereas in Aristobulus and certainly in Hellenistic philosophy at large the primary concern

---

[145] See Moriz Friedländer, *Geschichte der Jüdischen Apologetik* (Leipzig, 1906; Amsterdam, Philo, 1973), pp. 222–5. In *Rewards and Punishments*, Philo states straightforwardly that a faithful proselyte will be welcomed by God whereas the unvirtuous Jew will be eternally damned: "The proselyte ... has won a prize best suited to his merits, a place in heaven firmly fixed, while the nobly born who has falsified his high lineage will be dragged right down and carried into Tartarus itself and profound darkness. ... God welcomes the virtue which springs from ignoble birth, that He takes no account of the roots but accepts the full-grown stem, because it has been changed from a weed into fruitfulness." (*De Praemiis et Poenis*, p. 152). Philo emphatically denies the assurance of eternal reward on the basis of ethnic origin.

was the pursuit of a theoretical basis of unity, the reconcilability of seemingly differing theological systems and discourse, Philo was far more concerned to articulate the social implications for unity which the shared acceptance of One God afforded.

The question of the relationship between the Gentiles, specifically proselytes, and the Jewish community is the most significant context for Philo's use of this topos. In addition to the socio-political implications which Hellenistic Jewish theology had drawn from the affirmation of One God, there is the explicit theological function of the topos, on the one hand, in the polemic against polytheism and idol worship, and on the other hand, in the avowal that the God and gods to whom the Greek philosophers and poets refer is none other than the One God whom Israel worships.[146] Philo, however, is primarily concerned to encourage the native born Jews to embrace proselytes as equal members of the community. Similarly, Paul seeks to promote respect for Gentile Christians by Jewish Christians. In the wider context of Romans 1–3, one finds that all the above mentioned apologetic functions of the "One God" topos have relevance and thus the consummate appropriateness of Paul's concluding this section of Romans with explicit reference to the One God is apparent. Paul, as the Apostle to the Gentiles, affirms the full inclusion of the Gentiles and, as well, is concerned with the unity between Jewish and Gentile Christians. By the relative clause ὅς δικαιώσει of Romans 3.30, Paul conjoins his preaching of justification to the "One God" topos and thereby defends his gospel as the gospel of God (1.1).[147] The affirmation of One God is important to Paul's endeavor to assure Jewish Christians that his preaching is not blasphemous and that they should not consider him inimical to Jewish Christianity.[148]

---

[146] See excursus on Josephus, Sibylline Oracles, and Aristobulus.

[147] Accordingly, recall the polemic against idolatry of Romans 1.18–32 and Paul's concern in Romans 2 to argue for the impartiality of God towards Jews and Gentiles and the equivalence of function of the revealed Law and natural Law in God's judgment of Jews and Gentiles respectively. Further, Romans 3.1–20 sets up the antithesis between οὐκ ἔστιν δίκαιος οὐδὲ εἷς (3.10) and εἷς θεός. Paul affirms that God is the God of the Jews and the One God justifies both Jews and Gentiles (3.29–30). To be sure, however, for the immediate context of 3. 21–31, the function of the topos to promote the inclusion of the Gentiles is dominant and suggests that Paul and Philo shared a common Hellenistic Jewish tradition.

[148] Note my discussion on the relationship between monotheism and christology in Paul; see chapters 3 and 4.

EXCURSUS: THE "ONE GOD" TOPOS IN JEWISH APOLOGETIC LITERATURE

The "One God" topos in Jewish literature appears frequently in apologetic writings. By the word topos, I intend to denote a formulaic or stereotyped motif, in this case εἷς (ὁ) θεός often with the verb "to be" and the Hebrew equivalents. This fixed verbal formula provides an important control for the investigation which an attempt, for example, to look at the concept of monotheism, without such formal criterion could not offer. Such formulaic expressions or topoi, however, can and do have diverse functions in apologetic literature. It thus becomes indispensable to abide by the basic exegetical principle of understanding this topos by attention to the immediate literary context in which it is placed.

The "One God" topos in the Old Testament

Eric Peterson

Eric Peterson examined the uses of the εἷς θεός formula in early Christian, as well as non-Christian, epigraphic material.[149] He argues that the Christian use of this formula is not derived from the Old Testament or Jewish sources,[150] but rather from Hellenistic religious usage. Rejecting specifically the thesis that the Christian usage of εἷς θεός was dependent on Deuteronomy 6.4, Peterson points out the text reads εἷς κύριος, not θεός.[151] He observes the frequent employment of the εἷς θεός formula for religious propagandistic purposes especially in the context of miracle claims.[152] Peterson does not so summarily dismiss the possibility of a connection between the Shema and the liturgical type of the "One God" topos in Christian inscriptions.[153] The enduring value of Peterson's work is that it points us in the right direction as to the Hellenistic provenance of the "One God" formula. The limitations of his work which are in part inherent in his self-defined task are threefold: (1)

---

[149] Cf. Eric Peterson, *Eis theos: Epigraphische, formgeschichtliche und religionsgeschichtliche Untersuchungen* (Göttingen, Vandenhoeck & Ruprecht, 1926).

[150] The formula is similarly lacking in both The Old Testament Apocrypha and Pseudepigrapha.

[151] It is strange that Peterson omits any reference to Malachi 2.10 in his discussion.

[152] Peterson, *Eis Theos*, p. 304.

[153] The use of ἅγιος in such inscriptions was a decisive marker for Peterson in categorizing the liturgical use of the εἷς θεός formula. Peterson, *Eis Theos*, p. 135.

he overlooks the frequent use of the formula in Hellenistic Jewish apologetic literature and therefore does not consider its possible influence on the Christian use of this Formula;[154] (2) he fails to evaluate Malachi 2.10 which is the only instance in the LXX where εἷς and θεός appear together albeit in reverse order (θεὸς εἷς); and (3) he does not grant sufficient importance to the role of Deuteronomy 6.4 in preparing for the reception of the εἷς θεός formula in Jewish Hellenistic and Christian circles.

Deuteronomy 6.4 and its uses[155]

The most important distinctive feature of Deuteronomy in comparison to the Book of the Covenant is the impulse to centralize the cult.[156] The opening words of Deuteronomy 6.4 *šĕma' yiśrā'el* occur also at 5.1, 9.1, 20.3, 27.9 and constitute a stereotyped formula which was probably used to open the ancient qahal or the "assembly for worship of the tribes."[157] Michal Peter has suggested that the Shema was understood as a nationalistic text early in Israel's life and only during and after the exile did a more universal conception of the One Lord/God emerge.[158] The ambiguity of the Hebrew allows for two alternative meanings: "Yahweh is our God, Yahweh alone!" or "Yahweh, our God, is one Yahweh." The first translation suggests a confession which stands in opposition to the Canaanite cult of Baal.[159] In the second translation it is a confession of the oneness of Yahweh and is directed against the diversity within the traditions of Yahweh worship. That liturgical language may

---

[154] At the mention of the Jewish Hellenistic use of εἷς θεός, Peterson refers the reader to Eduard Norden's *Agnostos Theos* (Darmstadt, Wissenschaftliche Buchgesellschaft, 1956), p. 124, where Norden, however, makes only a passing reference to *3 Sib. Or.*

[155] Note that the discussion of this and other biblical passages in this chapter will be restricted to matters relevant to the development of the "One God" topos and does not purport to be an exhaustive study of issues in Old Testament scholarship on the same.

[156] Gerhard von Rad, *Deuteronomy*, trans. Dorothea Barton, Old Testament Library (Philadelphia, Westminster, 1966), p. 16.

[157] von Rad (*Deuteronomy*, p. 63) believes that Deuteronomy 6.4 belongs to the earliest stratum of Deuteronomy, and thus is from the pre-kingdom period. See further, Peter Höffken, "Eine Bemerkung zum religionsgeschichtlichen Hintergrund von Dtn 6,4," *BZ*, 28 (1984), 88–93.

[158] Michal Peter, "Dtn 6,4 – ein monotheistischer text?," *BZ*, 24 (1980), 252–62.

[159] von Rad, *Deuteronomy*, p. 63.

serve both purposes of separating from undesirable views and groups as well as of self-definition is certainly known.[160]

The later use of Deuteronomy 6.4 as a central confession of Judaism assures its prominence in the liturgical and the later synagogal context. The special place of Deuteronomy 6.4 in the religious life of ancient Judaism is testified to by the Mishna and the findings at Qumran, as well as the New Testament. Both Mishnaic and sectarian Judaism concur in affirming the creedal significance of Deuteronomy 6.4. The phylacteries discovered at Qumran show that Deuteronomy 6.4 was pivotal to pre-Mishnaic Jewish worship before the Christian era.[161] Although there is some dispute at least later in *Sifre Deut.* concerning whether the Shema should include the Decalogue and Exodus 13.1–16, these latter passages together with Deuteronomy 6.4–9 and 11.13–21 are contained in the phylacteries found at Qumran.[162] Another pre-Mishnaic reference to phylacteries is found in Matthew 23 amidst the material criticizing the high-sounding titles in verses 8–10, including a rejection of the title of father on the grounds that εἷς (γάρ) ἐστιν ὑμῶν ὁ πατὴρ ὁ οὐράνιος.[163]

Mark 12.8–34 and parallels give further testimony to the importance of Deuteronomy 6.4–5 for first-century Judaism. In response to the scribe's question as to which is the greatest commandment, Jesus

[160] See Lawrence A. Hoffman, "Censoring In and Censoring Out: A Function of Liturgical Language," in Joseph Gutman, *Ancient Synagogues*, Brown Judaic Studies 22 (Chicago, Scholars, 1981), p. 2.

[161] Cf. R. De Vaux and J. T. Milik, *Qumran Grotte 4*, DJD, 6 (Oxford, Clarendon, 1977), pp. 38–79. Phylacteries "C," "H," and "M" contain Deuteronomy 6.4. See also G. Vermes, "Pre-Mishnaic Jewish Worship and the Phylacteries from the Dead Sea," *VT*, 9 (1959), 65–72. Cf. also M. Sebu. 3.8,11, etc. From the fragments of the four phylacteries which were found in cave 4 it is known that all the passages contained in the rabbinic phylactery are at least partly represented in those of Qumran. Further, Vermes remarks that the longer quotation of Deuteronomy in the qumranic phylactery may have been the more common practice when before the Mishnaic legislation the phylacteries regularly contained five rather than four sections. It appears that this additional section included the decalogue (Deut. 5.6–21).

[162] See M. Friedländer, *The Jewish Religion* (London, Kegan, Trench, Trübner, 1891), pp. 331–4. Friedländer states that the tefillin expresses four teachings: (1) Ex. 13.1–10 expresses the belief that God is the King and Ruler of the universe; (2) Ex. 13.11–16 reminds of the way in which God delivered the forefathers from Egyptian bondage; (3) Deuteronomy 6.4–9 teaches the unity of God and to love and obey God; and (4) Deuteronomy 11.13–20 teaches that God's providence rewards and punishes people according to their merits.

[163] It is not unimportant to note for the history of conflict between early Christianity and Judaism that Matthew challenges the confession of the One God by adding in 23.10 ὅτι καθηγητὴς ὑμῶν ἐστιν εἷς ὁ Χριστός. See Bultmann, *History of the Synoptic Tradition*, trans. John Marsh (New York, Harper & Row, 1976), p. 148.

recites first Deuteronomy 6.4–5 (12.29–30) and then Leviticus 19.18 as the second commandment (12.31). The scribe approves of Jesus' answer (12.32), and Jesus in turn compliments his interrogator. The evangelist here imposes on the scribe a Hellenistic Jewish view of the Law which was critical of the sacrificial cult on the basis of the confession of monotheism and the double love commandment.[164] A fundamental aspect of this view is that the Law is reconcilable with human reason. Traces of this Hellenistic Jewish thinking are clear in Mark especially in his quoting of Deuteronomy 6.5 where διάνοια (Mk. 12.30) is read,[165] and in the use of the NT hapaxlegomenon of 12.34, νουνεχῶς (with Vaticanis). The confession of the One God is clearly a point of agreement between Judaism and the early Church in Mark, whereas the change to a controversy dialogue in Matthew and Luke makes for quite different theological use of the material.[166] Notably, Luke chooses to use this dialogue as the occasion to introduce the story of the Good Samaritan with its polemical edge against ethnocentrism.

Jacob Petuchowski allows that the Shema and its benedictions are "historically speaking, the earliest liturgical components of the synagogue service."[167] The liturgical use of the Shema antedated the synagogue which cannot be confidently dated before the second century BCE.[168] Petuchowski's theological analysis of the two benedictions which are recited immediately before the Shema and the one benediction immediately after it leads him to the conclusion: "the three benedictions which surround the recitation of the Shema supplement the Shema's formulation of ethical monotheism with a hymnic affirmation of the three cardinal doctrines of biblical relig-

---

[164] See Günther Bornkamm, "Das Doppelgebot der Liebe" in Walther Eltester, *Neutestamentliche Studien für Rudolf Bultmann* (Berlin, Töpelmann, 1954), pp. 89–90.

[165] Bornkamm, "Doppelgebot," pp. 86, 89.

[166] Bultmann, *Synoptic Tradition*, p. 51.

[167] Jacob Petuchowski, "The Liturgy of the Synagogue" in *The Lord's Prayer and Jewish Liturgy*, ed. Jacob Petuchowski and M. Brocke (New York, Seabury, 1978), p. 55. Elbogen had already concluded that as both the Schools of Shammai and Hillel on the rabbinic side and Josephus on the Hellenistic, are in agreement that the twice daily recital of the Shema was an ancient Mosaic institution that in the first century the practice must have already been long established in order that their exaggerated claim might be plausibly advanced. See "Studies in the Jewish Liturgy," *JQR*, 19 (1907); Jakob J. Petuchowski, *Contributions to the Scientific Study of Jewish Liturgy* (New York, Ktav, 1970), pp. 14–15.

[168] Joseph Gutman, *Synagogues*, pp. 3–4. Note that Sidney B. Hoenig points to the bamot of the city-square as the place of the democratic and laity-centered Pharisaic worship in "City-Square and Synagogue," *ANRW*, 19.1 (1979), 449–50.

ion: Creation, Revelation, and Redemption."[169] In the third benediction there is reflection on Israel's salvation history, particularly
Moses' leadership during the exodus. It should be noted that the
pattern of Paul's theological discourse in Romans bears direct
correspondence to this liturgical tradition. Paul speaks of God as
Creator (1.19–20) and Revealer (1.17, 18; 3.21) prior to his affirmation of εἷς ὁ θεός in 3.29, and then subsequently reflects on the
Christ event in relation to Abraham (Rom. 4), Adam (Rom. 5) and
the Mosaic Law (Rom. 5–8). It is, of course, certain that Paul knew
the importance of the Shema from its prevalent liturgical use in
Judaism. The Shema functioned in Jewish liturgy as the equivalent
of a creedal confession, not simply as prayer,[170] and it readily
became a central element of Jewish apologetics.[171] The close relation between εἷς κύριος (*yhwh 'eḥād*) *and* θεός (*'elōhîm*) which is
found in the text of Deuteronomy 6.4 encouraged the ready acceptance and prolific use of the Hellenistic εἷς θεός formula by Jewish
apologists. Paul, however, could not have known the εἷς θεός
formula as such from the Shema for it is not to be found there.

Malachi 2.10: the One God, Father, and the Fathers

From the point of view of New Testament scholarship, interest in
Malachi has been limited for the most part to two verses: Malachi
3.1, which is interpreted in the gospel tradition (cf. Mark 1.2) as a
reference to the messianic herald, and Malachi 4.5, wherein a
prediction regarding Elijah is transferred to John the Baptist (cf.
Mark 9.11–13). My attention to Malachi 2.10 is prompted by its
considerable importance for understanding an initial stage in the
trajectory of the "One God" topos. First and foremost, it is the only
instance in the Old Testament where *'eḥād* (LXX εἷς) modifies
directly *'ēl* (LXX θεός).[172] Second, the "One God" topos in Malachi
2.10 is used as a separating term to divide Jews from Gentiles. Third,

---

[169] Petuchowski, "Liturgy of the Synagogue," 49. He explains that the first
benediction deals with God's fashioning of light. The second benediction deals with
God's love manifested in God's providing Israel with the revelation of Torah. The
third benediction develops the theme of the Exodus from Egypt.

[170] Petuchowski, "Liturgy of the Synagogue," 49–50.

[171] On the relation between creed and apologetic cf. Helmut Koester, *Introduction
to the New Testament*, vol. 2 (Philadelphia, Fortress, 1982), pp. 341, 344. Also see
Arthur Marmorstein, *Studies in Jewish Theology* (Freeport, New World, 1972), p. 73

[172] As already noted the order in Malachi 2.10 is the reverse of the usual order εἷς
θεός.

Malachi 2.10 juxtaposes the "One God" topos and the Fathers (Patriarchs), and hence provides a parallel to a similar juxtaposition between Romans 3.29–30 and Romans 4.1.[173] Finally, and perhaps the most striking parallel to the use in Romans is that Malachi 2.10 places the θεὸς εἷς expression in a rhetorical question and then proceeds to utilize the formula to argue in favor of a point of the Law. It is important to note that the only other instance of the "One God" topos used in a rhetorical question is to be found in our text in Romans. Paul also follows up its use there in the next verse with the claim that "we uphold the law" (Rom. 3.31). The question arises: how significant are these parallels? Only a detailed analysis of the unit Malachi 2.10–16 will be able to provide an answer, discerning similarities as well as dissimilarities to Romans.

In the unit Malachi 2.10–16 the prophet condemns two acts of faithless behavior: mixed marriages (2.11–12) and divorce from an Israelite wife (2.13–16). Malachi 2.10 serves as an appropriate introduction to both topics.[174] The rhetorical character of the questions of 2.10a and b are underscored by the repetitive syntactical arrangement in both the MT and the LXX.[175] The questions function as statements of incontestable truth which serve to indict behavior which falsifies their implicit claims. The substantives *'āb* (LXX πατήρ) and *'ēl* (LXX θεός) appear without the article, and each is followed by the cardinal *'eḥād* (LXX εἷς). There can be little doubt that "father" in verse 10a (LXX 10b) refers to Yahweh and not to Abraham (cf. Isa. 51.1–2) or any other patriarch. The use of the word *'ăbōtênû* (covenant of our fathers) at the end of 2.10 eliminates any conceivable ambiguity, and the parallelism between *'āb* and *'ēl* prompts the same conclusion.[176] In Deuteronomy 32.6 Yahweh is identified as "your Father who created you." The near oxymoron in

[173] It should be noted that in two other uses of the εἷς θεός formula in the NT there is linkage specifically with the patriarch Abraham: James 2.18–23 and Galatians 2.16–19. Note also John 8.39–41 where Abraham is mentioned together with εἷς πατήρ ὁ θεός. See chapter 3.

[174] Wilhelm Rudolph states (*Haggai/Sacharja 1–8/Sacharja 9–14/Maleachi*, KAT, 13.4, [Gütersloh, Gerd Mohn, 1976], p. 271) "Es werden zwei Arten von ehelichen Missverhältnissen behandelt: Mischehen (Mal. 2.11f.) und Ehescheidungen (vv.13–16), während v. 10 die gemeinsame Einleitung für beides bildet." Rene Vuilleumier's division of the pericope is overly subtle: "un question de divorce (10–11a et 13–16) et une autre traitant du marriage mixte (11b-12)." *Malachie*, CAT 11c (Neuchâtel, Delachaux & Miestla ⅛, 1981) p. 237.

[175] Malachi 2.10a and b are transposed in the LXX from the order in the Hebrew text. It should also be noted that the second person pl. ὑμᾶς of the LXX differs from the first person pl. *lĕkullānû* of the Hebrew text.

[176] Rudolph, *Haggai*, p. 268 n. 10.

verse 10a with *lĕkullānû* and *'eḥād* (LXX 10b εἰς πάντων) stresses that the unity of the people is grounded in a shared divine paternity. The import of Malachi 2.10a,b is to affirm a transcendental source of unity for the Israelites on the basis of which (cf. *maddûar*) their treacherous behavior towards one another is understood to be all the more reprehensible (2.10c). In Malachi 2.10c a key term of the pericope 2.10–16 is introduced for the first of its five appearances: *bāgad* (LXX καταλείπω) which means "to act or deal treacherously, faithlessly, deceitfully" and is used in particular for family relations and covenants.[177]

In this first use of *bāgad*, its subject and object are expressed in the most general terms "each to his own brother." The objection is raised against the breaking of the bonds of trust and solidarity with the Israelite community. Malachi 2.10d specifies the Israelite covenant operative here as the "covenant of your fathers." The act of betrayal of 2.10c is tied directly to covenant – indeed it constitutes a violation (*ḥālal*) of the same.

The final words of Malachi 2.10, *lĕhallēl bĕrît 'ăbōtênû*, form a chiasm with the initial *'āb* and make clear that in the prophet's understanding, an individual's proper relationship to God and to the other members of the community are inextricably inter-related.[178] The verse does not advocate universalism, and all of 2.10a is similarly restricted to Israel.[179]

Malachi 2.11 provides the reader with a specific referent to the *'îs* of 2.10c. Judah, signifying the entire remnant community of Israel, has acted faithlessly *bāgĕdâ*. A most pronounced word of denun-ciation is uttered with the word *tô'ēbāh*, as R. Vuilleumier says: "C'est un des termes les plus violentes qu'il puisse utiliser pour qualifier la conduite qu'il condamne."[180] The same term is used elsewhere in the OT in invective against homosexuality (Lev. 18.22; 20.13) and idolatry (Deut. 7.25). The realm in which the abomi-nation is committed is described progressively: Israel, Jerusalem, and finally the sanctuary of the Lord (*qōdes yhwh*).[181]

More precisely, the MT states that the abomination has been

[177] Cf. *BDB*, p. 93.

[178] See Steven L. MacKenzie and Howard N. Wallace, "Covenant Themes in Malachi," *CBQ*, 45 (1984), 549–63.

[179] Th. Chary, *Les Prophètes et le Culte à partir de l'Exile* (Paris, Tournai Desclee, 1955) p. 164.

[180] Vuilleumier, *Malachie*, p. 238.

[181] Note that Smith (*Malachi*, p. 48.) judges "in Israel and in Jerusalem" to be an expansion by a later editor.

committed in Israel and Jerusalem because (*kî*) "Judah has pro-
faned the sanctuary of the Lord which he loved."[182] The final clause
of 2.11 explains the specific act which constitutes the profanation of
the sanctuary, namely, mixed marriages: "and he married the
daughter of a foreign god."[183] Racial and religious solidarity
become inseparable issues at this point. The whole community and
its relationship to God is threatened by the practice of mixed
marriages from the prophet's perspective.

Malachi 2.12 opens with the jussive verb *yakrēt*, which is appropriate to the form of a curse. This curse is limited to "the man who
does this" (*ya 'aśennâ*, LXX τὸν ποιοῦντα ταῦτα), and the referent
of "this" is to be found retrospectively in the mixed marriages of
2.11d. The content of the curse, that is, the nature of the sanctions
invoked, is necessarily both social and religious. The offender is to
be excluded from the community (from the tents of Jacob) and from
participation in cultic rites (from bringing an offering to the Lord of
hosts).[184]

Malachi 2.13 introduces the second objectionable social practice
which the prophet condemns, namely, divorce. The word *šēnît*
(again, second) is used of a similar but not identical act in a series.
What is precisely the referent of "you do this" is not made known
until 2.14, for the remainder of 2.13 speaks only of two consequences of the as yet unspecified act. Rene Vuilleumier understands the ritual in 2.13 to be a service of repentance or a ceremony
of lamentation.[185] Such an attempt to identify the historic example
of such a ritual of lamentation is itself misguided, for the rite

---

[182] Carroll Stuhlmueller ("Malachi," *JBC*, [1968], 400) understands the temple
(which Yahweh loves) to refer to the divorced – a most fantastic suggestion!

[183] It should be noted that LXX allows here for greater latitude of interpretation
than does the MT. *bā 'al* is a common Hebrew verb meaning "to marry" or "to take
possession of a wife" (*BDB*, p. 127), but is rendered by ἐπιτηδεύω in the LXX – a far
less common word in Greek for "to marry." *bat 'ēl nēkār* is rendered by θεοὺς
ἀλλοτρίους, which further enhances the construal of this passages as referring to
spiritual adultery, that is, idolatry. Cf. Abel Isaksson, *Marriage and Ministry in the
New Temple*, ASNU, 24 (Uppsala, Lund Gleerup, 1965), pp. 27–34.

[184] Cf. *BDB*, p. 1041. There is no entirely satisfactory solution to the question of
the meaning of *'ēr wĕ 'ō nêh*. For a review of some more recent attempts, see Rudolph,
Haggai, p. 269; and for some older gallant efforts see Smith, *Malachi*, pp. 50–1.
Vuilleumier (*Malachie*, p. 240) abides by the plurality opinion in stating that the sense
of the two expressions is that the individual's entire family shall endure punishment.

[185] Vuilleumier, *Malachie*, p. 238.

mentioned here is simply described as an offering, *minḥâ*.[186]
Moreover, lamentations were common in general worship of the
post-exilic period (cf. Zech. 7.2–3; Is. 58.2–9). The triple effort of
those making the offering – "you cover the Lord's altar with tears,
with weeping, and groaning"[187] – suggests the vehement exertions
which unsuccessfully (note in 2.13c *ôd*) aim to change God's stance
vis à vis the offering. Unlike Malachi 1.6–14 and 3.8, the prophet's
concern is not with inadequate or improper fulfillment of cultic
requirements, for on this level the ministrants in question are above
reproach. The verse ends on the intransigent note of Yahweh's
adamant refusal of the offering: *mē'-ēn ... wĕlāqaḥat rāṣôn
miyyĕdekem.*

The reason for Yahweh's obstinacy is given in Malachi 2.14 which
begins "You ask why?" and is followed by *kî*. The act which has
incurred Yahweh's disapproval is the man's infidelity to his wife.[188]
The affirmation of marriage as witnessed by Yahweh precedes the
accusation of divorce and underscores the vertical sanction for
marriage.[189] The emphatic final word of Malachi 2.14: *bĕrîteka*
expresses the prophet's fundamental understanding of marriage
between an Israelite man and woman as a covenantal relationship.[190] In spite of their correct offerings, they have been spurned by
Yahweh because of their disregard of the marriage covenant.[191]

There has been frequent skepticism concerning the possibility of

[186] For an example of such an attempt, cf. H. Winckler, *Altorientalische Forschungen* (Leipzig, Eduard Pfeiffer, 1899), 2. 531–39; wherein he relates the rite here
to the women's custom of weeping for Tammuz.

[187] The expression with weeping and groaning may be a later expansion; Smith,
Malachi, p. 51.

[188] Here the now familiar word *bāgad* in the present verse carries the particular
sense of divorce, as in Jer. 3.20a where the wife is the subject of *bāgĕdâ*: "as a faithless
wife leaves her companion."

[189] The use of the word *ḥaberet* in Malachi 2.14b to refer to wife is surprising
enough for BDB to make a single category entry and to give as its meaning "consort,
i.e. wife" (p. 289). The RSV is clearly correct to translate the same uninhibitedly as
"companion."

[190] Cf. Vuilleumier, *Malachie*, pp. 238–9.

[191] Malachi does not raise the issue of divorce as a solution to the problem of
mixed marriages as in Ezra 9–10. In my judgment, Malachi's position against both
divorce and mixed marriages may be seen as internally self-consistent if one understands that Malachi's over-riding concern is to bolster the view of marriage as an
institution sanctioned by the covenant of the "Fathers." It may even be the case that
Malachi was confronting a situation where Israelite men were divorcing their covenantal brides in order to marry foreign wives. Malachi's view of divorce with respect to
mixed marriages, however, remains unclear.

reconstructing the "thoroughly corrupt" text of 2.15a[192] and of making sense of the "obscure" beginning of the verse.[193] I suggest the following translation of Malachi 2.15: "Did not One make her (him) by a portion of his spirit and what does the One seek but godly offspring!" This construal does not depend upon major emendations of the MT.[194] It proposes the common correction of a mistaken division of words – *'āśā ûśĕ'ār* which should read as *'aśāhû šĕ'ār*. In my translation *lô* is understood as having its common possessive meaning "his" and modifies *rûaḥ*; *šĕ'ār rûaḥ* has an instrumental sense with the verb *'āśā*. Further, I take *hā'eḥād* as the subject of the participial clause *ûmāh . . . mĕbaqqēš*. Thus the *'eḥād* in both instances refers to God and is used in the rhetorical question form. This construal confirms that Malachi 2.15 forms a large scale enveloping chiasm with 2.10:

> 10: *hălô' 'āb 'eḥād . . . hălô' 'ēl 'eḥād bĕrā' anû*
> 15: *wĕlô' 'eḥād 'āśā(hû) . . . ûmāh hā'eḥād . . .*

In summary, Malachi 2.10–16 presents a coherent understanding of Israelite self-identity as grounded in the transcendent One God and Father as well as the covenant of the patriarchs. Proper social relationships, particularly marriage, are defined by this covenant. Mixed marriage is both a betrayal of the community and social responsibility as well as an offense against Yahweh. Divorce is hated by Yahweh as it is a violation against the covenant and the community. In Malachi, the "One God" topos functions to enforce social and religious exclusion and should in no way be construed as

---

[192] See e. g. Dumbrell, "Malachi and the Ezra-Nehemiah Reforms," *Reformed Theological Review*, 35 (1976), 47.

[193] Smith, *Malachi*, p. 54.

[194] J. M. P. Smith, "A Note on Malachi 2:15a," *AJSL*, 28 (1911), 204–6. Smith restores the text as follows: *wĕlô 'îš 'ăšer rûaḥ lô 'eḥād mĕbaqqēš zerā 'ĕlōhîm* and renders it in English accordingly: "There is not a man who has moral sense – one who seeks a godly seed." This bold emendation of John M. P. Smith remains the most imaginative attempt at reconstructing the text, but he relies almost exclusively on a Syriac reading which appears to be more blatantly interpretive than most text traditions. The RSV translation of Malachi 2.15a decides in favor of understanding *'eḥād* as the subject of verb *āśā*, but its marginal note acknowledges that it could as well be the object of this verb. The expression *ûśĕ'ār rûaḥ lô* may refer to the spirit dwelling in the flesh of men and animals as in Zech. 12.1 and Isaiah 42.5. The question is given that if the two become one flesh, then does the spirit of either continue in the new existence which is created by marriage. Rudolph suggests that the verse be interpreted in the light of Genesis 2.23–4, and takes *'eḥād* as the object of *'āśâ*. *'eḥād* expresses the unity of man and woman, a unity grounded in creation (Gen. 2.23) and realized in marriage (*Haggai*, p. 270).

supporting a universalist tendency. Although we find in Malachi a use of the "One God" topos which has several formal parallels with our text in Romans, particularly with respect to the juxtaposition of the "One God" and "the Fathers" topoi, and also the use of the "One God" topos in a rhetorical question form in order to sustain a point of Law, we must, however, search elsewhere to find an application of the topos which has similarity of content and intentionality. In this search, Malachi may also suggest a direction, as his own concern with ethnic and national solidarity in the context of foreign influences is a preoccupation of Jewish apologetics.[195]

Hellenistic Jewish apologetic uses of the "One God" topos

The infrequency of the use of the "One God" topos in biblical and other ancient Jewish literature already has been remarked, but this correct observation does not apply to Hellenistic Jewish apologetic literature. The topos expressed not only a central creedal element of Judaism which its apologists sought to promote against prevalent polytheistic and idolatrous beliefs and practices, but also provided these same apologists with a bridge between their religion and the growing theological consensus of the contemporary educated gentile of the Hellenistic period. The Greek philosophers from Plato onwards had critiqued both the anthropomorphism and polytheism of the popular religious thought and practice of their time.[196] Hellenistic Jews such as Aristobulus, and later Philo and Josephus could join their voices to this chorus. As will be noted, there were, however, differences between the Greek philosophers' theoretical affirmation of monotheism and the Jewish apologists' avowal of the One God who was to be worshipped in continuity with the tradition of their forefathers. In brief, Hellenistic Jewish apologetic uses of the "One God" topos were primarily : (1) to critique idolatry and proclaim the one divine source for all creation as alone worthy of human worship; (2) to propagandize for the superiority of Mosaic legislation over all alternative religio-socio-political worldviews;[197]

---

[195] As for example, Philo's *Hypothetica* and *Contra Apionem* of Josephus.

[196] As for example, Plato, *Republic*, 2.378. Before Plato, note Xenophanes' critique of the Homeric gods *frgs.* 23 and 26 *Diels.* See Edward Caird, *The Evolution of Theology in the Greek Philosophers*, 2 vols. (Glasgow, MacLehose 1904), esp. 1.58–79.

[197] Paul turns upside down the Jewish apologetic line of reasoning that the Law upholds the belief that God is one and says rather that by affirming that God is one that the Law is upheld (see above chapter 2).

and (3) to promote unity and equality between Jews and Gentiles as a direct implication of the affirmation of One God. Paul's use of the topos in Romans 3.29–30 is most analogous to this last mentioned function.

The One God and Creator: polemic against idolatry in *Sibylline Oracles* 3.8–45

3.8–16: Ἄνθρωποι θεόπλαστον ἔχοντες ἐν εἰκόνι μορφήν,
πίπτε μάτην πλάζεσθε καὶ οὐκ εὐθεῖαν ἀταρπὸν
Βαίνετε ἀθανάτου κτίστου μεμνημένοι αἰεί·
Εἷς θεός ἐστι μόναρχος ἀθέσφατος αἰθέρι ναίων
αὐτοφυὴς ἀόρατος ὁρῶν μόνος αὐτὸς ἅπαντα
ὃν χεὶρ οὐχ ἐποίησε λιθοξόος οὐδ᾽ ἀπὸ χρυσοῦ
τέχνης ἀνθρώπου φαίνει τύπος οὐδ᾽ ἐλέφαντος,
ἀλλ᾽ αὐτὸς ἀνέδειξεν αἰώνιον αὐτὸς ἑαυτὸν
ὄντα τε καὶ πρὶν ἐόντα, ἀτὰρ πάλι καὶ μετέπριτα.

A clear example of the apologetic use of the "One God" topos to critique polytheism, idolatry, and to affirm that God is the source of all things is to be found in the opening verses of *Sibylline Oracles* 3, and in particular 3.8–45.[198] This passage is typical of Jewish propaganda for monotheism and employs the apologetic theme of a spiritual idea of God that is in accord with Hellenistic philosophy: eternal (3.15), self-begotten and invisible (3.12, 17). Idolatry is false because it denies the unity and uniqueness of God in failing to acknowledge the hegemony of the One God who is the sole ruler (3.11). This passage has great similarity to Sibylline Fragments 1 and 3.[199] As in *Sibylline Oracles*, fragments 1 and 3, the εἷς θεός formula in 3.11 is placed in an immediate context (3.8–11) which represents God as Creator. The circumstantial participial clause of

---

[198] These verses are widely considered not to be originally integral to the main corpus of *Sib. Or.* 3. See Lanchester, H. C. O, "The Sibylline Oracles," *APOT*, 2. 371 (Oxford, Clarendon, 1963). John J. Collins "Sibylline Oracles," in James H. Charlesworth, *The O.T. Pseudepigrapha* (Garden City, Doubleday, 1983), 1.359–60. Johannes Geffcken, *Komposition und Entstehungszeit der Oracula Sibyllina* (Leipzig, J. C. Henrichs, 1902), p. 13. Valentin Nikiprowetsky, however, argues for the unity of the third book of Sibyl; *La Troisième Sibylle* (Paris, Mouton, 1970), pp. 217–25. On the matter of the apologetic character of *Sib. Or.* 3. See Hans Conzelmann, *Heiden–Juden–Christen* (Tübingen, Mohr/Siebeck, 1981), pp. 211–14.

[199] Collins believes that *Sib. Or.* 31–45 and fragments 1–3 are all part of the lost book two ("Sibylline Oracles," pp. 360–1, 469). He suggests a date in the late Hellenistic or early Roman periods and the provenance as most likely Egyptian.

3.8 describes human beings as having a form which God made according to his own image: ἄνθρωποι θεόπλαστον ἔχοντες ἐν εἰκόνι μορφήν.[200] This clause prefaces the admonitory question of verses 9: "Why do you wander in vain, and not walk the straight path?" *Sibylline Oracles* 3.10 ends this question with another participial phrase ἀθανάτου κτίστου μεμνημένοι αἰεί and thus reiterates the theme of God as Creator. The opening words of the next verse, "εἷς θεός ἐστι – there is one God," is followed by six predicates: μόναρχος ἀθέσφατος αἰθέρι ναίων αὐτοφυὴς ἀόρατος ὁρῶν μόνος αὐτὸς ἅπαντα which are heavily indebted to Hellenistic Jewish theology.[201] The oneness or unity of God is directly correlated to the affirmation of the unity of all creation which is derived from a single source (1 Cor. 8.4–6a).[202] An explicitly negative description of God in the vein of traditional Jewish refusal to depict God in human image is found in *Sibylline Oracles* 3.13–14. *Sibylline Oracles* 3.15–16 combine the attributes of God's eternity and God's self-revelation: ἀλλ' αὐτὸς ἀνέδειξεν αἰώνιον αὐτὸς ἑαυτὸν (cf. Rom. 1.20). The difference between mortals and God – τίς Θνητός and θεός is emphasized in verses 17–20, while verses 20–8 reiterate the two concepts of God as creator and fashioner already mentioned in the initial three verses of this passage, namely God as κτίστης or ποιητής (cf. *Sib. Or.* 3.20, 28) and God as πλάστης (see *Sib. Or.* 3.24, 25, and 27). Then 3.29–45 utilizes polemical topoi against specific traditions of idolatry: verse 30 refers to Egyptian idolatry, verse 31 critiques anthropomorphic idols, and verse 32 targets the Isis cult.[203] The traditional polemic against idol-makers and worshippers as immoral is exhibited in 3.36–45: "Alas for a race which rejoices in blood, a crafty and evil race of impious and false double-tongued men and immoral adulterous idol worshippers who plot deceit"(vv. 36–8). In *Sibylline Oracles* 3.8–45 as well as in fragments 1 (vv. 7–12) and 3 (v. 3) the "One God" formula is linked to the God as Creator theme, and the primary

[200] Marmorstein points out that the rabbis vehemently opposed the gnostics' use of the first person plural in Genesis 1.26 to deny the unity of God; *Studies*, pp. 98–9.
[201] Nikiprowetzky, *Sibylle*, p. 71.
[202] In Paul as well as in much Jewish theology the critique of idolatry and idol making appeals to an accusation of the implicit inversion of positions whereby the created being presumes to "create" the Creator (Rom. 1.23, 25; cf. also Wis. 13.10–19; Isa. 40.18–23). Paul is not concerned with atheism as a theoretical objection to the existence of God but rather with an "existential" atheism which manifests in the individual's conduct; immoral behavior leads to idolatry (Wis. 14.12) and God's retribution.
[203] *Sib. Or.* frgs. 1.5; 2.3.

function of these passages is to combat idolatry and to affirm monotheism.

One God and the Other Gods: Aristobulus

Fragment 4 (*Praep. Ev.* 13.12.5)

παλαιὸς δὲ λόγος περὶ τοῦδε φαείνει, εἷς ἔστ' αὐτοτελής, αὐτοῦ δ' ὕπο πάντα τελεῖται, ἐν δ' αὐτοῖς αὐτὸς περινίσσεται, οὐδέ τις αὐτὸν εἰσοράα ψυχῶν θνητῶν, νῷ δ' εἰσοράαται.

Alexandrian Hellenistic Judaism provides the most significant parallels to Paul's use of the "One God" topos in Romans. Anticipating Philo on a number of points,[204] Aristobulus (*c*.170 BCE) grappled with the issue of how the Jews' understanding of God related to other peoples' conceptions of God. He looked favorably upon the predominant Platonic philosophical conceptualization of God as universal, spiritual, and unitary. Although 2 Maccabees 1.10 refers to Aristobulus as a "Peripatetic," he is eclectic and shows influence from Stoicism and Platonism as well as Aristotle's school.[205] The primary apologetic intent of Aristobulus was to defend the Greek translation of the Mosaic Law, that is the LXX, as true philosophy and as compatible with philosophical canons of rationality.[206]

Indeed, Aristobulus may be the inventor of the apologetic topos that the Greek philosophers plagiarized Moses.[207] Aristobulus

---

[204] Helmut Koester notes in particular the use of the allegorical method of exegesis, in *Introduction to the New Testament*, vol.1 (Philadelphia, Fortress, 1982), p. 271. In frg. 5 (*Praep.Evang.* 13.12.9–16), for example, Aristobulus applies the allegorical method to penetrate to the meaning of the Sabbath. He begins this section by a reference to God described as "the Creator of the whole world" (13.12.9). Aristobulus assures that the significance of the biblical statement that God rested on the seventh day is not that "God henceforth ceases to do anything, but it refers to the fact that after He has brought the arrangements of His works to completion, He has arranged them thus for all time" (13.12.11). Aristobulus disagrees with the view that God restricts God's own creative activity to a once and only moment and rather affirms the concept of God's continuous sustenance of the creation.

[205] Martin Hengel, *Judaism and Hellenism*, trans. J. Bornden (Philadelphia, Fortress, 1981), p. 164.

[206] Cf. Hengle, *Judaism and Hellenism*, p. 164.

[207] Cf. frg. 3 (*Praep.Evang.* 13.12.1) where Aristobulus asserts that Plato followed our legislation – καθ' ἡμᾶς νομοθεσία. M. Joel, *Blicke in die Religionsgeschichte zu Anfang des zweite christlichen Jahrhundert I-II* (Breslau, Schottlaender, 1880), pp. 88–9. In the enumeration of fragments, I follow Nikolaus Walter, *Der Thoraausleger Aristobulos* (Berlin, Akademie, 1964), pp. 7–8.

allows that there is a revelatory source for the Greek philosophers'
correct understanding that God is both the Creator and Sustainer of
the world: "it seems to me that Pythagoras, Socrates, and Plato with
great care follow him (Moses) in all respects. They copy him when
they say that they hear the voice of God, when they contemplate the
arrangement of the universe, so carefully made and so unceasingly
held together by God."[208] Aristobulus further recommends the
insight of Orpheus that God is both immanent and transcendent,[209]
and proceeds to quote more than forty verses of an Orphic hymn. In
1.10 of this hymn there is an important variant of the εἷς ὁ θεός
formula: εἷς ἔστ' αὐτοτελής,[210] αὐτοῦ δ' ὕπο πάντα τελεῖται.[211]
Clearly, the import of the εἷς predicate is not only quantitative but
also qualitative, that is, the emphasis is upon the inner unity and
self-sufficiency of God which provides the common end point of all
things: "It is clearly shown, I think, that all things are pervaded by
the power of God" (fragment 4). Aristobulus joins the Greek philosopher who elevates the theology of the fellow poets and shares as
well the Greek philosopher's disdain for anthropomorphic concep-
tualizations of God.[212] Aristobulus changes the text of the poems of
Orpheus and Aratus,[213] which he quotes, by replacing the "Dis"
and "Zeus" with the word θεός.[214] The operative assumption of
Aristobulus' editing work in this instance is that the reality which
underlies all the various names for deity is one and the same. This
presupposition allows Aristobulus without qualms to alter the
divine names in the texts which he uses to the single title – θεός.
From the point of view of Aristobulus, although different peoples
and in this case some well-known poets use a multitude of names,

[208] Πυθαγόρας τε καί, Σωκράτης καὶ Πλάτων, λέγοντες ἀκούειν φωνῆς
θεοῦ, τὴν κατασκευὴν τῶν ὅλων συνθεωροῦντες ἀκριβῶς ὑπὸ θεοῦγεγονυῖαν καὶ
συνεχομένην ἀδιαλείπτως. Frg. 4 = *Praep. Ev.* 13.12.3–8.
[209] Frg. 4 (13.12.4): θείᾳ δυνάμει τὰ πάντα καὶ γενητὰ ὑπάρχειν, καὶ ἐπὶ πάντων
εἶναι τὸν θεόν.
[210] αὐτοτελής is replaced by αὐτογενής in Pseudo-Justin and the *Protrepticus.*
Cf. Clement, but the *Stromateis* agrees with Eusebius in reading αὐτοτελής.
[211] "He is one, complete in himself and by whom all things are completed."
[212] Cf. frg.2. = *Praep. Ev.* 8.10.2: "And I wish to exhort you to receive the
interpretations according to the laws of nature and to grasp the fitting conception
of God and not to fall into the mythical and the human way of thinking about
God."
[213] *Praep. Ev.* 13.12.6.
[214] *Praep. Ev.* 13.12.7 In *Ps. Aristeas* (vv.15–16) the need is obviated for such
editorial activity with regard to the use of these same epithets because the pseudony-
mous author is represented as a non-Jew.

one should never fail to recognize that their true referent is the One God.

Aristobulus confesses, nevertheless, his own pronounced concern as a Jew for proper expression *vis à vis* God, which may exceed that of other philosophers.[215] Even the Jewish apologist, Aristobulus, who intends to promote his religion as an attractive philosophical/ theological option for the Hellenistic world, feels compelled to acknowledge the greater piety which his religion enjoins. There are limits to the syncretism which Aristobulus will endorse.[216] Aristobulus exhibits an appreciation of other theological perspectives, but he remains intensely devoted to the particularities and superiority of his tradition.

One God and the best form of government:
Josephus'*Contra Apionem* 2.165-7

ὁ δ' ἡμέτερος νομοθέτης εἰς μὲν τούτων οὐδοτιοῦν ἀπεῖδεν, ὡς δ' ἄν τις εἴποι βιασάμενος τὸν λόγον, θεοκρατίαν ἀπέδειξε τὸ πολίτευμα, θεῷ τὴν ἀρχὴν καὶ τὸ κράτος ἀναθείς ... ἕνα γοῦν αὐτὸν ἀπέφηνε καὶ ἀγένητον, καὶ πρὸς τὸν ἀΐδιον χρόνον ἀναλλοίωτον ...

Contra Apionem 2.149–245 has been understood as an apology for the Law which utilizes in its effort Hellenistic theological and ethical concepts.[217] The section is introduced as a reply to the attack on the Mosaic Code by Apollonius Molon (2.147–49). Josephus makes an argument from the oneness of God to support the Mosaic Law (2.164–7). He has Moses representing God as: "One, uncreated and immutable to all eternity" (2.167).[218] Here the emphatic first place

---

[215] *Praep. Ev.* 13.12.8
[216] *Praep. Ev.* 13.12.8. It is precisely such limits of Jewish syncretism which were objectionable to the Greek universalist thinking of Hecateus and Posidoneus; cf. Hengel, *Judaism and Hellenism*, p. 261.
[217] See Ehrhard Hamlah, "Frömmigkeit und Tugend: Die Gesetzes-apologie des Josepheus in c. Ap. 2,149–295, 220–232," in *Josephus-Studien, Untersuchungen zu Josephus; dem antiken Judentum und dem Neuen Testament* (Göttingen, Vandenhoeck & Ruprect, 1974). See also Geza Vermes, "A Summary of the Law by Josephus," *NovT*, 24 (1982), 290–3.
[218] Adolf Schlatter, *Wie sprach Josephus von Gott?* (Gütersloh, Bentelsmann, 1910), and R. J. H. Shutt, "The Concept of God in the Works of Flavius Josephus," *JJS*, 31 (1980), 171–89. Note that Josephus is quick to follow this affirmation with the denial that the οὐσία of God is knowable (2.167).

positioning of the predicate εἰς (ἕνα) is consonant with Josephus' intention to argue for the superiority of Jewish doctrines, praxis and political constitution primarily on the basis of their universality and comprehensiveness. Josephus boasts that the Mosaic Law covers all aspects of human life: ὅλην τοῦ βίου τῷ νόμῳ περιλαβών ... (*C. Apion.* 2.156). The endless diversity (ἄπειροι αἱ διαφοραί) of customs and laws in the world is noted. This observable diversity, particularly of laws, is contrasted to the Law that is applicable to all which Moses espoused (*C.Apion.* 2.151). Accordingly, Josephus purports that Moses is unimpressed with the varieties of political systems, of which he selectively names monarchy, oligarchy, and democracy (*C.Apion.* 2.164). He coins the term theocracy to describe Moses' concept of government: θεοκρατίαν ἀπέδειξε τὸ πολίτευμα, θεῷ τὴν ἀρχὴν καὶ τὸ κράτος ἀναθείς ... (*C.Apion.* 2.165). Josephus allows that for God's reign to be effective, Moses must convince everyone that God is indeed the author of rewards and punishments (*C.Apion.* 2.166.). God is all-knowing, and no human thought or deed escapes notice: λαθεῖν δὲ τὴν ἐκείνου γνώμην οὐκ ἐνὸν οὔτε τῶν πραττομένων οὐθὲν οὔθ' ὧν ἄν τις παρ' αὐτῷ διανοηθείη (*C.Apion.* 2.166–7).

In this context, the "One God" topos argues for a single divine rule and implies rejection of the view that a number of forms of government are necessary to accommodate the various local societies (the Stoic option). By proposing that there is one ruler capable of knowing everything, the One God, Josephus intends to argue on behalf of the universal validity of the Mosaic constitution. In advancing this proposition, Josephus adopts for his own ends a traditional topos which ridiculed academics and compares the philosophers who speak only πρὸς ὀλίγους (to the few) to Moses who communicates effectively to the masses (εἰς πλήθη: to the multitude; *C.Apion.* 2.169). Josephus states that Moses' success in convincing others to abide by the Law is directly related to his refusal to subordinate religion to ethics: "for he did not make religion (εὐσεβεία) a department of virtue (ἀρετή) but the various virtues – I mean, justice, temperance, fortitude, and mutual harmony in all things between the members of the community – departments of religion" (*C.Apion.* 2.170). Those believing that the laws are the expressed will of God live according to them so as not to offend God (*C.Apion.* 2.184). Josephus considers Jewish uniformity in conceiving of God as a positive factor in promoting moral living whereas the contradictory statements about God which are espoused among other peoples accounts for their relative decadence (*C.Apion.* 2.179–80). In *Contra Apionem* 2.185 he raises the rhetorical question: "Could there be a finer or more equitable polity than one which sets God at the head of the universe?"

Josephus believes that the theological principle of monotheism should be reflected on the historical plane both in terms of political institutions as well as individual human behavior. It is this conviction which motivates his apologetic reasoning and argumentation throughout *Contra Apionem* 2.149. He enunciates this operative principle clearly at *Contra Apionem* 2.193: Εἷς ναὸς ἑνὸς θεοῦ, φίλον γὰρ ἀεὶ παντὶ τὸ ὅμοιον, κοινὸς ἁπάντων κοινοῦ θεοῦ ἁπάντων.

The Jewish Hellenistic apologists readily adopted the popular philosophical formula εἷς θεός in part because of its conceptual rapport with the Shema (Deut. 6.4) and Malachi 2.10. In turn the widespread use of the εἷς θεός formula is the immediate source of the formula in the New Testament and in other early Christian literature. It was shown above (see chapter 2) that Philo's apologetic employment of the "One God" topos for the purpose of including the Gentiles (proselyte) as equal members of the Jewish community offers a direct parallel to Paul's use of this topos in Romans 3.30.

3

ROMANS 4: THE CONTINUATION OF
APOLOGETIC ARGUMENTATION

The thesis of the present chapter is that Paul continues his apologetic argumentation in Romans 4 by bringing forth Abraham both as
a great testimonial figure and as scriptural confirmation. Paul's
apologetic line of argumentation has its climax at Romans 3.29–30
with the affirmation of the One God. Romans 4 provides scriptural
confirmation for his concern to manifest the continuity of the gospel
of God with that which "God promised before" (cf. Rom. 1.1–2).
The apologetic motifs here identified, it should be noted, are most
appropriate to the protreptic genre. Before presenting my analysis
of the apologetic motifs and logic of Romans 4, I will examine three
recent interpretations of this chapter.

Three representative approaches to Romans 4

Earle Ellis: Romans 4 as midrash

Earle Ellis has focused attention on the hermeneutical principles
informing Paul's use of the Old Testament.[1] Paul often combines
two or more quoted texts in various forms: a chain of passages (e.g.
Rom. 15.9–12); a commentary pattern (Rom. 9–11 passim), both of
which were commonly employed in Judaism; and composite or
merged citations (Rom. 3.10–18). He also makes ad hoc renderings
or interpretive selections from various known texts (cf. Rom. 9.33
and 10.11). Ellis argues that Paul, and the New Testament in
general, interprets the Old Testament in a midrashic mode:
"Explicit midrash appears in double entendre, in interpretive alter-
ations of Old Testament citations and in more elaborate forms."[2]

[1] E. Earle Ellis, *Prophecy and Hermeneutic*, WUNT, 18 (Tübingen, Mohr/Siebeck,
1978). In an earlier work (*Paul's Use of the Old Testament*, Edinburgh, Oliver and
Boyd, 1957), Ellis discussed the source and form of the Pauline scriptural quotations.
[2] Ellis, *Prophecy*, p. 152. Ellis reiterates the position he espoused in his *Paul's Use*.

This "explicit midrash" in the New Testament, Ellis asserts, has affinities both with the Pesher method of interpretation at Qumran and with midrash in rabbinic circles as well as in Philo.[3] Ellis is indebted to Peder Borgen for the proposal concerning the formal elements which constitute a homiletic midrash pattern which they believe is found in Romans 4.[4]

Borgen describes three basic characteristics of the homiletic pattern. The first is a correspondence between the opening and closing parts of the homily, in which the closing statement also sums up important points which appear throughout the sermon. Second, there is a main quotation from the Old Testament, which is presented at the outset and one or more subordinate quotations are added also from the Old Testament. Third, words from the text are paraphrased in the body of the homily. Borgen adduces several texts which exhibit this pattern, including John 6.31–58; Philo's *Mut. nom.* 253–263; *Leg. all.* 3. 65–75a, 162–68; as well as Romans 4.3–22 which is framed by the key words of Genesis 15.6: ἐλογίσθη αὐτῷ εἰς δικαιοσύνην. In addition to the main text of Genesis 15.6, Romans 4.1–22 has the subordinate quotations (Ps. 32.1–2; Gen. 15.5 and 17.5). In accordance with the third element of the homiletic pattern, Romans 4 quotes or paraphrases the central words of the text (Gen. 15.6) in 4.4–21. Borgen notes that the commentary in Romans 4 does not follow the sequence of the words in the text (i.e. Rom. 4.3). Instead, words are remarked upon as they "throw light on the problem which is being discussed."[5] Further, Borgen notes that the concentration on specific subject matter has caused the paraphrase to be less developed than in the homilies of Philo's *De Somniis* 2.17–30; *Legum Allegoriarum* 3.65–75a; and *De Legatione ad Gaium* 3.69 because the exposition is focused upon the problem which Paul links to the text. This problem takes precedence over the exegetical concern to clarify every word and phrase in the Old Testament text.

On several occasions, Philo alludes to exegetical lecturing in the synagogue (*Hypoth.* 7.12–15; *Omn. prob. lib. sit.* 80; *De vit. cont.* 30–31; *De spec. leg.* 2.61–2; *Vit. Mos* 2.215; *Som* 2.127). These references, however, cannot resolve the problem that there are no available sources to provide examples of Jewish homilies. Thus the

---

[3] Ellis, *Prophecy*, p. 154.

[4] Peder Borgen, *Bread From Heaven*, 2nd edn, *NovTSup* 10 (Leiden, Brill, 1981), pp. 169–73. Borgen argues that Romans 4 also evinces this pattern.

[5] Borgen, *Bread*, p. 50.

hypothesis of an ancient homiletic pattern is not verifiable. A further problem with defining Romans 4 as a midrash is that the term itself remains unclear, as Ellis admits.[6] Moreover, Borgen's suggestion that Paul's exegesis in Romans 4 does not follow the sequence of words but concentrates on topical concerns indicates that the homiletic midrashic model may be ill-suited to describe Romans 4. In sum, although the "midrashic" approach to Romans 4 may account for some general features of the text, it fails to accommodate several other important characteristics of this text, including the key Pauline hermeneutic in Romans 4 of drawing inferences from the narrative sequence of the Genesis account.

Hendrikus Boers: the central theological question of Romans 4

During the 1960s, a heated theological debate ensued between exegetes who read Romans 4 as affirming salvation–history theology and those who upheld the view that Paul's emphasis is on justification by faith.[7] Writing towards the end of this debate, Hendrikus Boers both summarizes some of the central arguments of the controversy and in some respects advances the discussion, particularly with regard to his delineation of the differences between Galatians 2–3 and Romans 4.[8] Boers agrees with Günther Klein's assessment of the central theological problem of Romans 4: if the possibility of experiencing the righteousness of God has its chronological start in the date of the death of Jesus, then how can a scriptural text which cites the case of Abraham serve to prove the point?[9] Paul

[6] Ellis, *Prophecy*, p. 192.

[7] Some of the main contestants in the debate were Oscar Cullmann, *Salvation in History*, ET (New York/Evanston, Harper and Row, 1967); Johannes Munck, *Paul and the Salvation of Mankind*, ET (Atlanta, John Knox Press, 1977); Günter Klein, "Romer 4 und die Idee der Heilsgeschichte," *EvTh*, 23 (1963), 424–47; Ulrich Wilckens, "Zu Römer 3,21–4,25: Antwort aus G. Klein," *EvTh*, 24 (1964), 586–610; Hans Conzelmann, "Die Rechtfertigungslehre des Paulus. Theologie oder Anthropologie?," *EvTh*, 28 (1968), 389–404; Krister Stendahl, "The Apostle Paul and the Introspective Conscience of the West," *HTR*, 56 (1963), 199–215, and Stendahl's response to E. Käsemann's critique (cf. below) of this article in *Paul among the Jews and Gentiles* (Philadelphia, Fortress Press, 1976), pp. 127–32; E. Käsemann, "Justification and Salvation History in the Epistle to the Romans," *Perspectives on Paul* (Philadelphia, Fortress Press, 1971), pp. 60–78.

[8] Hendrikus Boers, "The Significance of Abraham for the Christian Faith," in *Theology out of the Ghetto* (Leiden, Brill,1971), pp. 74–104.

[9] See Boers' quoting of Klein in "Significance of Abraham," 78, and also Käsemann, "The Faith of Abraham in Romans 4," *Perspectives*, p. 86.

unquestionably understands Abraham to have been justified by faith on the grounds of Genesis 15.6. Although Klein's question is legitimate, the thought may never have occurred to Paul. Boers understands Romans 4.2 as a "concession to the descendants in the flesh of Abraham," namely, that there is a certain justification in works.[10] He notes, however, that Paul immediately cuts off this line of thinking with the words: ἀλλ' οὐ πρὸς θεόν (4.2b) and substantiates this reversal with Genesis 15.6. Thus, Paul in 4.4–8 is opposing an interpretation of the Genesis verse which asserts a reckoning in accordance with what is owed on the basis of works to his own understanding of the verse as expressing the meaning in accordance with grace.[11]

There are several problems with Boers' construal at this point. It is not clear that the κατὰ σάρκα is more of a concession if applied to Judaism than when applied to Jesus (Rom. 1.3; 9.5). Moreover, προπάτωρ probably emphasizes that Abraham was, of course, not a Jew but a Gentile. This option becomes all the more plausible in light of the argument of 4.10. Further, it is not clear why quotation of Genesis 15.6 cuts off a presupposed plan of salvation, especially given Paul's undoubted conviction that Abraham was a historical figure.[12] Boers argues more cogently, although he does not offer any evidence for it,[13] that Paul is opposing an interpretation of Genesis 15.6 which presumes Abraham's meritorious achievement.

Observations concerning the differences between Romans 4 and Galatians 3.6–29 are instructive.[14] The structure of Abraham's faith is the key to Paul's argument in Romans 4. Paul establishes a positive relationship between the faith of Abraham and the faith of the Christian. In contrast to Romans, the structure of Abraham's faith was not significant to Paul's reasoning in Galatians 3. The presupposition of his argument in Galatians, namely, the identification of Christ as the "one" σπέρμα 'Αβραάμ (seed/offspring of Abraham) is precluded in Romans by the logic of 4.18–22. Boers suggests that in Romans, unlike Galatians, there is a "genuine dialogue" between the Christian Paul and the non-Christian

[10] Boers, *Theology*, p. 86.
[11] Ibid., p. 87
[12] Perhaps, Boers has in mind Käsemann's objection to an immanental view of salvation history; but this is already a rather distorted characterization of salvation history.
[13] Note E. P. Sanders' objection to a works' righteousness view of Palestinian Judaism is one of the central thrusts of his *Paul and Palestinian Judaism*.
[14] Boers, *Theology*, pp. 82–3.

Genesis account concerning the justification of Abraham.[15] Theocentrism is the distinctive characteristic of Romans 4, compared with the Christocentrism of Galatians 3. Nowhere in Romans 4 is the faith of Abraham interpreted either explicitly or implicitly as faith in Christ;[16] the primary feature of faith is trust in God, according to Romans 4.

Boers' theological insights have much to commend them. The major problem with his interpretation, however, is his overdrawn construction of a "Christian Paul." He imputes to Paul a lack of awareness that the Genesis account was pre-Christian.[17] But Paul never denied his Jewish heritage, although he was certainly aware that his interpretation of Scripture was rejected by many of his fellow Jews as service to another Lord. It is precisely for this reason that Paul in Romans 4 puts forth the apologetic theme of the continuity of God's acts in the past and now.

Stanley Stowers: Romans 4 and the diatribe

Early in this century, Rudolf Bultmann proposed that Paul's letters were related to the literary genre of the Cynic–Stoic diatribe.[18] Bultmann identified five elements of the diatribe style: (1) dialogical character; (2) rhetorical character; (3) constituent parts and arrangement; (4) manner of argumentation; and (5) tone and mood. For all of these elements Bultmann adduced copious examples from the Pauline corpus. In a recent dissertation, Stanley Stowers has re-examined the issue of the diatribe in relation to Romans.[19] Stowers focuses on one of these elements – the dialogical character of diatribe – and identifies this style in Romans at 2.1–5, 17–24; 3.27–4.25; 9.19–21; and 11.17–24.

In Romans 3.27–4.25 two major forms of discourse are fused:[20] a dialogical exchange in the mode of indictment or censure (3.27–4.2) is followed by an exemplum, providing a positive model for life

---

[15] Boers thinks that Paul allows a certain justification in works at Romans 4.2 and previously at 2.13b – the doers of the Law are justified. *Theology*, pp. 85–8.

[16] Boers, *Theology*, p. 91.

[17] "It was a fundamental assumption for him that it was Christian." Boers, *Theology*, p. 103.

[18] R. Bultmann, *Der Stil der Paulinischen Predigt und die kynish-stoische Diatribe* (Göttingen, Vandenhock & Ruprecht, 1910).

[19] Stanley Stowers, *The Diatribe and Paul's Letter to the Romans*, SBLDS, 57 (Chico, Scholars Press, 1981). One of the contributions of Stowers' work is to show conclusively that diatribe is not a genre designation.

[20] Stowers, *The Diatribe*, p. 155.

(Rom. 4.3–25). Thus, Stowers observes the protreptic mode marks 4.3–25. Moreover, several of the individual features of Romans 3.27–4.2 bear close similarity to the Dialogues of Epictetus,[21] particularly inquiring (3.27) and leading rhetorical questions (3.28b) as well as an objection (4.1–2a) and a false conclusion and its rejection (3.31). Romans 3.28 states a basic claim or thesis and 3.29a presents an undeniable basic principle. In general, the text is characterized by the lively paratactic question-and-answer style which is typical of Epictetus. The use of the first person plural in the objection, however, is atypical.[22]

Stowers points to the features of Romans 4 which resemble the exemplum as it is used in conjunction with the dialogical element in the diatribe.[23] Romans 4.2b–25 is a detailed answer to 4.1 and 2a, and also to the other questions which were raised in 3.27–31. The exemplum derives from the wider context of ancient rhetoric common to the diatribe and Romans 4. For instance, Paul rejects the implied interpretation of Abraham in 4.2b and puts forth the *auctoritas* (Gen. 15.6). In 4.4–5 the form of the argument resembles an enthymeme or rhetorical deduction. Romans 4.9–10 is another exchange of questions and answers. The warrant for applying the exemplum to the present argument appears in 4.9–11. Stowers' interpretation of Romans 4.3–25, however, omits verses 12–25 except to mention that 23–5 is an "admonition" concerning the applicability of the exemplum.[24]

Stowers' analysis leads him to the intriguing conclusion that the dialogical style of Romans is evidence for what could best be described as "Paul's school": "From Romans we would expect to find two basic, though not completely separate, activities in Paul's school. First, the exegesis and interpretation of the scriptures and second, ethical religious instruction in the style of indictment and protreptic."[25] This school hypothesis, however, might lead to the mistaken view of sedate and leisurely study and reflection. One needs to recall that Paul preached a gospel which was perceived as questioning the presuppositions of both the dominant religious and political power structures in his time. As his autobiographical asides

[21] Ibid., p.165.
[22] The use of the first person plural is indicative of the apologetic context; see my discussion of Romans 3.8 in the previous chapter.
[23] Stowers, *Diatribe*, p. 171.
[24] Ibid., p. 173. Stowers devotes only two pages (pp. 172–3) to this issue.
[25] Ibid., p. 183.

indicate, prison may be the more likely setting for his moments of profound reflection.[26] It should be noted, however, that Stowers' hypothesis need not be construed as excluding Paul's role as an apologist, and he has rightly suggested the protreptic character of the rhetoric in Romans 4. His school hypothesis, however, seems to be more apt for Justin, whose writings reveal more elaborate and abundant exegetical material.

Apologetic motifs in Romans 4

In Romans 4 Paul uses three apologetic motifs: (1) the testimonial use of "great name" figures; (2) the universalizing presentation of theological claims; and (3) the argument of the continuity of God's activity.

Traditional "great name" figures

In Romans 4 Paul adduces Scripture for support of various propositions and appeals to the status of "great name" figures therein. The repeated mention of Abraham throughout Romans 4 and the explicit use of the name of David in 4.6 should be seen in light of the apologetic traditions which commonly introduce these and other biblical names to testify to various causes. These and other figures functioned prominently in apologetic literature as testimonial figures and were put forth as guarantors of proposed theological and political positions. Accordingly, seeking to convince the Hellenistic world of the superiority of the Jewish culture, Philo used Joseph to represent the ideal political values embraced by Jews. Likewise the presentation of Moses as a divine man by Philo and Josephus served the purpose of commending the Law.[27]

In the New Testament frequent apologetic use is made of Abraham as a standard of comparison against which another figure's greatness is measured. In Hebrews 7.4 Melchizedek is proved to be great because Abraham acts towards him as a subordinate to a superior. This comparison is made on the way to establishing the main concern of the author of Hebrews: the ultimacy of the high priesthood of Christ. In John 8.53 the issue is the comparative greatness of Abraham and Jesus. The reply in 8.58 con-

---

[26] Cf. e.g. 2 Corinthians 11.23–33.

[27] See Erwin R. Goodenough, *An Introduction to Philo Judaeus*, 2nd edn (New York, Barnes & Noble, 1963).

tends that Jesus is the one with whom no historical individual can rightly be compared. Justin in his *Dialogue* (19.4) drew the battle line even farther back; he argued emphatically that Noah, not Abraham, is the "beginning of the race" (ἀρχὴ γένους).[28] In some Jewish literature, the *Book of Jubilees* for example, there seems to be concern to assert Abraham's paternal role over against that of Isaac, so that Isaac does not function as the father of Jacob but rather Abraham plays this role *vis à vis* both Isaac and Jacob (*Jubilees* 20; 22).

For Paul, Abraham afforded a positive figure from Judaism whom he could interpret to affirm his connection with his own past. Moses, because of that figure's inseparable identity with the Law, could not so readily be used towards this end (see for example 2 Cor. 3). In Romans 4 Paul does not make overt comparisons between Christ and Abraham in order to prove Christ's greatness. He refers straightforwardly to Abraham as our forefather κατὰ σάρκα in 4.1. Moreover, Paul's positive appropriation of Abraham in Romans 4 is in accord with the thrust of his reconciliatory theologizing, which is also his intention in 3.29–30 with his use of the "One God" topos. He uses the One God in Romans 3 to ameliorate the divisive consequences of his christology, which separates the Pauline communities from not only Jews but also Jewish Christians. As already suggested, Paul's appeal to the "One God" topos in Romans 3.29–30 has the central function of promoting unity between Gentile and Jewish Christians.

In Jewish Hellenistic apologetics, the Abraham figure functions to legitimize the inclusion of Gentiles in the Jewish community, as has also been shown of the "One God" topos. Philo explicitly uses Abraham as a warrant to affirm the dignity of the proselyte before his own kinspeople: "Abraham is the standard of nobility for proselytes who, abandoning the ignobility of strange laws and monstrous customs which assigned divine honours to sticks and stones and soulless things in general, have come to settle in a better land, in a commonwealth full of true life and vitality, with truth as its director and president."[29] In line with this correspondence of the functions of the "One God" topos and the figure of Abraham is the

---

[28] Note that ἡ ἀρχή carries the basic meanings of origin and ruler. The apologetic motifs of the great names and of the most ancient tradition often merge in actual usage.

[29] *De Virtutibus* 219.

tradition that Abraham was the first to believe in the One God.[30] As Josephus says: "He was the first boldly to declare that God, the Creator of the universe is one, and that, if any other being contributed aught to man's welfare, each did so by His command and not in virtue of its own inherent power."[31] Both Josephus and Philo allege that Abraham came to knowledge of the One God from the study of astrology.[32] Similarly, Philo says of Abraham: "And, therefore, he is the first person spoken of as believing in God, since he first grasped a firm and unswerving conception of the truth that there is one Cause above all and that it provides for the world and all that is therein" (*Virt.* 216). Philo pointedly says of Abraham in the section of *Virt.* just before the previous quotation that "The most ancient member of the Jewish nation was a Chaldean by birth, the son of an astrologer" (212). Hellenistic Jewish literature used Abraham internally to promote the dignity of proselytes as well as to overcome the stigma of past religious and ethnic affiliations, and externally to present Abraham as the master of all sciences and the teacher of other peoples.[33] Roy Ward has suggested that James 2.19 – "You believe that God is one" – may already be hinting at the πίστις (faith) of Abraham.[34] In sum, the close association between Abraham and the "One God" topos in apologetic literature as well as their equivalent sociological function (that is, to legitimate the inclusion of the Gentiles) strongly suggests that Paul's usage serves similar apologetic ends, namely, to promote the unity of Gentile Christians and Jewish Christians. Thus, Paul concludes his presentation of Abraham in Romans 4.11b–12 with the affirmation that Abraham is the Father of both the uncircumcised and the circumcised who follow in the footsteps of his faith (cf. 3.29–30; 4.16c,17,18).

The second significant biblical name which Paul adduces in Romans 4 is that of David (4.6). After quoting Genesis 15.6 in Galatians 3, Paul quickly moved to equate Christ with the seed of

[30] Most significant for understanding Paul's use of Abraham in Romans 4 is *Virt.* 214 where Abraham is referred to as achieving τὴν τοῦ ἑνὸς εὕρεσιν.

[31] *Antiquitates Judaicae* 1.155.

[32] *Ant.* 1.7.1; Philo, *De Gigantibus* 13–15. On the historical situation which prompted this apologetic tradition, see W. L. Knox, "Abraham and the Quest for God," *HTR*, 28 (1935), 55–60.

[33] Eupolemus in Alexander Polyhistor *apud* Eupolemus *Praep. Ev.* 9.17–18.

[34] Roy Warden, "The Works of Abraham Jas. 2:14–26," *HTR*, 61 (1968), 288.

Abraham.[35] In Romans 4, unlike Galatians, he follows up the quotation of Genesis 15.6 with another Old Testament citation (Rom. 4.7–8 = Ps. 31.1–2). Romans 4.6–8 continues the question of how righteousness is accounted to Abraham. More importantly, it introduces the question of how Abraham's righteousness is related to the rest of humankind – an issue which will be central in 4.9–12. In Romans 4.6 Paul uses the proper name David in the introductory quotation formula καὶ Δαυὶδ λέγει (also David says). Elsewhere he has quoted the Psalms (e.g. Rom. 10.18; 15.9), but does not use the name of David, although in these instances the Psalms in question were also attributed to David.[36] The only other instance where Paul uses the introductory formula καὶ Δαυὶδ λέγει is also in Romans (11.9–10), and here again the immediate context includes mention of other biblical names: Abraham, Benjamin (11.1), Elijah (11.2), and also Israel (11.7).[37] Moses, Abraham, and David represent the three most venerable figures in the view of Judaism in the first century.[38] By mentioning Abraham and David, Paul in Romans 4 has marshalled two superlative witnesses in support of his position.

In Romans 4.6–8, Paul adapts the theme of the benefactions of Abraham and the blessings which accrue from association with him. He emphasizes the word ὁ μακαρισμός by placing it immediately after the quotation formula in 4.6 (καὶ Δαυὶδ λέγει τὸν μακαρισμόν). Μακαρισμός is found in Greek literature since Aristotle as a technical term extolling personal fortune.[39] David and his kingdom were seen in Judaism as proof of the blessings the descendants of

[35] Galatians 3.6 is a complete parallel with LXX Genesis 15.6 except that the latter has "Abram" and the former "Abraam." Romans 4.3 also has the lengthened form of the personal name and adds a δέ before the name. James 2.23 is identical to Romans 4.3. It is possible that Paul consciously uses the lengthened form of the name anticipating his opponents' retort that it was only after Abraham's circumcision, and not after his merely believing God, that Abram received the new name which signified his new status before God (see Justin, *Dial.* 113.2–3). The δέ may then have been added without reflection in Romans, while James' retaining it may indicate, as his exegesis certainly does, that he has Paul's text in mind, and perhaps even in hand, as he advances his alternative interpretation of Genesis 15.6.

[36] At Romans 8.36 Paul quotes Psalm 43.23, accorded to the Sons of Korah by the Rabbis who accepted literally the scriptural statements concerning authorship. Paul's understanding of the authorship of the various Psalms also agreed with this literal reading of his day; cf. Toy, *Quotations in the New Testament* (New York, Scribner's, 1884), p. 29.

[37] Here, however, Israel denotes the nation and not the patriarch Jacob.

[38] See C. K. Barrett, *From First Adam to Last* (New York, Scribner's, 1962), p. 68.

[39] See Gustav L. Dirichlet, *De Veterum Macarismis*, Religionsgeschichtliche Versuche und Vorarbeiten 14 (Giessen,Töpelmann, 1914), p. 2; Bertram and Hauck, 'μακαρισμός', *TDNT*, 4 (1967), 362–70.

Abraham were capable of receiving. Paul's need to put forth a renowned figure to pronounce the blessing parallels the apologetic rationale for his explicit mention of David in Romans 4.6.[40]

The universalizing theme of Romans 4

The tendency to present Judaism as a universal religion whose import is without geographic or temporal restrictions is characteristic of Jewish apologetics, as Dieter Georgi has demonstrated.[41] The central thrust of this apologetic motif is that the professed claims are at least potentially consequential for all peoples. Paul is especially insistent to state in Romans that his gospel addresses *all* people.[42] In Romans 3, as has been noted, he makes both negative and positive universal statements: Ἰουδαίους τε καὶ Ἕλληνας πάντας ὑφ' ἁμαρτίαν (3.9) and δικαιοσύνη ... εἰς πάντας τοὺς πιστεύοντας (3.22b). The consequences of Adam's sin are universalized in Romans 5 in order to sustain the corresponding affirmation of the grace made available to all through Christ (5.12–19). Two subsidiary themes often accompanying the apologetic motif of universalism, namely that nature and humankind will enjoy a cooperative relationship and that the ideal of peace will be realized, are found respectively in Romans 8.19–25 and 5.1 (see chapter 4).

Romans 4 presents Abraham as the universal father figure of all who believe in God. In line with Jewish apologetics that pointed to the fact that Abraham lived before the time of the differentiation between Jews and Gentiles, Paul affirms that Abraham is the foundation figure for both Jews and Gentiles: as their common Father, Abraham is the basis for unity. Abraham as the first believer in the One God guarantees unity between all people despite ethnic and even religious differences (3.29–30).[43] Faith, not lineal descent, is the only qualification for the status of child of Abraham, since faith is an orientation of being towards God, before whom all such

[40] See *Ben Sira* 36.17 where the more common εὐλογία is used instead of μακαρισμός.

[41] Dieter Georgi, *The Opponents of Paul in Second Corinthians*, trans. and rev. edn (Philadelphia, Fortress, 1986), pp. 148–51.

[42] Paul uses the word πᾶς over thirty times in Romans. Ironically, Paul is painfully aware that the Christ event, which intended to overcome the barrier between Jews and the nations, has created further divisions – see below on Romans 9–11.

[43] See Knox, "Abraham," 55–60. The pluralism envisaged is intra-Christian. Thus a distinction between the prepositions in 3.30 would enhance this reading; see chapter 2, n. 124.

distinctions are void (2.11; 25–9, 3.29–30; 4.2). Paul uses the word πατήρ (Father) for Abraham six times in Romans 4 (4.11,12 [twice],16,17,18). The influence of the Roman *patria potestas* concept which was pervasive in the Hellenistic world should not be overlooked here.[44] Augustus in the *Res gestae* proudly reports that the Roman people gave him the title of Father of the country (*pater patriae*; πατὴρ πατρίδος) and that this same title was inscribed upon the vestibule of his house and in the senate house as well as in the Forum Augustum (*Res gestae* 6.35). Thus the term apparently was widely used in the "secular" sphere to render to the ruling elite the additional loyalty deriving from traditions of ancestral devotion. Paul plays on this common usage as he dwells on the promise to Abraham that τό κληρονόμον αὐτὸν εἶναι κόσμου (4.13). The presumed allusions here, Genesis 18.18 and 22.17–18, do not use the word κόσμος. Paul uses the word here as at 1.8 and 3.19 with its nonpejorative sense of the "whole inhabited world" or the entire earth.[45] This global meaning of the word is apposite in the context of Romans 4, which emphasizes the link between the Father Abraham and the topos of the "many nations" which is to be found already in the Genesis text (Gen. 17.5 = Rom. 4.17). Paul repeats the expression πατὴρ πολλῶν ἐθνῶν in 4.18, where he makes that role the telos of Abraham's believing (ἐπίστευσεν εἰς τὸ γενέσθαι αὐτὸν πατέρα πολλῶν ἐθνῶν).[46] With this theological modification, he adopts the Abraham of Hellenistic Jewish apologetic, the universal founding figure who not only guarantees the full inclusion of the Gentiles but presages the overcoming of all such social antagonism. Paul attempts a universalizing reinterpretation of σπέρμα 'Αβραάμ in Romans 4. In 4.13 the universal statement τὸ κληρονόμον αὐτὸν εἶναι κόσμου already mentioned is placed immediately after τῷ σπέρματι αὐτοῦ (Abraham's). In 4.16 Paul adds the universalizing πᾶς in attributive position to σπέρμα. In its final occurrence in Romans 4 σπέρμα is explained in the light of Genesis 17.5 'πατέρα πολλῶν ἐθνῶν'. In Romans 9, however, Paul uses the expression σπέρμα 'Αβραάμ as a restricting term. Σπέρμα 'Αβραάμ' is not equivalent to πάντες τέκνα (all children) for it excludes τὰ τέκνα τῆς σαρκός (children of the flesh; 9.7–8). Thus Paul argues against a

---

[44] Schrenk, 'πατήρ', *TDNT*, 5 (1967), 950–1.

[45] See Sasse, 'κοσμέω', *TDNT*, 3 (1965), 888.

[46] Note that Paul stresses the noetic dimension of Abraham's faith in Romans 4.19, in accordance with the apologetic emphasis on the knowledge of Abraham which allows him to discover God (cf. Josephus, *Ant.* 1.154–68).

purely ethnic definition of σπέρμα ᾽Αβραάμ but does not universalize it from the perspective of a secular worldview. In this sense the philosophical universalists should have the same disdain for Paul as was accorded to Aristobulus, for instance.[47] Paul still adduces a differentiating principle, albeit a theological one rather than a natural or social one. Thus the criticism of all apologetic universalizing arguments may also be made of Paul here. For this reason, I suggest that Paul's theological program be described as inclusive particularism rather than universalism. Yet, for the purposes of explaining the self-understanding of apologetics, the term universalizing as used in the description is accurate.

The motif of the continuity of God's acts

A focal theme of Jewish apologetics is that God continues to act on behalf of God's people in the present. For instance, in *De Legatione ad Gaium* 1.3, Philo answers the skepticism of some Jews who were unable to believe that God was still concerned with them. Thus, Philo speaks of God as working in specific acts to protect them in their present difficulties with Gaius (*Leg. Gaium.* 220; 367). The Christian appropriation of the apologetic motif of the continuity of God's acts is determined by the presentation and defense of its kerygma.[48] Christian apologetics affirm that God acts "now" in the Christ event and that this act is consistent with God's past acts in history. Christian apologetics emphasize the continuity of God's work so as to promote its novel theological claims. Thus, the prominence of the promise-fulfillment motif in Christian apologetics is not surprising. Accordingly, in Acts 3.25b; 7.5, 17 the "promise to Abraham" occurs in salvation history recitations which culminate in the proclamation of Christ (Acts 3.18–26; 7.2–53).[49]

The centrality of the promise to Abraham in Romans 4.13–25 is well known. The noun ἐπαγγελία occurs four times (vv. 4.13,14,16, 20) and the verb ἐπαγγέλλομαι appears in 4.21, where it emphasizes

[47] See Martin Hengel, *Judaism and Hellenism* (Philadelphia, Fortress, 1981), p. 261
[48] There is no dispute that a primary concern of NT apologetics is the presentation of the cross and resurrection of Jesus as the fulfillment of the Will of God. Towards this end, the synoptic Gospels are constructed and their appeal to Scripture (Old Testament) is in large measure to affirm this kerygma; Lindars, *New Testament Apologetic* (London, SCM, 1961); Bultmann, *History of the Synoptic Tradition* (New York, Harper & Row, 1976), pp. 180–2; Koester, *History and Literature*, pp. 174–5
[49] In Acts 26.6 the generic "to our fathers" replaces Abraham as the direct recipients of God's words of promise (cf. Luke 1.55).

the theme of God's power to do what God has promised (ὃ ἐπήγ-γελται δυνατός ἐστιν καὶ ποιῆσαι). Paul's affirmation of the δύναμις of God reflects the Jewish apologetic ambivalence towards the miraculous that arises from its commitment to rationality. Thus the validity of the promise (4.14), for Paul, is to be based on the potency of God. The giver of the promise is able to fulfill the promise. The correct human response is faith (2.19), but Paul does not relinquish the rational dimension of faith; he stresses that Abraham: κατενόησεν τὸ ἑαυτοῦ σῶμα νενεκρωμένον, ἑκατον-ταετής που ὑπάρχων (he considered his own body to be as if dead, being about one hundred years old; 4.19). Thus the rational acknowledgement of human limitations and weakness is com-plementary rather than antithetical to the affirmation of tran-scendent power operative in the human situation. Paul affirms a continuity between God's promise and God's act.

The second and main aspect of the apologetic theme of the continuity of God's activity is the relatedness to be established between particular events. In 4.17, Paul offers a striking definition of God that first emphasizes God's regenerative power: τοῦ ζῳο-ποιοῦντος τοὺς νεκρούς (making alive those who died); and second mentions God's creative capacity: καλοῦντος τὰ μὴ ὄντα ὡς ὄντα (calling into existence the things not existing). Why does Paul choose to emphasize God's regenerative powers in Romans 4.17? I suggest that this definition of God is critical for his apologe-tic affirmation of the continuity of God's activity. Paul's argument hinges upon his use of the root νεκρ- (i.e., death-words) four times in this pericope. After his programmatic definition of God in 4.17, Paul uses a form of νεκρ twice in 4.19. Abraham is said to be aware that his own body is νενεκρωμένον, and then Sarah is mentioned by name in a genitive construction dependent on the noun νέκρωσις (τὴν νέκρωσιν τῆς μήτρας Σάρρας). From the reference to Genesis 15.5 in Romans 4.18 (and especially 4.17), and the mention of Abraham's age (ἑκατονταετής)[50] as well as ἡ μήτηρ Σάρρα, it is apparent that Paul refers to the birth of Isaac – a birth, as he metaphorically puts it, through dead parents. The birth of Isaac is a demonstration of the power of God (ζῳοποιοῦντος τοὺς νεκρούς). Paul is not emphasizing the miracle of birth through the aged parents, but that God ὃ ἐπήγγελται δυνατός ἐστιν καὶ ποιῆσαι (is able to do what he promised; 4.21).

[50] See Genesis 17.17.

The apologetic argument of continuity does not culminate until Romans 4.24–5. Paul draws the analogy of the faith of Abraham to τοῖς πιστεύουσιν ἐπὶ τὸν ἐγείραντα Ἰησοῦν τὸν κύριον ἡμῶν ἐκ νεκρῶν. In this fourth and final use of νεκρ-words, Paul's argument achieves its rhetorical climax. In Romans 4.24 ἐκ νεκρῶν refers to Jesus' death on the cross and corresponds to the state of death ascribed to Abraham and Sarah, through whom God brought life. Likewise, the object of the participle τοῖς πιστεύουσιν in 4.24 is not Jesus but, emphatically, God – τὸν ἐγείραντα Ἰησοῦν.[51] Paul compares Abraham, who believed in God, to those who believe the gospel that Paul preaches. The same God who promised Abraham to give him a son in his time of "death" raised Jesus from the dead (διὰ τὴν δικαίωσιν ἡμῶν, 4.25). Paul affirms the continuity of God's activity by declaring that God's acts have consistent effects under the same circumstances, understood to be death from which God effects life.

The coherence of Romans 3.29–4.25

Paul not only employs several apologetic motifs in Romans 4; he also integrates them into a coherent and effective argument. The integrity of his argument is grounded in the leading monotheistic motif of Romans 3.29–30. Most commentators struggle to see a reasonable transition between Romans 3 and 4;[52] usually pointing to a connection with boasting in 3.27, while ignoring 3.29–30.[53] In contrast, the interpretation I am proposing resolves the problem by pointing to the centrality of 3.29–30 and understanding Romans 3.29–4.25 as a unitary argument. The following presents in outline form the logic of Paul's argument:

3.29–4.25:   There is One God who justifies all: thesis and
               scriptural witnesses.
3.29–31   I   3.29–31: The thesis: there is one God who will
               justify both the circumcised and the
               uncircumcised.

---

[51] In Romans 4.25, when ὅς refers to Jesus, it is the subject of passive verbs.

[52] See Hays, "A Reconsideration of Rom. 4:1," *NovT*, 27 (1985), 86.

[53] C. E. B. Cranfield understands Romans 4 to follow upon 3.27: "the function of this section [4.1–25] is to confirm the truth of what was said in the first part of 3.27" (*Romans*, vol. 1, p. 224). Käsemann also stresses the relationship between Romans 4.2 and 3.27 (*Romans*, p. 106). Otto Michel points to a connection between Romans 4.1–8 with its two scriptural quotations and 3.21 and 3.31, but he does not mention 3.29–30; *Der Brief an die Römer*, MeyerK, 4th edn (Göttingen, Vandenhoeck & Ruprecht, 1955), p. 98.

3.29–31			– One God of All – for the faithful	
29–30		(1)	The One God and the solidarity of humankind (a creedal acclamation and its social implication)	
29			(a)	rhetorical question and answer affirming that God is the God of Gentiles as well as Jews
30a			(b)	creedal acclamation – there is One God (the shared presupposition)
30b			(c)	consequences for both circumcised and uncircumcised – God justifies both through faith
31		(2)	Νόμος (Scripture) maintained	
31a			(a)	rhetorical question rejecting the accusation that Paul destroys the Law
31b			(b)	Scripture sustained (backward reference to One God and forward reference to Abraham)
4.1–12	II		Abraham as the scriptural witness that God is One and justifies both Jews and Gentiles	
1–5	A		The status of Abraham *vis à vis* God and people	
1		(1)	Rhetorical question regarding Abraham's discovery	
2		(2)	Boast of Abraham	
2a			(a)	based on contrary to fact condition
2b			(b)	negation of boast before God
3–5		(3)	Primary scriptural argument	
3			(a)	quotation of Genesis 15.6
4–5			(b)	exegesis of quotation: the basis of the reckoning: Abraham believed God (τὸν δικαιοῦντα τὸν ἀσεβῆ)
6–8	B		David as the second scriptural witness to God's blessing of humanity	
6		(1)	David: introductory quotation formula	
7–8		(2)	Quotation of Psalm 31.15 (cf. 3.25d–26a)	
9–12	C		Abraham as Father of the circumcised and uncircumcised	
9a		(1)	Question of inclusion (cf. 3.29)	
9b–11a		(2)	Question and answer as to whether Abraham was circumcised before or after he was reckoned righteous	

11b–12		(3)	Conclusion: Abraham is Father of all who believe, circumcised and uncircumcised (cf. 3.30)
4.13–25	III		Consistency between God's promise and act: past and present
	A		God's promise to Abraham (scriptural witness) and God's potency
13–14		(1)	Nature and basis of the promise
13a			(a) basis of the promise negatively stated
13b			(b) content of the promise
13c			(c) basis of the promise positively stated
14			(d) contrary to fact premise re. promise and its consequences
15		(2)	Digression on Law (perhaps, however, an allusion to the fact that Abraham lived before the time of the Mosaic Law)
16–22		(3)	Abraham's belief that God could do what He promised
16			(a) basis and content of the promise
16a–b			(i) positive basis of the promise
16c1			(ii) the recipients of the promise defined
16c2–17a1			(b) status of Abraham the Father of All (Gen. 17.5)
17a2			(c) conclusion: God defined whom Abraham believed
18			(d) goal of Abraham's belief (Gen. 17.5; 15.5)
19–21		(4)	God's potency and the circumstances of Abraham's faith
19			(a) awareness of bodily circumstances
20a			(b) relation between the promise and Abraham's faith
20b			(c) Abraham's active relation to God
21			(d) potency of the one who promised
22			(e) conclusion: Abraham is reckoned righteous because he believes God is able.
23–25	B		Application to the present
23		(1)	Negative statement re. application
24a		(2)	Positive statement re. application

24b–25   (3)   Basis of the application: believing in the
                      same One who acts

The entire argument in 3.29–4.25 hinges upon the shared presupposition that there is one God. Paul affirms that because there is one God, this God will justify both Jews and Gentiles according to a common standard of faith. He painstakingly demonstrates this in 3.29–4.25 with a heavy reliance on scriptural witnesses.[54]

The overriding significance of the "One God" topos can best be seen by Paul's choosing to attribute to εἷς ὁ θεός the last use of the verb δικαιόω (justify) in Romans 3. The christological assertions in Romans 3.24–6 led to theological objections by Jews and Jewish Christians who inquired how the proclamation of Christ crucified was to be reconciled with traditional beliefs.[55] In the earliest Christian community, Jesus had become an object of cultic veneration.[56] It was this fact that led Paul to persecute the Christian community before his "conversion" experience (Gal. 1.13–16). Larry Hurtado rightly notes that "early Jewish Christians, like Paul after his Damascus road experience, felt justified in giving Jesus reverence in terms of divinity and at the same time thought of themselves as worshipping one God."[57] Hurtado acknowledges in passing that this veneration of Jesus may have caused other Jews to regard such Christians as violating the most important test for true monotheism, that is, exclusivity in worship, but he does not explore the question further.[58] There can be no doubt that the exalted status of Jesus and the polemical comparisons with traditional Jewish figures (above all Moses but also Melchizedek, Abraham, David, Enoch, and others) led many Jews to question the authenticity of early Christian monotheism. Paul's christological affirmations were most problematic and required a response to those who objected that his christology was fundamentally inimical to monotheism and the Law.

Paul seizes the high ground by affirming the One God and building on well-known Jewish apologetic arguments that adduced

[54] See Cranfield, *Romans*, p. 202 n. 2. The twofold designation used here for the Old Testament as a whole is also found at Matthew 5.17, 7.12, 22.40.

[55] See Halvor Moxnes, *Theology in Conflict*, NovTSup, 53 (Leiden, Brill, 1980).

[56] See Larry W. Hurtado, *One God, One Lord: Early Christian Devotion and Ancient Jewish Monotheism* (Philadelphia, Fortress, 1988), p. 4.

[57] Hurtado, *One God*, p. 2.

[58] In fairness to Hurtado it should be noted his expressed concern in this work is to demonstrate that early Christianity derived from ancient Judaism the conceptual category of divine agency by which it was to construe the exalted Jesus at the right hand of God – *One God*, p. 12.

the "One God" topos as the guarantor of the status of proselytes.[59] He demonstrates the compatibility of his soteriological proclamation with traditional Jewish monotheism by attributing the significant verb δικαιόω το εἷς ὁ θεός (the One God will justify, 3.30). Thus, the rhetorical question in Romans 3.30 is intended to silence implicit objections that Paul's gospel diminshes the One God and slights the Jews – a concern present in Romans 4 and again explicitly in Romans 9–11.[60] Paul raises the social implications of the creedal acclamation that God is one in verses 29–30.[61] The oneness of God contrasts with the social dualism of the circumcised and uncircumcised (i.e. Jews and Gentiles);[62] Paul argues that monotheism assures the solidarity of the human race – solidarity to be realized in the Christian community.[63]

Romans 3.31 could mean either that the norm or law of faith is upheld or that νόμος referring to Scripture is upheld; the latter is more likely. A few verses earlier, Paul uses the word νόμος with precisely this sense, as in 3.21b where he claims that scripture bears witness to the righteousness of God. In 3.19 the word again unequivocally denotes Scripture. Paul's assertion that he upholds the Scripture in 3.31 refers both backward to a central affirmation of biblical faith in one God, and forward to David and, especially, to Abraham of Romans 4 with its several scriptural quotations. In typical apologetic fashion, Paul contends that he does not "destroy" (καταργέω) but rather upholds the Scripture. He will insist in Romans 4 that he has penetrated to the real meaning of the Scriptures and that he explains more of the Scripture and more correctly, as, for instance, why Abraham is circumcised only after he is said to believe in God.

Precisely here in Romans 4.3, 7, 8 Paul shows that he has scriptural grounds for his thesis that God acts impartially towards Jews

---

[59] See Philo, *Spec. Leg.*, 1.52
[60] See chapter 5.
[61] Betz's suggestion (*Galatians*, p. 173) of the application of the ancient rule τὸ ὅμοιον τῷ ὁμοίῳ φίλον to understand Galatians 3.20 may be more relevant to Romans 3.29–30. That Paul does not distinguish between the attributes and substance of God is seen by verses 30 and 26b: God is just and is justifying; God is one and acts as God towards all.
[62] See G. Schrenk, "Der Römerbrief als Missionsdokument," in *Studien zu Paulus*, Zurich, Zwingli, 1954, pp. 81–106.
[63] As already suggested, Paul is advocating for a diversified Christian community which is marked by respect among its constituent elements; see chapter 1.

and Gentiles.[64] Before that, however, he allows an objection to his position to surface at 4.1, namely a claim to preferential treatment that is based on the ancestral merits of Abraham and presumes mistakenly that Abraham, rather than God, effects righteousness.[65] This objection he emphatically denies,[66] arguing that it has no foundation in Scripture and contradicts the clear meaning of it (4.2). The One God justifies according to faith and not because of the works of Abraham.[67] Paul quotes Genesis 15.6 in Romans 4.3 in order to sustain the case that his gospel is in accord with Scripture. In 4.4–5 he juxtaposes the two conflicting interpretations of Abraham's justification – compensation for works rendered and faith in God who justifies the impious. Paul will now give further scriptural support to this second interpretation. In Romans 4.6–8 God alone is presented as the great benefactor who blesses individuals despite their unworthiness. God's blessing is given to those whose works do not warrant it and whose sins would undoubtedly preclude it. It is not the calculation (λογίζομαι) of human merit, but God's grace that grants the blessing. Before Paul will affirm Abraham's role as "Father" he intends to make clear that even Abraham has no claim to righteousness except that he believed God (ἐπὶ τὸν δικαιοῦντα τὸν ἀσεβῆ, 4.5).

Paul proposes to answer the question of whether the blessing is for the circumcised or the uncircumcised (4.9) by determining the condition under which Abraham received the blessing (4.10–11). He notes that Genesis 17.10–11 refers to circumcision as a sign (σημεῖον) of the relationship/covenant between God and Abraham.[68] Abraham's circumcision is also described as a seal of his righteousness and this implies that his status as righteous preceded his circumcision. Arguing from the order of the scriptural verses, Paul concludes that circumcision cannot have been a requirement of Abraham's blessing/justification. For Paul this conclusion is incontrovertible because of the priority of Genesis 15.6 to Genesis 17.10–11 where

[64] See Jouette M. Bassler, "Divine Impartiality in Paul's Letter to the Romans," *NovT*, 26 (1984), 43–58.
[65] Having raised an issue of the relation of God to the uncircumcised in verses 3.29–30, Paul's mention of Abraham in 4.1 is totally unsurprising. See above on the role of Abraham with respect to proselytes.
[66] Ulrich Wilckens, *Der Brief an die Römer*, EKKNT, 6 (Zurich, Neukirchen, 1978), vol. 1, pp. 261–2
[67] For a list of texts with Jewish and Hellenistic Jewish interpretations of Genesis 15.6 opposed to that of Paul – See Wilckens, *Brief*, n. 832.
[68] See Rengstorf, 'σημεῖον', *TDNT*, 7 (1971), 258.

Abraham's circumcision is first mentioned. Paul stresses that Abraham is the Father only of those among the cirumcised who follow the footsteps of Abraham's faith, that is, before his circumcision (4.12). Abraham is presented as an *exemplum* of faith; in holding forth this *imitatio fidei* interpretation of Abraham's true descendants, Paul rejects the notion of ancestral inheritance. The One God justifies all according to faith regardless of ethnic origins.[69]

The brilliant exegetical insight of Paul in 4.10–11 that Abraham was reckoned righteous before his circumcision parallels the argument of 3.29–30 and establishes the conclusion that Abraham is the Father of all who believe, whether they are circumcised or not. On the historical or horizontal plane, Abraham has a parallel relationship, with respect to both the "circumcised" and the "uncircumcised" of faith, as has the One God to these same two peoples. Indeed, Abraham stands in this position only because he was the first to believe in God. Paul has appropriated Abraham just as confidently as he has the One God to support his plea for the inclusion of Gentiles into the Christian community and to encourage mutual respect between Jewish and Gentile Christians.[70]

The question of God's promise to Abraham is addressed in Romans 4.13–21. Paul must confront renewed objections that his preaching "destroys" (καταργέω – cf. 3.31, 4.14) Scripture. In Romans 4, the issue is specifically his interpretation of Abraham and whether it implies a denial of the promise of Genesis 18.18, 22.17, namely, that his seed will inherit the world (4.13–14). Paul responds that the promise is still valid (βέβαια – 4.16) not only for the lineal descendants of Abraham but for all peoples. The content of the promise is the inheritance of the world (Rom. 4.13b; Gen. 18.18; 22.17–18), and in Genesis 17.5 it is further expressed that "Abraham will be the father of many nations." Paul argues that Genesis 17.5, which he quotes at 4.7, has already stated the universalism characterizing his understanding of the role of Abraham.

The central thread of 4.13–22, that the basis of the promise is not the Law but the faith of Abraham, is continuous with 4.1–12, where

[69] Paul's "universalism," of course, sets up another standard of exclusion as well as inclusion.

[70] On the identification of the "circumcised who are not merely circumcised but also follow the example of the faith" (Rom. 4.12) as Jewish Christians, see Francis Watson, *Paul, Judaism and the Gentiles: A Sociological Approach*, SNTSMS, 56 (Cambridge, University Press, 1986), p. 141.

it is affirmed that Abraham is justified on the basis of his faith and not his works. In Romans 4.13–22 the verb πιστεύω or noun πίστις (faith, trust) is attributed to Abraham at verses 13, 14, 16, 17, 18, 19, 20.[71] Verse 17b defines the object of Abraham's believing as θεοῦ τοῦ ζῳοποιοῦντος τοὺς νεκροὺς καὶ καλοῦντος τὰ μὴ ὄντα ὡς ὄντα. The potency of God is emphasized here over against the situation of the impotency of Abraham and Sarah (4.19). The promise that Abraham is to be the "father of many nations" was beyond human hope or expectations (4.18a) as Abraham and Sarah remained childless in their old age. Paul quotes Genesis 15.5 (= Rom 4.18b): "so shall your seed be," and makes clear that Abraham believed the promise of the birth of Isaac. This is the material content of the promise that Paul has in mind already in Romans 4.3 when he quoted Genesis 15.6.[72] He understands that there is a noetic aspect (κατανοέω) to Abraham's faith, namely, that he is aware of his own and Sarah's bodily condition, which are both pointedly characterized by the word "death." The reference to the announcement of the birth of Isaac is further confirmed by the ἑκατονταετής[73] and also the appositive to Sarah, μήτηρ (mother). Here the stress on God's potency is crucial, and the potency of God is defined by Paul very particularly *vis à vis* death. As Abraham believes in a God "who gives life to the dead and calls into existence the things that do not exist," the circumstances of Sarah's physical condition and his own are not cause for despair. The potency of God guarantees the validity of the promise (βεβαίαν τὴν ἐπαγγελίαν, 4.16). In telling a tale whose end is already known by his hearers, Paul without mentioning the name of Isaac, has already passed the last test of the apologist – the demonstration of the fulfillment of the promise (ὃ ἐπήγγελται δυνατός ἐστιν καὶ ποιῆσαι). Paul's apologetic intent is to apply the lesson of the ancient biblical story to the present situation of Christians.

In the final verses of Romans 4, Paul continues to rely on Scrip-

[71] Romans 4.15 may, however, be a digression unless it is an allusion to the fact that Abraham lived before the time of the Mosaic Law, in which case 4.16 would follow logically affirming that on the basis of his faith (in a time when there was no Law) Abraham confirmed the promise for Jews and Gentiles.

[72] See Käsemann, *Romans*, p. 110; Cranfield, *Romans*, 1.231. Note that Genesis 15.5 (Rom. 4.18b) is the last direct quotation of Scripture before the repetition of the clause ἐλογίσθη αὐτῷ εἰς δικαιοσύνην from Genesis 15.6 (Rom. 4.22).

[73] Cf. Genesis 17.17: "Then Abraham fell on his face and laughed, and said to himself, 'Shall a child be born to a man who is a hundred years old? Shall Sarah, who is ninety years old, bear a child?'"

ture (ἐγάφη, 4.23) in order now to establish the connection between Abraham and Christians. The righteousness accounted to Abraham is also to be accounted to them (vv.23–4). Paul's case for the extension of this blessing to Christians is predicated on a "not only ... but also" logic. In verses 23–4 it is made clear that the Abraham example is applicable to the present believers as indicated by the co-ordinate clauses: Οὐκ ἐγάφη δὲ δι' αὐτὸν (that is, Abraham) μόνον ὅτι ἐλογίσθη αὐτῷ ἀλλὰ καὶ δι' ἡμᾶς. In Romans 4.12 and 16, Paul has also used the same logic (οὐ μόνον, ἀλλὰ καί) to argue that Abraham is the Father of both Jews and Gentiles who "follow in the footsteps of Abraham's faith." This mode of argumentation was first put forth in Romans 3.29: "Is God the God of the Jews only? Is He not also the God of the Gentiles?"[74] Paul answered that query by appealing in 3.30 to the One God who justifies both Jews and Gentiles. Abraham and Christians are accounted righteous because they believe in the same God:

> 4.5b: πιστεύοντι δὲ ἐπὶ τὸν δικαιοῦντα τὸν ἀσεβῆ
> 4.24b: τοῖς πιστεύουσιν ἐπὶ τὸν ἐγείραντα Ἰησοῦν τὸν κύριον ἡμῶν[75]

There is an identity in terms of the agency which effects the central religious experience of both Abraham and Christians: the same God justifies them. Paul affirms that there is one God who has both promised and effected this promise under the same circumstances of "death" (vv.17, 19, 24) in Abraham and "now" in those believing that God has acted in Christ.[76]

Conclusion

The affirmation that there is One God who acts now in a manner consistent with past promises and under like circumstances is central to Paul's logic. Paul's application of the verb δικαιόω to the

---

[74] Note that Romans 3.29a is a rhetorical question, and thus "μόνον" has the same import as "οὐ μόνον" in 4.12, 16, and 23.

[75] The construction of πιστεύω with the preposition ἐπὶ followed by the accusative participle with article and concluded by the accusative direct object with article of the participle, is precisely paralleled in Romans 4.5 where the object of belief is also God – τὸν δικαιοῦντα.

[76] For a discussion of how Paul deals with conflict between the concrete promise of the land in Genesis and his spiritualized interpretation of this promise, see W. D. Davies, *The Gospel and the Land* (Berkeley, University of Californial Press, 1974), pp. 166–216.

"One God" formula in Romans 3.30 indicates that he is concerned with monotheism not as a metaphysical truth claim, but rather for its theological and sociological implication: that God acts toward humankind in an impartial and trustworthy manner. Romans 4 is an outstanding instance of the creative reinterpretation of Scripture, for the purpose of promoting a new community and its value system, evidencing its protreptic orientation. Throughout Romans 3.29–4.25 Paul speaks on behalf of his constituency, Gentile Christians, and pleads their case that the One God justifies them as well as Jewish Christians. The promise to Abraham included Gentile Christians and they fulfill the many nations of which Abraham is the Father. Paul argues effectively in Romans 4 that the new experience of justification of Christians is related to the ancient biblical event of Abraham's justification (Gen. 15.6). He thus claims that his gospel is not merely consonant with Jewish monotheism and Scripture but emphatically upholds them.

4

PAUL RECOMMENDS AND DEFENDS THE GOSPEL OF GOD

Introduction

Comparable to other λόγοι προτρεπτικοί, Romans 5–8 functions primarily in a positive manner as an ἐνδεικτικός (see glossary) and constitutes a commendation of the life made possible in Christ.[1] Romans 5–8 provides abundant evidence for the thesis that Paul is speaking with a primary concern for Jewish Christians, those who know the Law (7.1). Although Paul is unwilling to compromise on the essential elements of his Law-free gospel, he evinces significant interest in countering the accusation of antinomianism. His polemic against the Law and Moses in Romans is both tempered and nuanced (unlike either Galatians or 2 Corinthians). In focusing on the contrast between Adam and Christ, Paul avoids a direct contraposition between Christ and Moses. Moses is subtly contained and his relatively circumscribed historical role is indicated by the juxtaposition to the cosmic figures of Adam and Christ. While Abraham and the One God are symbols of Judaism which Paul may without ambivalence endorse, his evaluation of Moses and the Law is more complex. Thus, although the positive aspect of Protreptic is dominant in Romans 5–8, both a negative element and σύγκρισις common to the Protreptic are also present.

Three motifs: Romans 5.1–11

In Romans 5.1–11 three motifs dominate: (1) the ideal of peace and reconciliation (5.1,10–11); (2) the Maccabean theme of persecution (5.3b–4); and (3) the "sacrificial death" motif – who dies for whose sake! (5.6–8).

Although Paul's presentation of the theme of peace and recon-

---

[1] Aune, "Logos Protreptikos," pp. 36–7.

ciliation is undoubtably indebted to biblical traditions, it also reflects contemporary Roman heroic ideals. Thus a few words concerning Roman literary traditions extolling the imperial reign of peace are in order before examining Paul's treatment of the peace theme. Beginning with Augustus, imperial propaganda luxuriated in extravagant praise of the peace achieved by the *Princeps*. In Vergil and Horace, paeans to Augustus evinced a clearly eschatological emphasis, for the emperor was credited not only with ending an era of war and conflict but also with inaugurating the new age.[2] Pacification was accomplished by the strong yet clement hand of the savior, the emperor. The successors of Augustus expected similar accolades from their contemporary bards and were often obliged. A flatterer of Nero, the poet Calpurnius Siculus wrote:

> Amid untroubled peace, the Golden Age springs to a second birth; at last kindly Themis, throwing off the gathered dust of her mourning, returns to the earth; blissful ages attend the youthful prince.[3]

The more capable Seneca in the *Apocolocyntosis*, written in late 54 CE, compared Nero in voice and beauty to Apollo and celebrates Nero's reign as presaging the return to a golden age (*Apoc.* 4.1). Imperial propaganda exulted in the accomplishment of the *Pax Romana* that had not simply ended warfare, but reconciled antagonistic peoples in the warm embrace of the imperial father.[4]

Having presented Abraham in Romans 4 as the Father of all believers in contrast to the imperial father, Paul concludes the chapter by analogizing Abraham's faith with respect to the birth of Isaac to the faith of Christians in the resurrected Jesus (see chapter 3). It is not surpising that Paul in writing to Christians residing in the imperial capital cautiously contrasts the peace wrought by God through the death and resurrection of Jesus with the peace established by the Roman emperor. The main subject matter of Romans 5.1–11 is that "those who are justified are at peace with God" as is

---

[2] I am not intending to suggest that Paul read either Vergil or Horace. The orientation pointed to here is to be found in imperial propaganda popularized throughout the empire in the first century. See Helmut Koester, *Introduction to the New Testament, vol. 1: History, Culture, and Religion of the Hellenistic Age* (Philadelphia, Fortress, 1982), p. 369; For instance, the Roma-Augustus temple in Athens where the inscription on one of the epistyle blocks records the dedication by the "priest of the Goddess Rome and the Savior Augustus."

[3] See further Calpurnius Siculus 1.42–.

[4] See *Res gestae*, passim.

clear from verses 1,10,11.[5] As most exegetes acknowledge, Romans 5.1–2 is linked intentionally to 4.23–5 as indicated by the use of οὖν in 5.1. As a result of the justification based on the death and resurrection of Jesus Christ, believers have a new relationship with God which is defined as εἰρήνη (peace). The word ἡ προσαγωγή (5.2) suggests the privilege of being introduced to someone in high or royal station.[6] The rhetorical crescendo achieved in verses 3b–4 stresses the theme that "patience works all things" which Käsemann suggests has its origin in the context of the Maccabean persecution.[7] Paul clearly intends to distinguish the peace which he proclaims from imperial "peace" in terms both of its content and of the process by which it is achieved.

In Romans 5.6–8, Paul emphasizes that it is Christ's death that has made possible the new relationship with God that has renewed the human heart with the love of God (5.5). Four clauses in verses 6–8 end with the verb ἀποθνήσκειν (die). In 5.6, Paul makes a false start in contrasting the sacrifice of Christ with acts of heroism – "scarcely one will die for a just person" (5.6) but he allows that there are those who have given up their lives for the sake of their bene-factors.[8] The contrast to Christ, who is the good one who dies for those who are sinful as well as his inferiors, is unmistakable. The peace which God establishes is not wrought by the sacrifice of the many subjects (the legions) but rather God's own son is sacrificed to save his subjects (5.8): a stunning reversal from the normal course of "heroic" deeds and achievements which mark the successes of secular history. Here, Paul indulges the common protreptic stylistic feature of synkrysis, emphasizing the disparity between God's act and the accomplishments of an unregenerate humankind.

In Romans 5.10–11, Paul brings to a climax his portrayal of the achievement of God – God has reconciled his "enemy," sinful humanity, to God and in doing so has not sacrificed his subjects but rather his own son. A form of καταλλάσσω (reconcile) occurs three times in verses 10–11 and affirms God's definitive rule and sole effective action. Finally, Paul intends to make clear that there is, indeed, no real or positive comparison between the peace achieved by God through Christ and the much vaunted imperial peace of his

---

[5] Cranfield believes that this is the central theme for Romans 5–8, *Romans*, p. 255.
[6] See Cranfield, *Romans*, p. 259.
[7] Käsemann, *Romans*, p. 134.
[8] The phrase ὑπὲρ τοῦ ἀγαθοῦ may also mean "for the public good"; see Cranfield, *Romans*, pp. 264–5.

time. For the latter was by the emperor through the sacrifice of his subjects and is at best a temporary security whereas the peace achieved by God through Christ transforms human existence fundamentally. Paul may have two purposes in mind in distancing his gospel of peace from the secular ideals that predominate in the first century of the empire: to affirm the superiority of the gospel of Christ and at the same time to deny any intention to compete for earthly power with the Romans (see chapter 6 on Romans 13).

Romans 5.12–21: the two-fold comparison between "great name" figures: Christ and Adam

In Romans 5.12–21, Paul offers a two-fold comparison of Adam and Christ which is characteristic of the apologetic appropriation of "great name" figures: (1) Adam and Christ are seen as parallel in their impact on history (vv. 13, 14c, 18–19); (2) the superiority of the latter is asserted with respect to the former – πολλῷ μᾶλλον (vv. 15–17); and (3) the restricted purpose and subordinate status of Moses and of the Law are affirmed (vv. 13–14a, 20–1). Justin Martyr often employs such a two-step appropriation of "great name" figures in which positive association or equality with Christ is affirmed and then assertions of the inferiority of the same to Christ quickly follow (*Apol.* 1, 22. 2–4).[9] Likewise, Paul first asserts that Adam is a type of Christ[10] and that the two are similar in their univeral impact on human history (5.13, 14, 18, 19). Paul, however, qualifies immediately this assertion of similarity and claims the superority of Jesus over Adam in verses 15–17. In these verses, he will repeat the phrase πολλῷ μᾶλλον (much more) to assure that Christ's impact is, of course, much greater than that of Adam. Adam and Christ are, nevertheless, similar in that they determine the human condition – "one" over "many" or "all" (vv. 12, 15, 16, 17, 18, 19) and thus the extensiveness of their impact is comparable even if the direction of their impact is diametrically opposite.

---

[9] "If somebody objects that he was crucified, this is in common with the sons of Zeus, as you call them, who suffered, as previously listed. Since their fatal sufferings are narrated as not similar but different, so his unique passion should not seem any worse – indeed I will, as I have undertaken, show, as the argument proceeds that he was better; for he is shown to be better by his actions." Translation from Cyril C. Richardson, *Early Christian Fathers* (New York, Macmillan, 1970), p. 256.

[10] On typological exegesis and Paul, see Leonhhardt Goeppelt, *Typos: Die typologische Deutung des Alten Testaments im Neuen*, BFCTh, 2, Reihe 43 (Gütersloh, 1939; repr. Darmstadt, 1969).

Whereas classical Greek and Hellenistic philosophers were fasci-
nated with the metaphysical, or at least theoretical, question of the
relationship of the One and the many, Paul, and Philo before him,
raised the issue with a decidedly anthropological pitch: one cosmic
individual impacting all humankind.[11] Hellenistic Judaism has
already developed the motif of the Primal Man who is determinative
for all humankind. In conjoining the apocalyptic two aeons motif[12]
and that of the Primal Man, Paul creates his Adamic–Christ concept
that will not be significantly advanced again until Irenaeus (*Adv.
Haer*).[13] Käsemann has pointed to the complexity of Romans 5.12
deriving from the presence of the two contrary motifs of destiny and
personal guilt (vv. 12a–c and 12d respectively).[14] As already indicated, Paul presents both Adam and Christ as figures who impact
humankind willy-nilly. At the same time, he allows that within
either the Adamic or Christic spheres of influence individuals may
act wilfully (sinning and receiving grace, 5.12d, 17b). Paul is, nevertheless, much less resistant to allowing a role for destiny than is
Justin Martyr.[15] Herein may lie a partial answer to the philological
pecularity of 5.14–21 wherein Paul uses the verb βασιλεύω (reign,
14d; 17–2x; 21–2x) more times than in the entire rest of his correspondence.[16] The double use of the verb in verses 17 and 21 is
intended clearly to contrast the kingdoms of Adam and Christ. The
royal language is appropriate precisely because Paul understands
the two figures to exercise an authority or influence over all their
subjects, that is humanity. In verse 17 Paul chooses tenses carefully
and indicates in 17b that the reign of the saints is in the future. It is
likely that either Jewish or Christian Romans would readily see a
contrast implicit here between the imperial reign and this future
reign. Many exegetes of 5.12–21 have recognized that these verses
elaborate 5.1–11; one may also hear an echo therein of a suggested
contrast between the imperial peace and the peace achieved by God
through Christ in the dual uses of βασιλεύω. Paul, to be sure,

[11] See chapter 2 on Philo.
[12] As already mentioned, this motif is often employed in imperial propaganda.
[13] Gnostic use of the Adam–Christ motif is not infrequent but indicates two
inherently differentiated classes of human beings rather than alternative possiblities
of human historical existence as in Paul.
[14] The tendency of exegetes to dissolve too readily the antinomies is understandable but not warranted by the text.
[15] On this topic in Justin, see Erwin R. Goodenough, *The Theology of Justin
Martyr* (Jena,1923; Amsterdam, Philo Press, 1968).
[16] See Moulton and Geden, p. 144. Paul uses the verb in only four other instances
including once in Romans.

attempts to elevate the significance of the Kingdom of Christ so that it is not properly comparable to either the *imperium* and its peace or the reign of Adam.

Paul pointedly refuses to compare directly Moses and Jesus. Having set up the antithesis between Adam and Christ, he suspends Moses between these two determiners of the human condition. According to Paul, the only difference effected by the advent of Moses is that human sinfulness is enhanced (5.20a). After Moses introduces the Law, individuals sin in a manner more akin to Adam, who knowingly violated the commandment of God (5.14). Paul, however, admits to a positive if paradoxical role for the Law: the increase of sin resulting from Law-aware violators allows for the entrance of a countervailing grace. The "place" (οὗ) of greatest iniquity is also where grace most abounds (5.20a). Paul's theological and apostolic objections to the imposition of the requirements of the Law on Gentile Christians lead to a designed depreciation of Moses, the central revelatory mediator of Judaism. Paul's commitment to preach the gospel of Christ compels him to displace Moses who, from his perspective, is the figure that most hinders Jews from acknowledging the full significance of Christ (2 Cor. 3.12–16). Paul has deftly achieved the dethroning of Moses with his Adam–Christ typology which construes Moses as a secondary or intermediary figure. Moses is effectively contained between the cosmic poles of Adam and Christ.

Romans 6.1–14: "Shall we not sin that …": A legalist's objection and Paul's response

The apologetic character of Romans 6 has often been obscured by the dogmatic concern to exploit this text as a *locus classicus* for the doctrine of baptism. As most modern exegetes have realized, however, the purpose of this chapter of Romans is not the exposition of Paul's understanding of baptism but rather the response to two related objections to his preaching and accordingly Romans 6 is rightly divided into two parts: verses 1–14 and verses 15–23.[17]

The objection that Paul's teaching on grace leads logically to the conclusion that Christians ought to sin in order that God's grace

---

[17] In this division of the chapter, I concur with Barrett, Brunner, Cranfield, Nygren, et al. Käsemann, however, understands 6.12–14 as part of the second section.

may abound was already put forth in Romans 3.8.[18] However, Paul did not there enter into a full rebuttal of the accusation. The reappearance of this specific objection is prompted by what he has said in 5.20b: if grace abounds where sin increases, then one could reasonably conclude that it is, indeed, good to sin![19] In Romans 6.2 Paul provides his most basic as well as direct repartee to this objection which must surely be derived from previous encounters with opponents to his doctrine of grace (cf. 3.8).[20] He is no more likely to invent purely hypothetical objections to fundamental convictions than is any other ardent advocate of a cause. He is answering objections to specific positions that he has encountered previously and thus reasonably anticipates as likely to occur to the Jewish Christian recipients of his letter.[21] Paul asserts that Christians have "died" to sin and thus cannot continue to "live" in it (6.2). He adduces baptism in verse 3 as a demonstration of the thesis that Christians have died to sin (v.2). In other words, baptism is referred to as evidence for his central claim that his teaching is not antinomian. Paul, in Romans 6, is not contributing a unique doctrine of baptism, as is already clear from ἤ ἀγνοεῖτε, but rather is making reference to the understanding of baptism prevalent in Christian communities outside of Palestine.[22] In baptism Christians are freed from the power of sin by sharing in the death of Jesus. In verses 4–5 Paul draws a parallel between Christ's death and his resurrection, on the one hand, and Christians' baptism and the guarantee of their future resurrection, on the other. Romans 6.5–7 repeats the main thrust of Paul's argument in verses 2–4.[23] He is emphatic in his denial of the accusation of antinomianism.

Paul affirms again the noetic dimension of faith in Romans 6.8–9,

[18] It is interesting that Gerd Luedemann, who denied the possibility of determining whether Jewish Christians were part of Paul's audience in Romans, excepts Romans 3.8 and mentions that 6.1, 15 are answering similar accusations; see Gerd Luedemann, *Opposition to Paul in Jewish Christianity* (Minneapolis, Fortress, 1989), pp. 109–11. It seems to me highly improbable, if Paul's opposition is indeed Jewish Christian at Romans 3.8, that the same opposition is not also in mind when Paul elsewhere in Romans discusses Jewish Christian issues.

[19] So Cranfield, *Romans*, p. 296.

[20] So Brunner, p. 489; Barrett, pp. 120–1; Nygren, p. 253; Käsemann, p. 165.

[21] Given Paul's specific and detailed knowledge of both the political situation in Rome (see chapter 6) and the Roman Christian community (see chapter 1), it is likely, in my view, that Paul knows this objection to be circulating among his audience.

[22] Günther Bornkamm, "Baptism and New Life in Paul: Romans 6" in *Early Christian Experience*, trans. P. L. Hammer (New York, Harper & Row, 1969), p. 85 n. 6; Cranfield, *Romans*, p. 300.

[23] Pace Käsemann, *Romans*, p. 167.

namely that there is an essential cognitive component of faith.[24] The verbal elements of 8b and 9a – πιστεύομεν (we believe) and εἰδότες (knowing) as well as the subsequent ὅτι-clauses indicate the noetic dimension constitutive of the Pauline concept of faith. The τύπος διδαχῆς (type of teaching) of Romans 6.17 suggests further the intellectual component of faith as a body of knowledge to which Christians have given assent.[25]

It should be no surprise that Paul evokes the motif of the *militia Christi* in Romans 6.12–14, as Victor Pfitzner has already demonstrated that the apostle employs the motif when he is defending his apostleship and gospel (see e.g. 2 Cor. 10–13).[26] In Romans 6.12–14, Paul presents the battle explicitly as internal/spiritual – against ταῖς ἐπιθυμίαις (desires) – this modification reflecting an adaptation of the battle motif already achieved in Stoicism and Hellenistic Judaism. For Paul, of course, the war has already been won by God through Christ (6.11) and the battles in which Christians participate are only to preserve the victory. Pfitzner has shown how Paul conjoins the slave and soldier roles (6.16–20, 22.).[27] After extended development of the slave analogy in 6.15–22, he readily returns to the military metaphor in 6.23 where the term τὰ ὀψώνια has the explicit meaning of "soldier's pay."[28]

Romans 6.15–23: continuing the defense

In Romans 6.15–23 a second objection to Paul's doctrine of justification is confronted: "Are we to sin because we are not under the law but under grace?" At first it may seem surprising after the lengthy refutation of 6.2–14 that Paul continues to find a need for further defense of his position but the preoccupation suggests how seriously the apostle took the objections to this element of his preaching. In the first part of Romans 6, the legalist objection is set forth and now the false inference of the libertine arises. We know that there were, indeed, members of Paul's communities who

---

[24] See chapter 3.
[25] Käsemann is right to point to the parallel here with ἡ μόρφωσις τῆς γνώσεως of Romans 2.20; see his *Romans*, pp. 181–2.
[26] See Victor Pfitzner, *Paul and the Agon Motif*, NovTSup 16 (Leiden, Brill, 1967), p. 160. Pfitzner observes "the image of the στρατεία pictures the life and work of the apostle in its loyalty, together with his present struggle against the Corinthian opponents."
[27] Pfitzner, *Paul*, p. 162.
[28] Pace Käsemann, *Romans*, p. 185.

accepted his teaching on justification and concluded to the libertinist ethic (1 Cor. 5). In Romans 6.15–23, the libertinist assertion follows directly upon the ending of the previous section: "for you are not under the law but under grace" (6.14b). Paul allows that the Law functions only to enhance the accountability of the sinner in 5.13. By eliminating the Law, Paul may plausibly be accused of promoting the notion that Christians are no longer to be held responsible for their misconduct, as the criterion for identifying sin is lacking. He is aware that Jesus believers may expect God to be "partial" because they are "under grace" just as the Jews expected special treatment because they are "under the Law" (cf. 2.11).[29] Paul does affirm that Christians are freed from the power of sin (6.18), but this freedom demands that they willingly submit as slaves to righteousness! Christians although liberated from sin can again fall prey to its power if they do not struggle against it and submit to God's power (6.16). It is precisely because of this ambiguity of Christian existence as understood by Paul that both the paranetic components (vv.12–14,19–22) and the martial images of Romans 6 are necessary and appropriate.[30] Both elements are, however, presented as evidence that Paul does not advocate a libertinist position, as is apparent from the introductory statement of Romans 6.15. His response to the clearly annoying legalist and libertine objections urges that the hearer take into account other elements of his teaching and not view the doctrine of justification out of context and in isolation. Paul argues that if his admonitions to Christians to combat the power of sin are not conveniently forgotten then a "blasphemous" (3.8) interpretation of his teaching on grace is wholly untenable.

Romans 7: "Law and gospel"

Paul in Romans 7, particularly verses 7–13, has appropriated an apology for the Law. His purpose, however, is not to defend the Law but rather the gospel that he preaches which has been routinely criticized for condemning God's Law. In this sense, Romans 7 shares the onus of Romans 6, wherein Paul confronts the accusation of antinomianism.

---

[29] See Nygren, *Romans*, p. 250.
[30] Paranesis is a prominent feature of Protreptic; see Aune, "Logos Protreptikos," 4–5.

Rom.7.1–6: thesis and analogy

In terms of the development of the argument, Paul moves to the last item in the triad of "death, sin, and law" which are for Paul all characteristic of the old age.[31] He explicitly picks up the assertion made in 6.14b that "we are no longer under the law." This central corollary of his preaching must be clearly explained and defended. In Romans 7.1, Paul reiterates that the effective reign of the Law is temporary. In light of his explanation that Christians have "died" with Christ in baptism in Romans 6, the assertion that the dead are freed from the constraints of the Law in 7.1 reaffirms that Christians are no longer under the Law. It is possible that the νόμος of 7.1 refers to the Old Testament as Cranfield believes, or more narrowly to the Mosaic Laws, but in either case it is an issue of particular concern to Jewish Christians (cf. 2.17–18).[32] Paul offers in 7.2–3 an analogy taken from the realm of secular law with respect to marriage and applied to Christians' relationship to the Mosaic Law. In secular law, a wife is relieved of marital obligations upon the death of her husband (7.2–3). The analogue is the death of Christ and the believer's resultant liberation from the Law of Moses (7.4–6). The use of secular legal material to illustrate an item of religious teaching is characteristic of both Jewish and Christian apologetics and may have seemed particularly appropriate to Paul when writing to those in the capital of the Roman Empire.[33] In Romans 7.6 Paul employs the value-laden language of "new and old": the "new life of the spirit" versus the "old written code" by which contrast the superiority of the new order in Christ is affirmed (cf. 6.4).[34] Paul is aware that this kind of advocacy will be annoying and used as evidence for critics so he quickly proceeds to foreclose such criticism.

---

[31] Käsemann, *Romans*, p. 186.
[32] Cranfield, *Romans*, pp. 332–3.
[33] See e.g. Athenagoras *Supp.* 1.1.
[34] As an early Christian apologist, Paul inverts the traditional theme of "old and new" (see chapter 1). It is precisely in such instances that Paul often turns immediately to more traditional apologetic argumentation (so Rom. 7.7–13; cf. 6.1 ff).

Romans 7.7–25: an apology for the gospel

It has been remarked that Romans 7.7–13 is an apology for the Law.[35] It may be more accurate, however, to describe this section as Paul's apology for the gospel. Paul must respond to the objection that a direct implication, perhaps even explicit assertion, of his gospel is that the Law is sin (7.7). This conclusion follows logically from his statements of 5.20, 6.14, and most immediately 7.1–6. Paul seeks once again to eliminate the "reasons" for Jewish Christian opposition to his gospel and his proposed ministry in the West. In the course of this apology for the gospel in 7.7–25, he employs numerous Hellenistic Jewish motifs and significantly again adduces Scripture in support of his position. Having denied in 7.7 that the Law is sin (μὴ γένοιτο), Paul quickly adds that the Law is, nonetheless, the means by which we come to recognize sin as sin (7b–c; 13b). In addition to this noetic function, the Law also awakens or intensifies the power of sin. Paul argues the truth of this last point by returning to the exegesis of Genesis.[36] In Romans 7.8 sin is personified and the serpent who introduces the commandment in the Genesis fall story (Gen. 2.17) is invoked by Paul. The allusion to Genesis 2.17 is made apparent by the reference to "the commandment for life that leads to death" in 7.10. In Romans 7.11, Paul characterizes sin as "deceiving" (ἐξηπάτησεν), which is the word used in the LXX (Gen. 3.13) to describe the serpent's relationship to Eve. Before drawing the necessary conclusion from this exegesis, he reverts to the apologetic motif that the Law is holy and also asserts, to make no mistake, that the commandment (ἐντολή) is "holy and just and good" (7.12). By this piling on of laudatory modifiers, Paul intends to reinforce his affirmation with respect to the divine origin of both the Law and the commandment. He now returns to the issue at hand, namely the effects of the Law, and reasserts that the consequence of transgression is death (7.13) as expressed in the Genesis account (Gen. 3.3). Paul acknowledges that sin used the Law but in so doing two, albeit secondary, purposes of God's giving the Law are realized: (1) sin is exposed (v. 13b), and (2) the full measure of sinfulness is completed. This last point is particularly

---

[35] See Günther Bornkamm, "Sin, Law and Death: An Exegetical Study of Romans 7," in *Early Christian Experience*, trans. P. L. Hammer (New York, Harper & Row, 1969), pp. 88–9.

[36] Paul interprets the fall story recorded in Genesis 3; see Cranfield, *Romans*, pp. 350–1.

noteworthy as we find Paul here adducing an apocalyptic motif, namely the intensification of sin immediately preceding God's eschatological activity, to buttress the apologetic argument that he does not teach that the Law is sin. Thus Paul once again subordinates an apocalyptic motif to his paranetic and apologetic ends.

In Romans 7.14, Paul affirms that the Law is spiritual and humankind is "sold under sin." His approval here for the Law is emphatic as he characterizes the Law as πνευματικός (spiritual) while at the same time he declares Christians to be σάρκινος (fleshly).[37] Verses 15–23 serve to explain this surprising statement by Paul. The opposition between the ego willing good and effecting only evil is adduced as indirect proof that the Law is good (v.17). Romans 7.18–20 reinforce the same point. In verse 21, Paul returns to the use of νόμος as meaning ruling power or principle (cf. 7.5) and asserts there is a contrary law or power vying within the individual. Romans 7.22–3 explain verse 21. The crowning point of Paul's apology for the Law is the distinction drawn between ὁ νόμος τοῦ θεοῦ and ὁ νόμος τῆς ἁμαρτίας. Paul makes clear that he fully respects the Scripture which is the Law of God and expresses the Divine Will, but also that there is another "law" (v.23) that is the principle of sin. In verse 22 he affirms that the Law of God is good and that the "inner man" agrees with it. He states in 7. 23 that ὁ νόμος τοῦ νοός is in conflict with ἕτερος νόμος ἐν τοῖς μέλεσίν. The terms "inner man" (ἔσω ἄνθρωπος, v.22) and ὁ νόος approximate the meaning of the word conscience in 2.15 (ἡ συνείδη-σις).[38] Moreover, ὁ νοῦς is asserted to be subordinate (enslaved, 7.25b) to the νόμος τοῦ θεοῦ which is also approved by the "inner man" (7.22). Paul's use of the expression ὁ νόμος τοῦ νοός in 7.23, however, suggests that he understands it to be not only consistent with ὁ νόμος τοῦ θεοῦ but perhaps identical. On the other hand, the "law of sin" is the "other law in my members" (7.23). This dual conception of the Law as well as the dual terminology allows Paul to affirm his appreciation of the Law and to use the Scripture as a weapon to defend and explain the gospel while yet maintaining his long-standing opposition to the Mosaic legislation. The references to the rational dimension of human life are not intended to affirm

---

[37] Cranfield's arguments for understanding ἐγώ as referring to the believing Christian are decisive and help render the entire pericope of 7.14–25 comprehensible. See Cranfield, *Romans*, pp. 341–6.

[38] Plato used the expression ὁ ἐντὸς ἄνθρωπος (R 589a) and Philo in *Congr.* 97 refers to νοῦς as ἄνθρωπος ἐν ἀνθρώπῳ.

unimpaired innate human goodness, for Paul forecloses this line of interpretation in 7.24a, but rather are essential to the tradition of the apology for the Law, since it is spiritual and recognized as such by the human mind. The culmination of this line of reasoning is found in Philo, *Abr.* 5 and *Mos.* 2.5 wherein the ideal person is equivalent to the Law. While Paul acknowledges that the mind or inner man affirms the Law as good, it is not capable of effecting the good which it demands and indeed such knowledge only intensifies the power of sin or the culpability of the knowing sinner. Thus the cry for redemption of 24a and the confident assurance of a *future* redemption from the "body of death" (24b–25a) introduce as well as nuance his affirmations in Romans 8. Paul accomplishes a brilliant apologetic feat in Romans 7 by affirming, on the one hand, that the Law is "good," "spiritual" and "holy" but, on the other hand, that it is to no avail in freeing humankind from bondage to sin. Thus he has approved the divine origin of the Law and at the same time prepared for the introduction of the central theologoumenon – the gift of the Spirit, thereby demonstrating further the truth and significance of the gospel which he preaches.

Romans 8: evidences for the gospel

A common view among exegetes is that Romans 8 does not logically follow upon the more immediately preceding verses of Romans 7, but rather returns to 7.1–6.[39] It is here once again that reading Romans from the perspective of the apologetic tradition, both Jewish and Christian, and their appropriation of the Protreptic, elucidates Paul's argumentative strategy. The two-stage approach of apologetics is evident in 7.7–25 and Romans 8: (1) the affirmation of the values of the other tradition(s) and the relation of one's own commitment positively to such traditions; and (2) the assertion that one's own confession transcends and is, indeed, vastly superior to or at the least completes/fulfills the other tradition(s). Thus the second-century Christian apologists may speak, on the one hand, so favorably of the Logos, Socrates, and even of Greek philosophy in general, and, on the other hand, would seldom fail to point to the impotence of this philosophy to realize the ideals which it promul-

---

[39] For those who understand Romans 7.7–25 as a digression (as e.g. Käsemann) this is a natural conclusion but even for Cranfield who argues that 7.7–25 is critical to Paul's gospel the tendency is to argue for a gap between Romans 8 and 7.7–25. See Käsemann, *Romans*, p. 192, and Cranfield, *Romans*, p. 372.

gated. In other words, the appreciation of tradition even when guarded and nuanced, if not intentionally ambivalent, is allowed because it is finally construed as the preparation for the new and better philosophy.[40] Likewise, Paul's appreciation of the Law in Romans 7 discussed above prepares the hearer for his culminating exposition of the gospel in Romans 8.[41] Here again the protreptic character of the Christian apologetic tradition and Romans is palpably evident.

Objective proof of salvation is offered in Romans 8.1–11: the Spirit is able to do what the Law cannot! After affirming in Romans 7 that the Law is "spiritual" or "divine" in origin and purpose but that no one is able to fulfill its demands, Paul proclaims in Romans 8 that the Spirit alone enables Christians to be free. He echoes a theme that he has sounded throughout Romans, namely that the Law brings only condemnation, but Christians have been liberated from it (8.1–2).[42] What is new, of course, in Romans 8 is the explicit emphasis on the Spirit which is mentioned in this chapter twenty-one times while only five times in the seven preceding chapters. The Spirit is this enabling and liberating agency that is now active in the present aeon. The impotence of the Law is contrasted with the central efficacy of God's sending his own Son in 8.3. Christ is fully human but is without sin and by his death on the cross sin is contained and condemned.[43] Christ's death empowers Christians to fulfill the Law "according to the spirit" (8.4). Just as the term "flesh" indicates the objective power that leads to death and conflict with God, for Paul, the Spirit is not a psychological factor but an objective power. The Spirit is the power of God to effect life and peace and to make persons pleasing to God (8.6–8). In Romans 8 as in Romans 4 (see chapter 3), we enter into the realm of the supernatural and the miraculous; the Spirit is the crowning piece of evidence for the truth of the gospel of God that Paul preached.[44] Indeed the gospel is precisely this objective power of the Spirit that enables Christians to live in accord with the divine purpose (cf.

[40] A prime example is, of course, Justin *Dial.* 1–8.

[41] It may be worthwhile to recall that it was Paul who coined, perhaps, the dominant Christian apologetic motif with respect to Judaism, namely the "Old Covenant/Testament" – ἡ παλαιὰ διαθήκη – 2 Cor. 3.14.

[42] See Cranfield, *Romans*, p. 371.

[43] τό ὁμοίωμα of Romans 8.3 should be read in the light of Philippians 2.7 which limits the parallel to humanity by affirming that Christ is without sin.

[44] According to Käsemann, "pneuma is the power of miracle and ecstasy" which works in all who are baptized; see his *Romans*, p. 212.

1.16). Paul ends this paragraph by a reference to the "one who raised Christ from the dead and also renewed your mortal bodies" (8.11) that recalls the supernatural argument of Romans 4 (cf. esp. 4.24). In this paragraph where Paul appeals so strongly to the supernatural dimension of the gospel, he nevertheless maintains the emphasis on human rationality and responsibility by repeated use of such words as φρόνημα (8.6 twice; 8.7) and φρονέω (8.5) which stress mental judgment.[45] Paul is steering a very steady course in Romans between the extremes of enthusiasm and rationalism which he knows to be ready distortions of his preaching to which respectively Gentile and Jewish Christians are prone.

In Romans 8.12–17 Paul refers to the new family of God who are co-heirs with Christ. A cluster of familial motifs dominate this section of Romans: ἀδελφοί (brothers); υἱοὶ θεοῦ (sons of God); υἱοθεσία (adoption); ἀββὰ/ὁ πατήρ (father); τέκνα (children); κληρονόμοι/συγκληρονόμοι (heirs/co-heirs). In Romans 8.12, Jesus believers are directly addressed as ἀδελφοί which begins the chain of familial words that serve to reinforce the identity of the new social entity. To be sure, Paul's understanding is that this community is established by the Spirit of God (8.14). Note how the thoroughly Hellenistic concept of "adoption"[46] in 8.15 is transformed by its ascription as a function of the πνεῦμα. It is this πνεῦμα υἱοθεσίας ("Spirit of Adoption") that enables Christians to address God as ἀββὰ ὁ πατήρ. Thus, Paul appropriately correlates the motifs of υἱοὶ θεοῦ (8.14) and of the Father (8.15) through references to the mediating agency of the Spirit. According to 8.16, it is the mutual testimony of the divine and human spirit that Christians are "children of God." The emphasis on divine and human cooperation is also consonant with the exhortatory theme of suffering with Christ as the condition for sharing in his glory that ends the pericope in 8.17. The motifs of adoption (8.15) as well as "children"[47] prepare for the transition to the concept of inheritance (κληρονόμοι) in 8.17. In Romans 8.17 Paul clearly reiterates the subordinationist Christology prevalent throughout Romans; Christians are co-heirs with Christ (συγκληρονόμοι). The moderating christological

[45] Käsemann notes this emphasis and concludes that Paul is delineating his position in Romans 8 over against enthusiasts, but the noetic dimension, as I have shown above, is a constant of Paul's understanding of faith; see Käsemann, *Romans*, p. 212.

[46] The practice was not current among Jews in Paul's time but was so among Greeks and Romans; see Cranfield, *Romans*, p. 397.

[47] Note τέκνα (Rom. 8.16) is interchangeable with υἱοὶ θεοῦ (8.14).

expression is, in my view, another indication of Paul's purposeful reconciliatory approach to Jewish Christians in Rome. In Romans, Paul elaborates the foundation myth of the new nation of God while remaining peculiarly sensitive to his kinsmen by race, especially those who are already Christian.[48]

Paul develops in Romans 8.18–39 a rhetoric of social solidarity and superiority. The motifs of suffering (τὸ πάθημα – 8.18) and persecution (ὁ διωγμός – 8.35) are dominant in this pericope. To be sure, the suffering and persecution of the present time will be far outweighed by the future glory to be gained by those oppressed. Christians will receive the martyr's recompense for perseverance (δι᾽ ὑπομονῆς – v. 25) in their trials. The suffering is extended to the whole creation (vv. 19–22) and yet all such suffering is anticipatory of the manifestation of "the glory of the children of God" (v. 21). Apocalyptic motifs in this section are made subservient to the protreptic concern to encourage the minority and often persecuted Christian community. Philosophical Protreptic is often put forth under adverse conditions. Aristotle's *Protreptic* makes clear the general disdain for philosophy that characterized the contemporary attitude and shows his efforts to overcome popular objections to the study of philosophy and further to recommend it.[49] The word λογίζομαι which opens this section underscores that rational thought is involved – the reckoning of the expected reward far exceeds the present suffering.[50] Indeed, hope itself must be rationally and precisely defined. Hope is inherently related negatively to the present and visible order of reality, and instead posits a favorable future transformation of this order (vv. 24b–5).[51] The noetic dimension is also evident in 8.28: οἴδαμεν᾽ (also cf. vv. 22 and 26b) which introduces the Hellenistic motif of determinism: τοῖς ἀγαπῶ-σιν τὸν θεὸν πάντα συνεργεῖ εἰς ἀγαθόν (for those who love God all things work together for goodness). As has been acknowledged, this statement is reminiscent of Socrates' declaration at his trial: "But you too, gentlemen of the jury, must cherish a good hope with regard to death and be convinced of this one truth, that no evil

---

[48] See chapter 5 for further on this topic.

[49] See Ingmar Dühring, *Aristotle's Protrepticus: An Attempt at Reconstruction* (Göteborg, Elanders, 1961).

[50] See Cranfield, *Romans*, p. 408.

[51] The emphasis here in Romans 8 serves further to support our reading of Romans 7 that Christians through baptism are not freed from the powers of "sin, flesh, and death."

befalls a good man, either in life or after death, nor are his affairs neglected by the gods" (Plato's *Apol.* 41c–d).[52]

Paul's predestinarian leanings are further evidenced in 8.29–30. Thus Paul reinforces the idea already expressed in verses 26–7 that it is not finally human hope and perseverance but God's gracious decision that assures the well-being of the "saints." The ground of this assurance is stated in the rhetorical question of 8.31: "if God is for us, who can stand against us?" The battle line as drawn by Paul puts God on the side of the Christians and this is more than enough to counter the angelic and other powers of the opposition (8.38–9). Romans 8.32 adduces the event of God's willingness to sacrifice his son as proof of God's commitment to "all of us." Paul here, no doubt, consciously echoes the language of Genesis 22.16,[53] Abraham's sacrifice of Isaac, so that the apostle here once again appeals to Abraham and Isaac as testimonial figures for his gospel, as he has previously done at the end of Romans 4.

The divine calculus of the sacrificial system is also apparent wherein *one* victim becomes the instrument of salvation for *many* or *all* (ὑπὲρ ἡμῶν πάντων, 8.32). The long list of afflictions in 8.35 includes not only generic terms of ill-happenings but also specific terms of natural disasters ("famine") as well as of government oppression ("persecution" and the final: "sword").[54] The quotation of Psalm 43.23 in Romans 8.36 seeks to place definitively the persecution of the community under the perspective of the divine will and to remove doubt about the outcome. The persecuted are not vanquished; such confidence is characteristic of the Maccabean as well as later Christian apologetic literature (see e.g. 2 Macc. 7; Justin *Apol.* 1.68.2). In 8.18–39, Paul complements the rhetoric promoting social solidarity of 8.12–17 (cf. also vv.19, 21, 29b) with rhetoric that affirms the anticipated rewards of membership in the community over the immediate hardships.

The Protreptic again best describes the generic features of this section of Romans wherein Paul continues his negative criticism of alternative view(s) while making a more emphatic positive presentation of the value of life in Christ. Christian apologists of the second century will follow Paul's lead in proclaiming the future long-term benefits of membership in the now persecuted community. The response to the objection of antinomianism first raised in

---

[52] See e.g. Cranfield, *Romans*, p. 429 n. 1.
[53] James D. G. Dunn, *Romans*, WBC, 38ab (Dallas, Word, 1989), p. 501.
[54] See chapter 6 on Romans 13.1–7.

Romans 3.8 is elaborated in Romans 5–8. Paul is careful to balance his criticism of the Law with acknowledgments of its divine origin and purpose, though restricted. He is both unwilling to compromise his conviction that Gentiles in Christ are justified apart from the Law and concerned to express the gospel in a manner least offensive to Jewish Christians.

5

ROMANS 9–11: PAUL DEFENDS HIS MISSION TO THE GENTILES FOR THE SAKE OF THE JEWS

Introduction

Romans 9–11 offers strong support for the thesis that Paul is concerned to present his gospel and ministry and even himself as not inimical to the interests of Jewish Christians. The promises to the forefathers, the Law and most of all the potency and fairness of the God of Abraham, Isaac, and Jacob are central convictions of Jewish Christians. In Romans 9–11, Paul will challenge head-on the implicit objections to his gospel and ministry as constituting a rejection of God's promise to Abraham and covenant with Israel. Several exegetes have suggested that Romans 9–11 is Paul's further response to the objection raised in 3.1–9.[1] Romans 9–11 returns to the primarily negative aspect of Protreptic, countering alternative proposals.[2]

It may be that many Jewish Christians called into question the very premise of Paul's ministry, namely that there should be a Christian mission to the Gentiles at that time.[3] Even a Jewish Christian who had no objection to the Gentile mission in principle, might sensibly ask: since there are still so many Jews who have not received the gospel, should Christian missionaries (and such an effective one as Paul) ignore the unredeemed Jews and turn their attention to Gentiles?[4] Above all, might not the same Jewish Chris-

[1] See e.g. J. A. T. Robinson, *Wrestling with Romans* (Philadelphia, Westminster, 1979), pp. 108–9.
[2] Aune, "Logos Protreptikos," 41. Aune understands the unit as a "delayed answer" to an earlier objection.
[3] See J. W. Drane, *Paul: Libertine or Legalist?* (London, SPCK, 1975), p. 24. E. P. Sanders disagrees with Drane and thinks all Jewish Christians accepted the mission to the Gentiles; see E. P. Sanders, *Paul, the Law, and the Jewish People* (Philadelphia, Fortress, 1983), p. 18 and pp. 49–50 n. 8.
[4] Luke, of course, maintains that Paul did not neglect the Jews but rather first approached them and turned to Gentiles in each locality only after the former rejected his gospel. Yet the standard caution when Acts stands without confirming

tians object and assert that it is Paul's reputed disdain for Jewish tradition that has made the conversion of Jews virtually impossible! It seems to me that a close reading of Romans and in particular Romans 9–11 suggests Paul is seeking to convince his readers that his gospel neither impugns the God of Abraham, Isaac, and Jacob nor denies the elect status of Israel. A response to this visceral reaction of Jewish Christians is the onus of much of Paul's defense of the gospel and his mission in the letter to the Romans, and most particularly Romans 9–11. Paul is answering the objection to his apostleship to the Gentiles and particularly to his gospel as contradicting the Scripture. He has already answered objections regarding his supposed rejection of monotheism, the Patriarchs, and the Law. Now, the issue relates to Paul's ministry itself and whether his gospel entails a rejection of biblical history and the promise to Abraham.[5] Does Paul's gospel close the door to salvation for πᾶς Ἰσραήλ? This is the question that Paul attempts to answer for Jewish Christians in Rome in Romans 9–11.

Excluding at present references and allusions to Scripture, one finds Paul directly quoting the Bible at Romans 9.7, 9*, 12*, 13*, 15*, 17*, 20, 25–6*, 27–8*, 29*, 33*; 10.5*, 6–8*, 11*, 13, 15*, 16*, 18, 19*, 20*, 21*; 11.2, 3*, 4*, 8*, 9–10*, 26–7*, 34, 35. (The asterisk indicates that the verse is preceded by an introductory quotation formula and thus is intended indisputably as an explicit quotation by Paul.) That is, 35 of the 90 verses comprising Romans 9–11 contain direct quotations of biblical texts; 39 percent of Romans 9–11 consists of Scripture quotations. This frequency of quotation is striking and is approached nowhere else in the Pauline corpus. In terms of density of biblical quotations in Paul"s writings, Romans 4 comes in second place at 28 percent, and Galatians 3 next at 25 percent. Moreover, 51 of the 89 Scripture quotations in Paul's letters occur in Romans.[6] In addition, if one takes into account the numerous biblical references and allusions in Romans 9–11, the

evidence from Paul's writing should also be invoked in this instance. See Sanders, *Paul, the Law*, pp. 179–82.

[5] We know from the letter of James that Jewish Christians continued to object to Paul's gospel even after his death (James 2.14–26).

[6] See Richard B. Hays, *Echoes of Scripture in the Letters of Paul* (New Haven, Yale, 1989), p. 34. In a recent monograph, Christopher D. Stanley has dealt with the question of how to determine what constitutes a citation in *Paul and the Language of Scripture*, SNTSMS, 69 (Cambridge, University Press, 1992), pp. 33–7. He excludes for the purposes of his study a few passages such as Romans 10.13; 11.2, 25 listed above, but he indicates that he will treat them in a future work; p. 37, n. 14.

appeal to Scripture by Paul is most impressive.[7] For instance, the pericope 9.6–13 contains, as already indicated, direct quotations in verses 7, 9, 12 and 13; and verses 8 (τοῦτ' ἔστιν) and 10 are elaborations of the biblical texts preceding them respectively. The extraordinary recourse to Scripture in these chapters provides another reason to affirm that Paul has centrally in mind the Jewish Christians in his audience.[8]

Romans 9.1–5: self-defense: pathos

Paul has previously responded to the accusation that his gospel effectively impugns the πίστις of God (3.3–4; cf.9.6). In 9.1–3, he describes the situation which leads to the emphatic denial of 9.6 that "the word of God had failed!" Most of Paul's compatriots have rejected Christ. The issue is so charged that Paul rhetorically reverts to pathos; no callous, "objective" review of the present circumstances is allowable. In a passage reminiscent of Moses' plea to God to forgive the sinful Israelites and rather to "blot my own name from thy book" (Ex. 32.32), he prays to be separated from Christ ὑπὲρ τῶν ἀδελφῶν. Rhetorically, Paul is attempting to preclude any doubt regarding his concern for his kinsmen's present plight as viewed from a Jewish Christian perspective. In 9.4–5, he acknowledges the elect status of the Jews, whom he refers to as Ἰσραηλῖται (4a).[9] That which distinguishes the Ἰσραηλῖται, as the people of God is spelled out by Paul in 4b–5a. The first three terms: υἱοθεσία (sonship), δόξα (glory), and διαθῆκαι (covenants) indicate more general possessions than the following three – "the legislation, the worship, and the promises." Note that διαθῆκαι is plural and includes the several covenants of Noah and Abraham, as well as that of Moses. The next set of three, νομοθεσία[10] (Mosaic legisla-

---

[7] Hays is particularly astute in identifying such allusions. See his monograph mentioned in the previous note.

[8] Sanders leaps to Romans 11.13 (see chapter 1 on this verse) so to deny that the address of Romans 9–11 is primarily to Jewish Christians. Sanders' uneasiness about this part of his argument is evident when on the next page he asserts that one should not make any assumption about the addressees of Paul's other letters on the basis of Romans – an obvious point, which I suspect he makes only because the evidence for Paul's intent to address Jewish Christians in Romans is so abundant; see Sanders, *Paul*, pp. 183–4.

[9] See Cranfield, pp. 460–1; Dunn, p. 526. In Hellenistic Judaism, Israel is used infrequently and almost always in religious contexts. The term indicates that they are the chosen people of God.

[10] See *BAGD*, p. 541.

tion), λατρεία[11](worship, sacrificial cultus), and ἐπαγγελίαι (promise) are all contained within the Scripture. With designed association, Paul concludes his list with the Patriarchs *and* Christ, which are seen by Paul as the gifts of God to Israel greater than even the Scriptures. The reference to Christ as belonging to the "Israel-ites" κατὰ σάρκα is critical and returns to Paul's opening description of Christ as born ἐκ σπέρματος Δαυίδ (descended from David, 1.3). The Davidic identification assures the relation of the Christ event to Israel and is essential to Paul's intention to reassure Jewish Christians that he affirms the continuity between God's acts in the past and that in Christ.

Romans 9.6–29: the prophetic guarantee

The negative formulation of 9.6a: ἐκπέπτωκεν ὁ λόγος[12] τοῦ θεοῦ (it is not as though the word of God has failed) anticipates the reaction to Paul's expression of intense grief over the rejection of Christ by his kinsmen in 9.1–5. The present disbelief of Jews does not invalidate God's biblical assurances with respect to Israel. S. K. Williams has argued ὁ λόγος τοῦ θεοῦ refers specifically to God's promise to Abraham that through him "all people of the earth would become the children of God through faith."[13] It may, however, more naturally be understood to refer generally to the gifts of God mentioned in 9.4b–5a. The first line of support for the denial of 6a is given immediately in 6b by distinguishing between the empirical Israel and the true Israel.[14] A parallel distinction is drawn in 7a between τέκνα (children) and σπέρμα Ἀβραάμ (descendants of Abraham). Biological descent is not a decisive criterion for Paul. Romans 9.8 points the way to an allegorical interpretation to

[11] See Strathmann, "Λατρεύω", *TDNT*, 4 (1967), 61–5.

[12] The oracular sense of λόγος should be considered (LSJ, s.v. λόγος) as certainly the expression ὁ λόγος τοῦ θεοῦ carries here the import of determining/shaping the future course of events. The repeated emphasis on the predictive/prophetic validity of scripture in Romans 9–11 demands attention to this nuance of the word λόγος. Paul uses the expression "oracles of God" in Romans 3.2 in a context where again the issue of whether the apostle's assessment of the present situation of the Jewish people implies God's assurances to them recorded in the Scripture are now withdrawn. Paul, of course, will argue that the Scripture has "foretold" even the present disbelief of the majority of Jews and thus this turn of events, on the contrary, should give further credence to the biblical promises.

[13] See S. K. Williams, "The Righteousness of God," *JBL*, 99/2 (1980), 281. Williams points appropriately back to Romans 4 and forward to 9.9 in support of his contention.

[14] On this type of distinction, see my remarks on 2.28–9 in chapter 2.

explain the distinctions mentioned already, but unlike Galatians (4.22–31) Paul does not elaborate, as he is here more concerned with advancing an historical apologetic argument. The case of Isaac is cited in 7b (Gen. 21.12). In 9.9, Paul coalesces Genesis 18.10 and 14 as he seeks to remind the reader of the extraordinary (and, for Paul, nonetheless actual or historical) circumstances of the birth in question.[15] He provides a second biblical historical witness in Jacob and Esau (9.10–13). Paul's emphasis on Rebecca's κοίτην ἔχουσα ἐξ ἑνός (having conception from one man, Isaac), suggests sensitivity to the logical objection that the case of Isaac and Ishmael is vitiated by the two different mothers responsible in conception. Within the brief span of seven verses (9.7–13) he has adduced the central Patriarchs of Abraham, Isaac, and Jacob and most importantly has intimated a paradigm of divine election through the historical exemplars of Isaac and Ishmael and, more clearly, of Jacob and Esau.

The double predestinarian perspective enunciated by Paul in Romans 9.11–13 leads to the false inference in 9.14 (cf. οὖν) that God is unjust. If it is, as Paul suggests, from birth that individuals are called to the positions of beloved and hated of God (9.13), then should not God be deemed unjust? This inference is followed by the familiar emphatic denial: μὴ γένοιτο. Paul thinks that he has provided a rationale for this denial in the Scriptural quotation of 9.15. Moses, who is first to be mentioned in the sentence, is depicted as being addressed by God.[16] One may wonder how Paul could think that the quotation of Exodus 33.19 sustains his denial of divine arbitrariness. The issue of the justice of God is for him quite different from the accent of modern theodicy. Whereas modern theodicy focuses primarily on the issue of the unjust suffering of innocent people, Paul believes all to be sinners and worthy of condemnation (cf. 3.10,19). Thus for Paul the issue is quite the opposite of modern theodicy, for he is prone to ask: why does a righteous God allow sinners to go unpunished? From this perspective, one begins to understand how the Exodus quotation provides Paul an answer: it is God's mercy that explains the divine restraint towards human iniquity (cf. 3.25). It is not human striving but

---

[15] Paul has dwelt already on these circumstances in Romans 4.17–19.

[16] It is worthwhile to note that Paul moves from Abraham (Rom. 9.6–9), to Isaac (9.10), to Jacob (9.13) and then turns next to Moses (9.15). Has Paul explicitly passed over Joseph for political reasons given his recorded governing authority in Egypt?

divine mercy that accounts for all forbearance (9.16).[17] In 9.17, Paul depicts Scripture addressing Pharaoh, the antitype of Moses. As Paul sees it, both the fate of Moses and that of the Pharaoh are equally determined by the will of God. Paul in 9.18 introduces the biblical notion of the divine hardening; the Pharoah's resistance to relenting in his mistreatment of Israelites in Egypt is divinely determined. Paul is not unaware that his own further illustrations do not resolve the problem but rather magnify it. In 9.19, he is confronting a real objection: why does God find fault with human beings if he is so fully in control? Paul's response is to move from biblical history to biblical imagery, analogizing God to the potter and humankind to his clay (9.20–1).[18] In 9.22–3, he again asserts the significance of God's mercy, which may be the only true historical cause for the apostle, countervailing his penchant for determinism.

At Romans 9.24 Paul returns to the realm of the historical and relates the image of the vessel of mercy to the Christian community, which comprises "not only Jews but also Gentiles." He now wishes to resume the litany of "great name" biblical testimonial figures and begins somewhat awkwardly with ἐν τῷ Ὡσηέ (in Hosea) in 9.25. The subsequent two quotations from Hosea seek to demonstrate God's prior decision to make the Gentiles part of His people. A chain of quotations is contained in 9.27–9 wherein there is a double reference to Isaiah. Having established the biblical warrant for the inclusion of the Gentiles in verses 25–6, Paul tries now to do the same for the remnant or Jewish Christians.[19] It is for this purpose that he quotes from the twice named Isaiah. Romans 9.27–8 provides a biblical covering for the real situation of the relatively few Jews who have become Christians and the great majority who reject Christ.[20] In 9.29, Paul's clear apologetic intent is evident in the use of προείρη-κεν (predicted). Paul wishes to underscore that Isaiah foretold the current situation of the few Jewish Christians and the majority of non-believing Jews. It is this use of Scripture as predictive of and

---

[17] See Victor C. Pfitzner, *Paul and the Agon Motif*, *NovTSup*, 16 (Leiden, Brill, 1967), pp. 135–8. Pfitzner notes that τρέχειν and θέλειν are general Hellenistic terms for human striving and endeavor.

[18] Paul makes the same move in Romans 11.16–24 where he is explicitly addressing Gentile Christians.

[19] See François Refoulé, *"...Et Ainsi Tout Israël Sera Sauvé": Romains 11,25–32*, LD 117 (Paris, Cerf, 1984), pp. 144–52.

[20] "La citation d'Isaïe en 9,27 souligne simplement le contraste entre la multitude du peuple et le petit nombre des sauvés." Refoulé, *"...Et Ainsi"*, p. 149.

corresponding to present historical events that Justin Martyr will come to use so masterfully in his First Apology.[21]

Romans 9.30–10.21: Scripture testifies to the present Jewish and Gentile responses to the gospel

In 9.30–3, Paul states the paradoxical situation, namely that the Gentiles have accepted the gospel, whereas the majority of "Israel" have not, and offers two reasons for this turn of events. First, the Gentiles (ἔθνη) and Israel have pursued δικαιοσύνη in opposed ways, respectively the familiar ἐκ πίστεως and ἐξ ἔργων.[22] Second, God has intervened and caused those ἐν Σιών (in Zion) to stumble. The confirming scriptural quotation in 9.33 is a combination of Isaiah 28.16 and 8.14.[23] The motif of the "stone,"[24] symbolizing Christ, which causes those who deny to stumble (Is. 8.14), is introduced in the middle of the quotation from Is. 28.16, with its reassuring note of salvation for Jesus believers, changing drastically the meaning of the latter verse. Paul maintains its hopeful conclusion: "and he who believes in him will not be put to shame."

In Romans 10.1–13, Paul provides further explanation of "Israel's" rejection of the gospel. The rhetorical pathos of 10.1 reminds one of 9.1–3; Paul dares not speak matter-of-factly to his audience concerning the Jews' rejection of Christ. In 10.2, he acknowledges that his kinsmen have ζῆλον θεοῦ (zeal for God), but that it is not κατ' ἐπίγνωσιν (in accordance with knowledge; s.v. *BAGD*). The affirmation of a noetic dimension to faith is a constant of Pauline theology and is especially prominent in the letter to the Romans.[25] Romans 10.3 maintains this noetic element (ἀγνοοῦντες) and, in characteristic Pauline fashion, links it to obedience to God. Paul's elusive evaluation of his kinsmen in 9.31 and 10.2–3 can only be understood by reference to the decisive criterion of Christ as

---

[21] See Oskar Skarsaune, *The Proof From Prophecy: A Study in Justin Martyr's Proof-Text, Provenance, Theological Profile*, NovTSup, 56 (Leiden, Brill, 1987).

[22] There is much to be said for the suggestion that these are formulae which indicate simply those who follow Christ and those who do not. See Sanders (*Paul, the Law*, pp. 17–48) for whom Paul's use of the term ἐκ πίστεως signifies the apostle's understanding of the entrance requirements to the community of Christ.

[23] See Käsemann, *Romans*, p. 278.

[24] The λίθος in early Christian tradition became a widely used symbol for Christ – cf. Mt. 21.42; Acts 4.11; 1 P. 2.4–8. But E. Elizabeth Johnson suggests that here λίθος refers to the gospel; see her *The Function of Apocalyptic and Wisdom Traditions in Romans 9–11*, SBLDS, 109 (Atlanta, Scholars, 1989), p. 154.

[25] See chapters 3 and 4.

τέλος νόμου (10.4). There are three argued meanings for this phrase: (1) "end of the law," (2) "fulfillment of the law" and (3) "goal of the law."[26] The datum hard to evade is that Paul proclaims salvation to Gentiles without obedience to the Law as a consequence of the Christ event. Paul's view of the Law for Jewish Christians is more complicated, but I see no reason for denying that he allows Jewish Christians to abide by the Law as long as they center themselves in Christ – contra Watson. Sanders also argues that Paul would demand Jewish Christians in community with Gentile Christians to abandon the Law,[27] but Sanders' argument is based on the incorrect assumption that Paul, at least in this matter, is a pragmatist.

Romans 10.5–13 is a proof from Scripture for the bold assertion of 10.4, namely that Christ is the "goal of the law."[28] As already discussed in Romans 7 and 8, Paul presents the Law as the preparation for the gospel (see chapter 4); likewise this motif is used again in 10.5–9. Paul associates Moses and the wrong kind of pursuit of δικαιοσύνη (righteousness, 10.5),[29] and in 10.6, δικαιοσύνη ἐκ πίστεως (righteousness from faith) is contrasted with Moses. Despite this negative valuation of Moses, Paul will continue to quote from the Pentateuch to uphold his argument in the immediately succeeding passage (cf. v. 6b);[30] He can be hostile to the legal requirements of the Pentateuch but he affirms the authority of the scriptural narrative. The gospel that Paul preaches is readily accessible to all (10.8). Romans 10.9–13 begins to articulate the rationale for Paul's ministry and his Law-free gospel.[31] Scripture is once

---

[26] See Cranfield, *Romans*, pp. 515–20.

[27] Sanders, *Paul, the Law*, pp. 177–8.

[28] Contra Käsemann, *Romans*, p. 284 and Dunn, *Romans*, p. 597. Pace Johnson, *Romans 9–11, pp. 151–5*. Johnson also suggests that Christ stands as synecdoche for the entire gospel, n. 133, 155.

[29] For another reading of Romans 10.5, see Cranfield (*Romans*, pp. 521–2) who understands the verse as pointing to Christ, who by his "perfect obedience in life and death" alone fulfills the Law.

[30] Paul negatively evaluates Moses to the extent that he is identified with the legal requirements of the Pentateuch, but he is positively viewed as the author of the books of Torah – Romans 9.15,17.

[31] I do not rule out the possibility that in Romans 10.9–10 Paul is directing his comments to encourage Jewish Christians (who may be mumbling, in his view, an attenuated christology in the company of other Jews) to be more forthright in their expression of faith. The repetition of Isaiah 28.16 ("no one who believes in him will be put to shame") in this context would be instrumental. No doubt, Jewish Christians would find it convenient to omit mention of Christ in such circumstances; cf. Romans 1.16a.

again the sanction for Paul's preaching: "The Scripture says, 'No one who believes in him will be put to shame.' For there is no distinction between Jew and Greek; the same Lord is Lord of all and bestows his riches upon all who call upon him" (cf. 3.29–30). Paul is not only defending his gospel at this point, but also putting forth the fundamental theologoumenon which undergirds his central exhortation for mutual respect between Jewish and Gentile Christians (see chapter 1 on 15.7–13).

In Romans 10.14–21, Paul argues the justness of God's present judgment against Israel and further underscores the significance of his own apostolic ministry. In verses 14–15a, the necessary sequence of conditions for "calling on the name of the Lord" is delineated in reverse order: believing which necessitates hearing the Word of God, which in turn requires someone to preach it, and finally that God commissioned this someone (v.15a). In 15b Paul pays further tribute to his own designated mission by again quoting selected biblical material. He makes two points in 10.16–18, namely (1) that the gospel has been widely proclaimed; and (2) that many who have heard have not obeyed. In other words, the necessary preconditions for believing have been fulfilled by God and his ministers. As Paul would have his readers understand, it is not Paul and certainly not God who has ignored His people but the people who have turned away. Paul, however, wishes to argue that even this present turning away is within the sphere of God's Will. Thus he concludes the chapter with witnesses from Moses and Isaiah, demonstrating that the present situation is encompassed by the purpose of God. Romans 10.19 begins to intimate the extraordinary suggestion (to be developed in Rom. 11) that the success of Paul's Gentile mission is intended to lead to the "conversion"[32] of "Israel" by way of a provoked jealousy. The final two quotations from Isaiah give scriptural warrant for the Gentile mission (10.20) and for Israel's current rejection of the gospel (10.21). Thus Paul intends his reader to conclude that his ministry is directly ordained by God and that he has been sent by God to the Gentiles because of the rejection of the gospel by the majority of Jews, and most astonishingly that this ministry to the Gentiles will eventually serve to bring Israel to Christ. Moreover, Paul's copious appeal to Scripture is intended to prove that God has predestined every stage in this tortuous course of Israel.

---

[32] See Sanders' nuanced discussion of the appropriateness of this word to express Paul's understanding of the phenomenon of individuals' joining the Christian movement (*Paul, the Law*, pp. 176–8).

Romans 11.1–10: the present corresponds to the biblical past

In Romans 11.1–10, Paul confronts the objection deriving from 10.19–21 (note the οὖν) that he is proclaiming God has renounced His chosen people. He provides immediately two rationales for the μὴ γένοιτο (by no means) of 11.1b. First, he points out that he himself is an "Israelite, from the seed of Abraham, of the tribe of Benjamin" and after all that he not only has accepted Christ but also is the chief apostle to the Gentiles.[33] Second, he adduces a scriptural passage indicating that God has already sworn off such rejection (11.2). The extended appeal to the story of Elijah[34] provides further scriptural warrant for the present relationship of the majority of Jews to Christ. Elijah's complaint to God concerning the iniquity of His people meets with the divine rejoinder that God has kept for himself seven thousand who have been faithful.[35] In 11.5 Paul makes the direct application to the present (ἐν τῷ νῦν καιρῷ) and affirms the correspondence between the remnant in Elijah's time and the Jewish Christians "now." In Romans 11.7–10, Paul once again acknowledges that the majority of Jews have rejected Christ and the hardening motif re-emerges in order to affirm God's sovereignty.[36] The biblical quotations in verses 8–10 assure that God is still directing this part of the historical scenario. Notably, in 10.9, David is adduced as another "great name" testimonial figure.[37]

Romans 11.11–24: Paul's intention to "save some of the Jews"

Paul insists that the present rejection of Israel is not permanent.[38] Even the rejection of Israel has served the divine purpose of opening the way to salvation for the Gentiles, which in turn will provoke

---

[33] Here I agree with the consensus of commentators that this verse offers the first piece of evidence for the rejection of the thesis implicit in Romans 11.1: so Barrett, Cranfield, Dunn, Käsemann, Nygren, et al.

[34] On ἐν Ἡλίᾳ, see Cranfield, *Romans*, pp. 545–6.

[35] Note that in Romans 11.4 Paul has changed the future tense of the verb in the biblical verse to aorist and has also added ἐμαυτῷ.

[36] Refoulé argues that the "hardening" and "election" themes are not antithetical but rather the latter encompasses the former; see *"... Et Ainsi,"* pp. 164–7.

[37] David will emerge again in Romans 15 as the figure who first acknowledged that Gentiles can worship God (cf. 15.9, 12).

[38] Cranfield, *Romans*, p. 553; Refoulé, *"Et Ainsi,"* p. 237.

Israel to accept the gospel. This subsequent salvation of Israel will have even greater benefits again for humanity at large (11.12,15). In 11.13, where Paul explicitly addresses the Gentiles, he remains eager to affirm that his Gentile mission does not represent a turning away from Israel, but rather he carries out this mission to the Gentiles so as to "save some of them" (i.e. Jews; 11.14). Some rather questionable conclusions have been drawn from this fact, e.g. that throughout Romans 9–11, Paul is addressing primarily Gentiles and that in the Roman Christian community Gentiles were predominant. As already discussed, both suggestions are unjustified. It cannot be ruled out that the direct address here to Gentile Christians is intended primarily to assuage Jewish Christians' fears that Paul is disdainful of Jews and their traditions. The most convincing proof of Paul's respect for Jewish Christians would be his discourse to others about them, not his direct discourse! Further, the fact that Paul must make a point of calling Gentile Christians to attention in this part of Romans 11 may as easily lead to the conclusion that in the rest of Romans 9–11 he assumes the main audience are Jewish Christians. It is noteworthy that the only time in Romans 9–11 that a major segment of the writing is non-biblical is in this section specifically addressed to Gentile Christians, namely in 11.17–24 as Paul draws an extended metaphor from the natural world.

Paul returns, in 11.16–24, to the discourse of natural imagery – root, branches, wild olive tree. In 1 Enoch 93.5 Abraham is the root, and Paul is thinking of the Patriarchs in using this metaphor of the root.[39] The wild olive tree represents the Gentile Christians, and the branches broken off, the unbelieving Jews. The admonition to the Gentile Christians to avoid pride (11.20) lest they be "cut off" (11.22) and the concluding remarks affirming that the "natural branches" will be grafted back (11.24) are consonant with Paul's central concern throughout Romans 9–11 to promote unity within the Christian community and to establish his own credentials as the apostle worthy of the support of the entire Roman Christian community – Jewish and Gentile.

Romans 11.25–36: Summary of argument and the mystery of God's salvation/historical plan revealed

The use of the word τό μυστήριον (mystery) in Romans 11.25 has led some exegetes to suggest that Paul thinks of himself as an

---

[39] See Calvin, Cranfield, Käsemann; but Barrett thinks the root refers to Jewish Christians.

eschatological prophet who is unfolding secrets hitherto unknown to humankind.[40] Paul's understanding of the content of τό μυστήριον, already expounded, is summarized here in 11.25b–26, namely that a "hardening" has come upon part of Israel until the full number of Gentiles "come in,"[41] after which "πᾶς Ἰσραήλ will be saved." The meaning of this last clause, in my view, is that Paul expects the majority of Jews who presently reject the gospel to come to believe in Christ.[42] So familiar to us by now, the biblical quotations (composite in nature) in 11.26b–27 are intended to confirm Paul's explanation. He provides in this Isaian quotation an unequivocally spiritualized conception of the Messiah, which was no doubt difficult for the majority of Jews to recognize. Salvation has now nothing to do with the restoration of national sovereignty.[43] Indeed, in 11.28a, Paul is clear that the majority of Jews are ἐχθροί (enemies)[44] as far as their posture towards the gospel, but he is quick to add that they are ἀγαπητοὶ διὰ τοὺς πατέρας (beloved for the sake of their ancestors, v. 28b). Jewish Christians could respond affirmatively to this account of the status of their kinsmen. Paul confirms in 11.29 that God's election and blessing of Israel are not revoked. In 11.30–2, he concludes that God used the disobedience of Israel as an occasion to show mercy to Gentiles. There can be little doubt after 11.32 that Paul believes God's mercy to have priority over divine wrath: "in order to have mercy on all" (11.32). It cannot

[40] The speculation is, in part, spurred on by the fact that τό μυστήριον is closely associated with ἡ προφητεία in 1 Corinthians 13.2 and Ephesians 3.3. See the thorough treatment of this issue by Refoulé, "...*Et Ainsi*," pp. 257–67. However, it is not recognized that the claim to prophetic powers here serves the protreptic end of winning support for the apostle's ministry.

[41] Jesus traditions make abundant use of the verb εἰσέρχεσθαι often followed by the object "kingdom of God" or "life" (cf. Mk. 9.43,45,47; Mt. 5.20, 7.13; Jn 3.5).

[42] Pace Sanders, *Paul, the Law*, pp. 193–5. Sanders' criticism of the widespread ecumenical reading of this passage is incisive: "But for the present question, whether or not Paul thought of the salvation of Israel apart from Christ, it matters little whether he understands 'the Deliverer' to be God or Christ; for it is incredible that he thought of 'God apart from Christ', just as it is that he thought of 'Christ apart from God'. This is where the interpretation of Romans 11.25 f. as offering two ways of salvation goes astray. It requires Paul to have made just that distinction." The question whether this event will take place at the eschaton or simply later is not made clear by Paul; he does state clearly, however, the order of events, namely this event is to occur after the full number of Gentiles come in. See Refoulé, who concludes Paul intends to say the salvation of "all Israel is an eschatological event" – "...*Et Ainsi*," pp. 135–89.

[43] See W. D. Davies, *The Gospel and the Land: Early Christianity and Jewish Territorial Doctrine* (Berkeley, University of California, 1974).

[44] Paul, one should recall, is addressing Jewish and Gentile Christians, and they would both agree with the apostle on this point.

be overlooked that even in these theological and pious reflections, Paul is inexorably advancing his purpose – as the necessary condition for God's mercy to be extended to "all Israel" is "the coming in of the full number of Gentiles" and we know whose employment is required therein! Here and even in the concluding doxology,[45] wherein the expression of the unfathomable depths of God's ways would appear to enhance the significance of Paul's gift of explaining τό μυστήριον (11.25), Paul remains fully in command of his rhetoric.

In conclusion, Paul in Romans 9–11 has asserted that his own ministry to the Gentiles is vital to the fulfillment of God's plan of salvation for all humankind. He has assured Jewish Christians that he is not indifferent to the status of Israel and the majority of Jews who have rejected the gospel. Paul maintains that the successful completion of his mission to the Gentiles, which he seeks to realize by his proposed efforts in the West, is the necessary precondition for the salvation of πᾶς Ἰσραήλ. Further, Paul has expressed throughout Romans 9–11 considerable appreciation for Jewish traditions: the Patriarchs, the Promises and Scripture. Indeed, the abundant use of biblical quotations is outstanding, exceeding that in all other genuine Pauline texts. He has attempted to demonstrate that the course of Christian missionary expansion is repeating a pattern of rejection and salvation discernible in the biblical record. Furthermore, he has argued that the stages of the history of the Christian mission – beginning with a small number of Jewish Christians, then a greater number of Gentiles following the rejection by the majority of Jews, and finally the inclusion of "all Israel" after the completion of his mission to the Gentiles – are all "events" testified/predicted by the Scriptures. Paul hopes that the Roman community will conclude from this argument that his ministry is ordained by God and that they ought to support his forthcoming mission to the West.

[45] The influence of Stoicism via Hellenistic Judaism has been thoroughly documented in this passage. The concluding doxology in Romans 11.33–6 is not surprising; after claiming some capacity to explain τό μυστήριον, that Paul should feel obligated to acknowledge the source of all Wisdom and to affirm the ultimate inscrutability of God is to be expected.

6

ROMANS 12–13 AND 16: THE "ROMAN FACTOR"

Introduction

Our reading of Romans thus far has strongly suggested that Paul writes with an image in mind of two groups i.e. Jewish and Gentile Christians. In the chapters of Romans remaining to be discusssed, another aspect of Paul's image of his audience becomes apparent. Most significant in this section of Romans is the explicit political apologetic (13.1–7) which indicates Paul's attention to what I am calling the "Roman factor." Paul is not only sensitive to the assumed Roman consciousness of Christians in the capital city but also concerned to protect the Christian community against civil disciplinary action as was experienced in the past. He must convince both Christian groups that he is a loyal subject of the Emperor and will not bring political catastrophe on the Roman Christian community, though this explicit political agenda should not overshadow the wider protreptic concern that continues to dominate even in this section of Romans. Thus, the persistent philosophical/rational characterization of Christian worship reflects Paul's appeal to the Roman consciousness and values which he presumes of the community addressed, and accords well with the protreptic task to promote a preferred way of life as both consistent with mainstream values, and also superior to them.[1]

Romans 12.1–2: the rationality of Christian worship

From the opening verses (12.1–2) which serve as an introduction to the entire section (12.1–15.13),[2] Paul insists that the worship of the

---

[1] See Stephen Benko, "Pagan Criticism of Christianity during the First Two Centuries AD," *ANRW*, II.23.2 (1980), 1055–118.

[2] This section constitutes the explicit paranetic section of the letter. Note Aune's correct judgment that the verb παρακαλεῖν in 12.1 is not simply an "epistolary

Christian community in Rome be rational. Moreover, this insistence is presented by Paul as a natural conclusion from the previous chapters of Romans, as shown by the use of οὖν at the beginning of 12.1.[3] The vocabulary of 12.1–2 reflects the technical terminology of religious ritual: παραστῆσαι ... θυσίαν and λατρεία. Paul distinguishes Christian worship from that of others on two counts, indicated respectively by the words "living" and "rational." In the first instance, he intends to contrast the worship of Christians to that of the ancient sacrificial system typified by bloody animal offerings.[4] In the second case, the final words of 12.1: τὴν λογικὴν λατρείαν ὑμῶν (your rational worship) bring to mind the already described "irrational" pagan worship (cf. Rom. 2.20–5). The aforementioned phrase derives from Stoic formulations most likely mediated to Paul by the Hellenistic synagogue.[5] A central term of Stoicism, λογικός (rational), was used by Epictetus in the context of worship of God: "Were I a nightingale I would do what is proper to a nightingale, were I a swan, what is proper to a swan. In fact I am λογικός: so I must praise God."[6] Philo also uses this word in a passage concerned with the worship of God: "what is precious in the sight of God is not the number of victims immolated but the true purity of a rational (λογικόν) spirit in him who makes the sacrifice."[7] The word is frequently employed in the philosophical criticism of ancient sacrificial systems.[8] It should be noted that in 12.2 the eschatological perspective serves to underscore the Christian renewal of the rational mind and the consequent enhanced capacity of its function of critical judgment (τὸ δοκιμάζειν). For Paul, and most especially in Romans, apocalyptic views do not serve as an excuse for "transcending" the temporal responsibility of rational judgment but rather provide hope that Christians may better fulfill this responsibility.[9]

formula, but is used with the meaning 'exhort' (synonymous with προτρέπειν)"; see Aune, "Logos Protreptikos," 41. Recall that exhortation is the third, though optional feature of Protreptics (see chapter 1).

[3] Cranfield suggests that Paul has in mind the previous eleven chapters of the epistle; cf. Cranfield, *Romans*, p. 596.

[4] Pace Käsemann, *Romans*, p. 327.

[5] Cf. Barrett, *Romans*, p. 232.

[6] Cf. Arrian, *Epict.* 1.16.20.

[7] Philo, *Spec. Leg.* 1.277.

[8] Behm, s.v. θύω, *TDNT*, III, 187–9. The use of this tradition in later Christian apologetic writings is extensive; cf. for example Aristides, Justin.

[9] Käsemann here (*Romans*, pp. 330–3) acknowledges the paradoxical consequence of Paul's eschatological orientation but he fails to see how consistently and radically Paul revises the apocalyptic world view throughout Romans.

Romans 12.2–8: the urging towards social virtues

Philosophical Protreptic is characterized by an emphasis on exhortation and was defined by Stobaeus as an "urging towards virtue."[10] The strong assertion of authority that opens the appeal for sober self-estimation in Romans 12.3 suggests that Paul understands this to be a real problem in the Roman community.[11] The heavily noetic vocabulary remains prominent in 12.3: the root word, φρονέω (think), occurs four times including ὑπερφρονέω and σωφρονέω. The latter word is one of the four cardinal virtues of Greek philosophy.[12] Paul has just warned Gentile Christians in 11.17–22 not to think of themselves too highly (cf. 11.20 μὴ ὑψηλὰ φρόνει; cf. also 12.16) and specifically of arrogance towards Jewish Christians. Thus, it would seem natural to conclude that Paul proceeds with this same scenario in view. He offers the fundamental reason why Christians should not be arrogant, namely it is God who gives to each his share of faith which is the individual's real measure of value (12.3d). In 12.4–5 Paul employs the metaphor of the one body and its many members to refer to the right relationship among Christians in Rome. Livy has Menenius Agrippa use the same metaphor to advocate unity when the plebs rebelled (Livy 2.3.21). Paul is, no doubt, right to point to those with special talents, position etc., as the source of real and potential trouble within the community. He stresses that the capacity to fulfill the functions of prophesying, teaching, etc., is a gift given by the grace of God (12.6). Paul's theological doctrine of charismata and grace, as well as his earlier admonition, serves the same purpose of discouraging disunity within the Christian community which in the Roman context may be perceived as more susceptible to civil reprisals. It is noteworthy that the last three functions Paul mentions (12.8) pertain to social benefactions. It not only gives further evidence that social welfare characterized the early Christian communities but also may reflect Paul's awareness of the Roman social consciousness which approved highly of the philanthropic ideal.[13]

---

[10] Stobaeus, *Anthology*, 2.7.2; see Mark D. Jordan, "Ancient Philosophical Protreptic and the Problem of Persuasive Genres," *Rhetorica*, 4 (1986), 316–17.

[11] Barrett, *Romans*, p. 235.

[12] Cf. e.g. Aristot, *Eth. Nic.* 1117b. 13.

[13] See, for instance, the *Res Gestae* or Seneca's *De Clementia* written in late 55 or 56 CE to praise as well as exhort Nero to embrace the virtues most appropriate to a ruler.

Romans 12.9–21: poverty and persecution

Immediately following the mention of the three welfare functions of the community (12.8), Paul admonishes to "love without hypocrisy" (12.9). He speaks in this section of love both towards the "insiders" (vv. 9–13) and the "outsiders" (vv. 14–21) – from the brethren to the vehement persecutors. Romans 12.13a (ταῖς χρείαις τῶν ἁγίων κοινωνοῦντες) implies that some members of the Christian community were in fact in need of the assistance promoted. In verse 14 the instruction with repect to "outsiders" commences with the command: "bless those who persecute you."[14] The emphasis on disavowing revenge (vv. 17–21) confirms that the focus remains on persecution throughout the section.[15] Given the references elsewhere in Romans to withstanding persecution (e.g. 8.31–9), and in the light of Romans 13.1–7, it is natural to conclude that Paul has in mind the past instances of persecution in Rome and the always present danger of further persecution.[16]

The "Roman factor": Romans 13.1–7 as political apologetic

The passage 13.1–7 has caused perhaps the greatest perplexity on the part of exegetes of Romans. Cranfield finds it inexplicable that Paul could write "so positively about the authorities."[17] Käsemann refers to the passage as "surprising" and as an "independent block."[18] The highly resourceful Paul Minear admits with reference to this section: "I am unable to find particular reasons in the Roman situation for Paul's including of this teaching."[19] A particular reason, however, becomes obvious as soon as one acknowledges the "Roman factor," that is, that Paul is addressing specifically *Roman* Gentile and Jewish Christians. It is this factor that has been ignored in the exegesis of Romans and the results have been nowhere more

[14] Cranfield, *Romans*, p. 629; Käsemann, *Romans*, p. 345.

[15] The classical Greek tradition already strongly condemned the law of retaliation; cf. Sophocles, *Phil.* 679; Plato, *Crito*, 48.

[16] Mark Jordan has noted that concrete circumstances of urgency are often the context for Protreptic; see Jordan, "Ancient Philosophical Protreptic," 322. Although intriguing, Leenhardt's suggestion, that already in Romans 12.19 Paul envisions the "wrath" being exercised "through the medium of the civil power," seems uncertain at best. Cf. Leenhardt, *Romans*, p. 319.

[17] Cranfield, *Romans*, p. 653.

[18] Käsemann, *Romans*, pp. 350, 352.

[19] Paul S. Minear, *The Obedience of Faith: the Purpose of Paul in the Epistle to the Romans*, SBT, 19 (London, SCM, 1971), p. 88.

distorting than in the analysis of 13.1–7.[20] Robert Grant has rightly
pointed to Romans 13.1–7 as the clearest instance of political
apologetic that the New Testament affords us.[21] It is the sustained
nature of the argumentation in 13.1–7 that requires the serious
student of Romans to consider that this section was no thoughtless
repetition of tradition but rather was intended to fulfill a significant
purpose of Paul's communication to Rome.[22] Is it not likely that
Paul would be especially concerned with the addressed community's
relationship with the governing authorities considering its location
in the capital of the Empire? The answer to this question is certainly
to be given in the affirmative. In 49 CE Claudius expelled from
Rome some Christians deemed to be rabble rousers.[23] The impact of
this expulsion by the emperor must have echoed loudly throughout
the fledgling Christian community. That Paul in writing Romans
would have forgotten this event is far from credible. Moreover, he
would have received a firsthand account of the entire episode from
Aquila and Priscilla, who are the first individuals to whom Paul
extends greetings in 16.3.[24]

An examination of the structure of the argument and language of
13.1–7 is required to understand the explicit political concerns of
Paul. Romans 13.1a makes the unqualified assertion that "everyone
should be subject to the governing authorities." Virtually all commentators agree that the word ἐξουσία refers to government

[20] Barrett thinks there were many good reasons for Paul using the "practical
example" of Romans 13.1–7 but says they are unknown to us; in a parenthesis,
however, he adds that the disturbances "impulsore Chresto" come to mind but then
moves on to criticize Cullman's reading of the passage. See Barrett, *Romans*, p. 244.

[21] Robert M. Grant, *Greek Apologists of the Second Century* (Philadelphia, Westminster, 1988), pp. 19–21.

[22] Käsemann, *Romans*, p. 355.

[23] The probability that we have come upon a real concern of the Christian and
Jewish communities as well as Paul himself in 13.1–7 seems to me significantly
enhanced when one considers that at least some Jews and Jewish Christians were
expelled from Rome by Claudius for disturbances related to the preaching of Christ.
Suetonius' very brief statement: "Iudaeos impulsore Chresto assidue tumultuantes
Roma expulit" (Claudius 25.4) has engendered a prolonged debate. M. Stern concludes there can be little doubt that Chrestus stands for Jesus (*Greek and Latin
Authors On Jews and Judaism*, 2.116). Considerable debate continues as to the date of
Claudius' act; the two options are 41 or 49 CE. Dio Cassius lends support to the
earlier dating (LX, 6.6) whereas Acts 18.2 and Orosius (*Adversus Paganos*, VII, 6.15)
support the later dating, which I follow here. There is also disagreement concerning
the nature of Claudius' response although the consensus stands that there was at least
a partial expulsion of Jews/Jewish Christians. Acts 18.2 makes clear that Aquila and
his wife Priscilla, whom Paul met in Corinth, were among those expelled from Rome
by Claudius.

[24] See below on Romans 16.3.

authorities (Wilckens, Cranfield, Käsemann, Barrett, Leenhardt, Nygren). A few maintain that the word contains a double reference to angelic as well as human power (Cullmann, Morrison). In either case, there is no escaping the fact that Paul is speaking at the least of the individual's relationship to the political authorities and that he affirms the latter as instituted by God. Further, he not only affirms that citizens must fulfill their obligations to the state but also claims that the state's coercive power is divinely sanctioned (13.1bc; 4). In 13.2a, Paul equates rebelling against the authorities with defiance of God, while 2b draws the consequence. Verse 3a reaffirms the propriety of the ruler's authority, followed by verse 3b which speaks concretely of the official practice of commending citizens and communities deemed good by the Roman administration.[25] Paul may have in mind here public inscriptions in praise of benefactors.[26] As ἔπαινος (praise) is the authorities' response to good conduct so ἡ μάχαιρα (the sword) represents their reaction to bad conduct (4b–d). The expression "bearing the sword" has either of two meanings (and possibly both): (1) a general statement concerning the ruling authorities' wielding of military power[27] and/or (2) a specific reference to the dagger worn by the Emperor as "Imperator."[28] In either case, Paul points to the coercive and punitive powers of the Roman state. Romans 13.5 summarizes the argument of the previous four verses with the central exegetical issue in this verse being the meaning of συνείδησις.[29] The phrase διὰ τὴν συνείδησιν is clearly set forth by Paul as a contrasting parallel (οὐ μόνον/ἀλλὰ καί) to the preceding διὰ τὴν ὀργήν. Thus, συνείδησις must indicate a source of punishment which, unlike the divine ὀργή, arises from human consciousness or self-awareness (cf. Wisd. 17.10). Therefore, Pierce's earlier construal of this phrase as "on

[25] Käsemann, *Romans*, p. 353.

[26] So suggests Leenhardt, *Romans*, p. 330.

[27] Barrett (*Romans*, p. 247) makes reference to the *jus gladii* and the magistrate's inflicting the punishment of death (cf. Tac. *Hist.* 3, 68).

[28] Cranfield favors the first of the two options but my reading of Romans would suggest that a reference directly to the Emperor would not be out of the question for Paul here (see below on 13.7); cf. Cranfield, *Romans*, p. 667.

[29] Nygren understands the phrase διὰ τὴν συνείδησιν in context to mean "for the sake of God." Nygren, *Romans*, p. 431. Leenhardt makes a desperate attempt here to override the distasteful implications of the present passage but Romans 13.5 cannot be used to present Paul as an advocate of civil disobedience; cf. Leenhardt, *Romans*, p. 335. Cranfield prefers the bare sense of "knowledge"; see Cranfield, *Romans*, p. 668.

account of bad conscience" is to be maintained.[30] Johannes Friedrich, et al., have demonstrated that verses 6–7 are the climax of
Romans 13.1–7 as well as that the exhortation here reflects Paul's
knowledge of concrete socio-political conditions in Rome at the
time of his writing.[31]

In Romans 13.6a, Paul makes an observation concerning the
current practice of Christians, namely that they do pay taxes, in
order to support further the section's fundamental premise of obedience to the civil authorities. He underscores the statement by calling
those who collect the taxes "ministers of God" in verse 6b. In verse
7, Paul concludes his thought with the universal statement: "pay all
of them their dues," and then lists: taxes (φόρος), revenues
(τέλος),[32] fear (φόβος), and honor (τιμή).[33] This emphasis on taxes
(direct and indirect) and on the tax collector reflects an actual state
of affairs in Rome at the time. For under Nero there were agitated
protests by the Roman populace against perceived abuses on the
part of tax collectors.[34] Tacitus reports that the outburst of protest
against private agencies commissioned by the government to collect
indirect taxes and against the abuses of the tax collectors prompted
Nero in 58 CE to reform the system of collecting taxes (*Ann.*, 13, 50
f). Nero's response strongly suggests that the complaints had been
vociferously expressed for some considerable period and thus were
heard before and at the time of Paul's writing to the Roman
community. In 56 CE Obutronius Sabinus, a quaestor in charge of
the aerarium, was accused by a Tribune of the plebs with undue
severity in collecting taxes due to the treasury; Nero responded by
replacing quaestors with praefecti of praetorian rank (which, incidentally was Augustus' practice that Nero's predecessor Claudius
had changed). [35] The situation of Roman Christians with respect to
taxation may have been complicated at least in the eyes of the
populace. For the Jewish community had received an exemption
which permitted them to send their annual tax to the temple in

[30] C. A. Pierce, *Conscience in the NT* (Chicago, Allenson, 1955), p. 71.

[31] Johannes Friedrich, Wolfgang Pöhlmann, Peter Stuhlmacher, "Zur historischen Situation und Intention von Röm 13, 1–7," *ZThK*, 73/2 (1976), esp. 156–66.

[32] The distinction between φόρος and τέλος is that of direct and indirect taxes; see
Dunn, *Romans*, p. 766, where, however, the *vectigalia* is incorrectly referred to as
"direct taxes."

[33] The use of φόβος (fear) may indicate specifically the respect due to the highest
official, i.e. the Emperor; Cranfield, *Romans*, p. 670.

[34] Cf. Suetonius, *Nero*, p. 44.

[35] See Miriam T. Griffin, *Nero*, p. 57. Also cf. Tacitus *Ann.* 13, pp. 28–9. Romans
was most probably written in early 56 CE; see Koester, *History and Literature*, p. 104.

Jerusalem instead of to the imperial coffers.[36] This fact had long created resentment towards Jews in the general population. Since during the first few centuries Christianity was perceived by others as just another branch of Judaism, Paul may have also been concerned that the fledgling Christian community avoid any further hostility from either the authorities[37] or the populace.

In conclusion, Romans 13.1–7 is an exhortation which is directed at the concrete historical situation of the Christians living in Rome in the mid to late fifties CE, when the issue of taxation is a critical point of irritation and conflict between the people and the ruling authorities. Paul is probably also aware of the especially strained relations between the Jewish community and the wider populace concerning the issue of taxation. Moreover, Paul's full awareness that some seven or eight years previous the Emperor Claudius had officially expelled Christians from Rome compels the apostle to be attentive to the addressed community's relationship to the Roman authorities. Thus, in affirming the state's coercive powers and in encouraging loyalty and dutiful fulfillment of civic obligations, above all the payment of taxes, Paul echoes the themes of traditional political apologetic. Paul's expression of loyalty to the state, unique in his extant writings, indicates how the location and past history of the community addressed is a determining factor in his communication.[38]

Romans 13.8–10: the Law and love

It is generally suggested by exegetes that 13.8a is connected to the previous section which ends with the command: "pay all of them their dues," but that verse 8b moves emphatically on to a theme unrelated to the former thought.[39] It seems more likely, however, that Paul in typical fashion moves logically to discuss the next level of human relationship: beyond fear, honor and obligation is the command to love. Paul adduces a catechetical tradition of Jewish

[36] The exemption was, in fact, first granted by Julius Caesar.

[37] See above on Claudius' expulsion of Christians from Rome.

[38] Although it is not incorrect to say with Käsemann that obedience is encouraged so as not to discredit Christianity in the eyes of the world, it is inadequate (Cf. Käsemann, *Romans*, pp. 331–2). Paul's concern is with explicit official repression already experienced by the community and always a present danger.

[39] A notable exception is Leenhardt, who understands τὸν ἕτερον as the object of ὁ ἀγαπῶν and accordingly translates Romans 13.8b: "as he who loves has fulfilled the other law." Cf. Leenhardt, *Romans*, p. 337 n.

Christianity:[40] that to love others is to fulfill the Law, thus returning to a familiar defensive explanation that the gospel is not antinomian.[41] He quotes the negative commands of Torah in 13.9 with full approval for he has never changed his mind regarding the correctness of the ethical requirements of the Law.[42] Paul has been consistent in affirming that he "upholds the law" (Rom. 3.31; see also above on Rom. 7.7–12) and he is also consistent in maintaining his apologetic reinterpretation of the Law (see above on Rom. 2.25–29 and Rom. 7).[43] Without compromising his theological integrity, Paul continues to try to present his gospel in the least offensive manner to Jewish Christians by expresssing respect for the Law.[44]

Romans 13.11–14: eschatology and daily obligations

Romans 13.11–14 may provide the strongest evidence that Paul's eschatological/apocalyptic convictions do not exclude a primary protreptic aim for Romans.[45] Paul's claim that: "our salvation is now closer than when we first believed" (v. 11c) suggests he shares a sense of eschatological imminence.[46] However, he employs the motif of eschatological urgency here to encourage believers to live now in an ethically exemplary manner; it serves to support the moral exhortation of the entire section (12.1–13.10). Paul does not appeal to eschatology in order to trivialize the present but rather to undergird his insistence that good social conduct and love of others should characterize the Christian life style. The construction of 13.13–14 evinces his apologetic intent. The clause: "But put on the Lord Jesus Christ" (v. 14a) is situated between two clauses; the first rejects several named vices ("not in revelling and drunkeness, not in

[40] Pace Käsemann, *Romans*, p. 361.

[41] Käsemann's remark that Romans 13.8–10 is problematic because there is "no polemicizing against the law" reveals how totally he has misunderstood Paul's intention; cf. Käsemann, *Romans*, p. 361.

[42] Moreover, these same commands are nicely in agreement with Roman sentiments as well as Law, of which Paul's knowledge should not be too readily dismissed in light of 7.1–3.

[43] There are two senses in which Paul unequivocally upholds the Law – namely in terms of the narrative of Scripture and also with respect to its ethical aspect.

[44] Paul is also consistent here in asserting that the Law cannot be fulfilled (13.8,10b; cf. 7.14–25).

[45] Recall that Aristotle's *Protrepticus* very likely ended with an eschatological invitation to take up philosophy, which offers the greatest hope of reaching "the Isles of the Blest" after death.

[46] Cranfield's hesitancy with repect to this issue, however, should not be peremptorily dismissed; cf. *Romans*, p. 682.

debauchery and licentiousness, not in quarreling and jealousy,"
13.13b) and the second expresses the generalized moral exhortation
not to gratify fleshly desires (14b). Paul effectively identifies Christ
and those "who put on Christ" with the virtuous and, from the
viewpoint of popular philosophy, with the truly wise. Paul's apologetic interest in equating Christ and his movement with the accepted
moral values of his day was apparently heightened and was thought
by him to be a significant requirement in his communication to the
capital city where Republican and now imperial propaganda promoted self-restraint, sobriety, and moderation.

Romans 16:[47] further evidence for the "Roman factor"

The greetings in Romans 16.3–16 confirm that Paul is knowledge-
able about the situation and composition of the Roman community.[48] He knows several of its most prominent members who,
undoubtedly, were a ready and willing source of information for
him regarding past and present tensions and problems both within
the community and in its relationships to the wider society.[49] The
prosopographic evidence in verses 3–16 suggests there are a number
of Christians in Rome who are of Jewish descent. It cannot be
simply concluded that all or any of the latter are "Jewish Christians" in the sense of Christians who insist on abiding by the ritual
and dietary laws in part or *in toto* as do the "weak" in Romans
14.1–15.13.[50] Paul is, of course, ethnically Jewish but clearly identifies himself with the "strong" who reject all such legal restraints. It

[47] The arguments for denying that Romans 16 was part of the original correspondence that Paul sent to Rome have been, in my view, on the whole neutralized; see
Harry Gamble, *The Textual History of the Letter to the Romans*, Studies and
Documents 42 (Grand Rapids, Eerdmands, 1977) and the commentaries of Wilckens,
Cranfield, and Dunn. For those who still maintain that Romans 16 was not part of
the letter to the Romans, I suggest that the interpretive thesis of this work is tenable
without recourse to this chapter. At the same time, it should be noted that Romans 16
provides further support for the interpretation proposed here.

[48] Romans 16.1–2 is a recommendation to the Roman congregation for Phoebe
who may be the bearer of the letter to them. So Wayne A. Meeks, *The First Urban
Christians: The Social World of the Apostle Paul* (New Haven, Yale, 1983), p. 16. In
any case, as Phoebe is not a member of the Roman congregation, she is not relevant
to the issue of its composition. In the ancient period such recommendations were
often placed at the conclusions of letters; see Harry Gamble, *Textual History*, pp.
84–7.

[49] See above chapter 1 on Romans 14.1–15.13 with respect to the specifics of the
conflict within the Roman Christian community known to Paul.

[50] See chapter 1. It is in this sense that I have been using the term "Jewish
Christians" in this work.

is most likely that Prisca and Aquila are Jewish by descent but are to be identified with Gentile Christians in Rome.[51] Mary mentioned in 16.6 is also likely to be of Jewish descent,[52] but it is not possible to determine her religious orientation. Both Andronicus and Junias (v. 7) are Jewish, as is made clear by συγγενεῖς μου ("my kinsmen"). The fact that Andronicus is a Greek name suggests that some of the other Greek names in Romans 16 (perhaps excluding names derived from those of various deities) may also belong to individuals of Jewish descent. Appeles, for instance, in verse 10 is a Greek name that was commonly used among the community of Jews in Rome.[53] Both Cranfield and Dunn think that Aristobulus, whose household is mentioned in verse 10b, is likely to be the grandson of Herod the Great and brother of Agrippa. If this is the case, then the household mentioned presumably not only includes other Jews but also may be linked to the imperial household. Herodian of verse 11 is also indisputably of Jewish descent, and most probably so is Rufus and his mother in verse 13.[54] Excluding these last two, there are seven names in the list of twenty-four names, or roughly one third of those mentioned, which are of Jewish descent. Paul especially at verse 7 uses the opportunity of mentioning Jews in order to indicate his own ethnic identity and to underscore, as he does in 9.3, his affection for his "kinsmen," thus deflecting Jewish Christian accusations.

In addition to the household of Aristobulus already mentioned, an extraordinary number of the names listed by Paul are common to slaves in the imperial household. In this category are to be included both Urbanus and Stachys[55](v. 9), Appeles[56] (v. 10), Narcissus[57] (v. 11), Tryphaena and Tryphosa[58] (v. 12). Asyncritus (v. 14) is a name attested of an imperial freedman; likewise Philologus (v. 15) appears in lists of members of the imperial household.[59] Julia (v. 15) is the

---

[51] Meeks, *Urban Christians*, pp. 26–7.

[52] See Cranfield, *Romans*, p. 787, and Dunn, *Romans*, p. 893, who grant the possibility that Μαρία may be a feminine form of the Roman name "Marius." This point is denied by Käsemann (*Romans*, p. 413) who rejects altogether the Roman destination of Romans 16.

[53] Dunn, *Romans*, p. 896.

[54] Ibid., p. 900.

[55] See Cranfield, *Romans*, pp. 790–1.

[56] Ibid., p. 791; Dunn, *Romans*, p. 896.

[57] Lightfoot suggested Narcissus was the notorious freedman of Claudius; see Cranfield, *Romans*, pp. 792–3.

[58] These names appear in inscriptions of the imperial household; Cranfield, *Romans*, p. 794.

[59] Dunn, *Romans*, p. 898.

name of a woman of the Julian gens and is also a slave name particularly used in the imperial household.[60] Nereus and Olympas (v. 15) are common to the imperial household. Among this list, the name of Stachys is to be especially noted because it is rarely used outside the imperial household.[61] Although an assessment less enthusiastic than that of Cranfield and Dunn may be warranted, it does seem likely that one or more of the names were mentioned by Paul precisely because of the imperial connection. The interest for Paul with such connections may not be simply another case of classic name dropping. As already noted in the interpretation of Romans 13.1–7, Paul may have been concerned specifically with the Roman Christian community's perception of his own stance toward imperial authority, but also with the potential use of his communication as a pretext for imperial police action against the Christian community or Paul himself. The personal greeting to one-time, and possibly present, loyalists of the emperor such as imperial freedmen might be considered by Paul as politically useful. Prisca and Aquila (vv. 3–5), first to be greeted in this long list, are to be identified with those mentioned by the same name in Acts 18.2, who were expelled by the emperor Claudius in 49 CE. The impact of an imperial edict expelling Christians as well as Jews must have been tremendous upon the tiny Christian community throughout the empire. The impression would have been even more marked upon the apostle, as he would have been informed of it directly by two persons who were in fact exiled by the edict; their presence (Paul lived with them in their house in Ephesus; see 1 Cor. 16.19) would in itself be a constant reminder of imperial authority. It should be recalled that Paul is writing to Rome only seven or eight years after this expulsion.

There are reverberations of the expulsion throughout the letter. It is in this light that the severe warning against those who create dissensions in Romans 16.17–20 should be read. Paul is aware of real conflict within the community at present (see above on 14.1–15.13) and is painfully aware of the possibility for even greater divisiveness.[62] He is especially concerned that the Jewish Christian

---

[60] Cranfield, *Romans*, p. 795.

[61] Ibid., p. 791.

[62] This reading of Romans 16.17–20 seems to me superior to the two widely held alternatives: (1) the referents here are to the "strong" and "weak" (14.1–15.13) – so Minear, *Obedience*, pp. 28–9; and (2) the warning has nothing to do with the present situation of the Roman community but is an anticipation of "libertinizing" or "gnosticizing" Christians who are about to enter the community – so Käsemann, *Romans*, pp. 417–18 and Dunn, *Romans*, pp. 900–4. My proposal affirms (1), but also

element in Rome will become more radicalized and that he will then be confronted with opposition similar to that encountered in Galatia. Thus his efforts to demythologize circumcision and the Law throughout the early chapters in Romans (Rom. 2–7) are understandable, even though the Jewish Christian faction in Rome apparently does not presently insist on the former (see above on 14.1–15.13). Fully aware of the present conflict as well as the past belligerence between Jews and Christians leading to expulsion, Paul is highly motivated to express a warning that seeks to avoid a repetition of the past conflict and especially of the state response to it. For Paul to receive assistance either spiritually or materially from the Roman Christians, the minimum requirement is that there be such a community in Rome and further that they avoid the highly fractious behavior which could lead to either imperial repression or the emergence of an activist group inimical to Paul's mission. Thus the plea for mutual respect between Jewish and Gentile Christians, the expressions of respect and concern for his Jewish heritage, as well as the conservative political rhetoric, all point to Paul's determination to decrease the likelihood of conflict within the Roman Christian community that could lead to its elimination from the Roman scene.

adds that Paul is aware that this conflict can be intensified, especially by the "weak" becoming radical Judaizers resulting in the enhancement of antagonism between the two Christian groups in Rome.

7

SUMMARY AND CONCLUSION

Summary

In chapter 1, our analysis of both primary and secondary writings concerning the classical genre, *protreptikos logos*, affirms that the Protreptic functions as an invitation to a way-of-life, espousing a comprehensive world view setting forth its advantages and replying to objections. The aim of protreptic writers is to bring their readers to a new or renewed commitment to pursue a particular life path. This defining purpose of the genre accounts for its two basic structural components as well as an occasional third element: (1) a positive section presenting the doctrines and practices of the championed cause; (2) a negative section criticizing rival causes potentially or actually vying for the allegiance of the audience; and (3) sometimes, a final section encouraging the acceptance of the invitation. It is noted that of the few New Testament scholars who have suggested that Romans is a protreptic work, David Aune has made the best case for the proposal. However, by ignoring the historical context of Paul's communication, Aune is prevented from seeing Romans integrally as a Protreptic, and instead he argues unconvincingly that Romans is composed of three and possibly four independently written Protreptics while failing altogether to see the protreptic function of Romans 9–11, which he persists in characterizing as a digression.

It is argued that second-century Christian apologetic literature offers the closest parallels to the content, function and structure of Paul's communication to Rome. The examination of central modes of argumentation evidenced in second-century apologetic literature corroborates the emerging consensus of scholarship with respect to its protreptic character. Eight of twelve motifs from apologetic literature are identified as primary indicators of protreptic literature and the remaining four are consonant with the genre's concern to respond to objections against the recommended way-of-life. A determination that Romans is a Protreptic has consequences for both the reading of Romans and its influence upon the development of later Christian literary tradition.

In Part II of chapter 1, the opening sections and closing of the body of the letter are examined. Romans 1.1–7 commences the two lines of defense that preoccupy Paul throughout much of his communication to Rome, namely the promotion of his apostolic mission as well as of the gospel that he preaches. The correlations between the thanksgiving section (1.8–15) and the concluding section of the body of the letter (15.14–29) suggest the apostle's awareness of his audience's potential to resist Paul's authority and even to deny his veracity and sincerity. The view that Paul's audience in Rome consisted entirely of Gentile Christians is shown to be without decisive textual support. The verses (1.5–6, 13; 11.13 and 15.15–16) that are commonly adduced in defense of this position are at best ambiguous and cannot sustain the intended thesis. Thus a mixed audience of Jewish and Gentile Christians is most likely, and it is natural to conclude that Paul is referring to these two groups also when he offers guidance to the "weak" and "strong" in Romans 14.1–15.13. The burden of proof for this view of Paul's Roman audience is carried throughout the exegesis of the entire text, but critical points are made at this stage of the analysis, including that the focus on the biblical cogency of Paul's argument in 15.7–13 is consonant with the concern to allay fears of Jewish Christians and the available external evidence attesting to Jews exhibiting behavior similar to that ascribed to the "weak" in Romans 14–15. The central exhortation for mutual respect between the two groups of Christians is repeated throughout this section. This exhortation is directed to both groups and its central place in the letter is similar to the role of exhortation in other protreptic writings.

In chapter 2, it is shown that in Romans 1–3, Paul pursues the protreptic task of criticizing alternate world views (Jewish and Gentile) and affirming the superiority of a preferred perspective (the gospel). Frequent use is made of σύγκρισις, as is common in protreptic literature. In addition to the generic or formal correspondences with the Protreptic, the thesis is argued that Romans 1–3, inclusive of 3.21–31, is best understood as apologetic theology. Several apologetic motifs are identified in Romans 1–3. In Romans 1, these include: (1) natural knowledge/revelation of God (1.19–21); (2) the critique of idol worship (1.23); and (3) the corresponding polemic against immorality as a disordering of nature (1.26–7). The use of philosophical/ethical terminology and the emphasis on noetic language such as ἡ ἐπίγνωσις further evince the reliance on Hellenistic Jewish apologetics in Romans 1. Likewise, in Romans 2, Paul appropriates motifs from Jewish apologetics for the Law, including the affirmation that the Gentile has an innate understanding of the Law (2.12–14). Also in Romans 2, Paul employs the common apologetic critique of other peoples/religions. Corresponding to the polemic against the Gentiles in Romans 1, he now engages in such critique with respect to Jews. Paul, however, transforms the characteristic thrust of ethnocentric apologetics, as his intent is not to argue for the superiority of one race over the other, but rather to assert human solidarity in Christ. Further, he employs the common Hellenistic Jewish reinterpretation of circumcision, which denies significance to its literal meaning and points instead to a spiritualized reading (Rom. 2.2–9). In Romans 3, two typical apologetic themes are noted, namely, the answering of objections and the use of Scripture to prove one's position. Thus, in Romans 3.9–18, Paul answers three objections which are laid against his gospel : (1) that it implies that God is unfaithful to God's own promises to Israel; (2) that it makes God appear to be an unjust judge; and (3) that it encourages moral libertinism. Paul uses, in Romans 3.9–18, a catena of scriptural quotations to prove his conviction that all humanity is sinful. This method of proof texting was to become prominent in later Christian apologetic literature with its evidenced propensity toward Protreptic. Paul continues in Romans 3.21–31 to utilize apologetic motifs in the further appeal to Scripture (3.21, 31), to martyrological tradition (3.24–6), and finally to the One God (3.30).

The neglectful and mistaken exegesis of Romans 3.30 in past and present commentaries on Romans necessitates extended consideration of this issue. The nearly universal consensus of interpreters that Paul is appealing to the Shema (Deut. 6.4) in Romans 3.30 is demonstrated to be incorrect. The εἷς ὁ θεός formula which is used by Paul in Romans cannot be found in Deuteronomy 6.4. Indeed the only place in the LXX that εἷς directly modifies ὁ θεός is in Malachi 2.10. The concern in Mal. 2.10–16 is with the relationship between the people of Israel and other peoples (specifically, the issue of mixed marriages is at issue). Peterson's conclusion that the "One God" topos is Hellenistic in origin is well taken, but he did not take it as his task to pursue the use of the topos in Hellenistic Jewish literature. In Jewish apologetics, the theological implications (in polemic against polytheism and idol worship) and the socio-political implication of this topos are fully exploited.[1] It is demonstrated that Philo's use of the "One God" topos specifically to argue for the inclusion and full acceptance of the Gentiles (proselytes) into the Jewish community is the proper parallel to Paul's use of the topos in Romans 3.30. The "One God" topos also functions in the context of Romans 3.21–31 to combat objections that Paul's christology effectively denies monotheism.

In the third chapter, it is demonstrated that the line of argumentation into and throughout Romans 4 is continuous with that of Romans 3. Once the significance of the "One God" topos in Romans 3 is understood, the coherence between the opening of Romans 4 and the closing of Romans becomes apparent. In appealing to Abraham in Romans 4, Paul buttresses his position that Gentile Christians should be considered as equal members of the community of Christ by Jewish Christians. In Hellenistic Jewish literature, Abraham played a central role as the father of proselytes as well as the "first proselyte." Particularly, Philo describes Abraham's alien ethnic and religious origins and his "discovery" of the One God to advocate acceptance and respect for proselytes. Paul is also supporting his contention *vis à vis* Jewish Christians that his gospel is consonant with the central tenet of Judaism – monotheism. The apostle's intent to convince Jewish Christians of the legitimacy of his gospel and to promote mutual acceptance between Jewish and Gentile Christians is center stage. Paul appropriates the motifs and arguments of Hellenistic Jewish apologetics in a manner determinative for later Christian literature, especially the second-century Greek Christian apologetic tradition.

In chapter 4, Romans 5–8 is demonstrated to be Protreptic in terms of both form and content. Corresponding to the positive aspect of the λόγος προτρεπτικός, Romans 5–8 constitutes a commendation of the life made possible in Christ. Criticism of alternative world views (especially the Law and Moses) and response to objections (antinomianism) continue, nevertheless, to play a role in this fundamentally affirmative section of Romans. In Romans 5.1–11, three apologetic motifs are noted: (1) peace propaganda (vv. 1, 10–11); (2) sacrificial death popular in imperial propaganda (vv. 6–8); and (3) the Maccabean persecution theme (vv.

---

[1] I review the uses of the "One God" topos in Hellenistic Judaism in the excursus of chapter 2.

3b-4). In Romans 5.12–21, Paul employs a typical apologetic two-fold comparison wherein the initially stated similarity between Adam and Christ (vv. 1, 14; cf. also vv. 18, 19) is countered by a claim of superiority of the latter over the former (vv. 15–17). Paul pointedly refuses to compare Moses and Christ directly and instead suspends Moses by juxtaposing him to the two determiners of the human condition, that is, Adam and Christ. In Romans 6, the response to two objections is at center stage; both objections are related to antinomian accusations which have been briefly encountered already (3.8). After asserting in Romans 7.1–25 that Christians are freed from the Law, Paul immediately presents in 7.7–25 an "apology for the Law." While maintaining the limitations of the Law, Paul affirms for it a divine origin and purpose (namely, to expose sin). The assertion of the incapability of the Law to free one from the bondage of sin prepares for the introduction of the central role of the Spirit in Romans 8. Herein is the key to the continuity (so often contested) between Romans 7.7–2 and Romans 8. This continuity is made apparent from the perspective of the two-stage argument of apologetics: (1) the affirmation of the value of the other tradition(s) and relation of one's own commitment positively to it (them); and (2) the assertion that one's own confession is superior to or at least completes/fulfills the other(s). In Romans 8.1–11, the Spirit is presented as the crowning piece of evidence for the truth of the gospel. The claims to power of the Spirit must, however, be made coherent with the present suffering of the community (8.18–37). Thus Paul complements his rhetoric promoting social solidarity (vv. 12–17) with rhetoric that affirms the anticipated rewards of membership in the community over the immediate hardships and persecution (vv. 18, 21, 23, 28, 31–9). In addition to providing some evidence for the "Roman factor," much of the material in Romans 5–8 indicates Paul's sensitivity to the position and likely reaction of Jewish Christians.

In chapter 5, it was seen that in Romans 9–11 Paul most fully discusses issues of special interest to Jewish Christians.[2] In doing so, he returns to the primarily negative aspect of Protreptic, i.e. countering alternative proposals. Consonant with this reading of Romans 9–11 is the overwhelming recourse to Scripture; 39 percent

---

[2] Recall that this group may include ethnic Gentiles and most likely a significant number of proselytes; see chapter 1 above.

of 9–11 consists of scriptural quotations.[3] In 9.1–3 Paul attempts rhetorically to suppress any suspicion with respect to his concern for his kinsmen's plight as viewed from a Jewish Christian perspective – those most prepared have rejected Christ nearly en masse. He acknowledges the elect status of the Jews (9.4–5), and further that Jesus Christ himself was a Jew, in order to affirm the continuity between God's acts in the past and that in Christ. Paul repeatedly asserts that scripture has foretold this rejection by Jews (as e.g. 9.27–9). In 9.30–10.3 he again acknowledges the obvious situation of a positive Gentile response to the gospel and the Jews' rejection of it. At the horizontal level Paul explains that the Jewish people have failed to understand the righteousness of God and "their own" (10.3). Gentiles, however, are justified apart from the Law in the present time when Christ has come as the goal of the Law (10.4). Both Jews and Gentiles have equal access to the gospel but only the latter have received it (10.5–13). Moreover Paul assures his readers that the gospel has been preached to Jews but they have not responded as the Gentiles have. This scenario of Gentile response and Jewish rejection has been foretold by Scripture (10.14–21). In 11.1–10, Paul responds to the objection that God has forsaken God's own people. He begins by correcting the presumed statement of facts; Paul himself is evidence that not all Jews have rejected the gospel. Most have, but God foreknew this (11.2–10). In Romans 11.11–24 Paul claims that the rejection of Israel is not permanent and has served the divine purpose of opening the way to salvation for Gentiles whose response will in turn provoke Israel to accept the gospel. He insists that he carries his mission to the Gentiles so as to "save some of them" (i.e. Jews; 11.14). In 11.16–24 Paul invokes imagery from aboriculture in his admonition targeted to Gentile Christians which encourages an attitude of respect for Jews conducive to unity within the Christian community. If Gentile Christians understand God's plan of salvation, then they will not be arrogant or disdainful of Jewish Christian concerns (11.25–32). Having explained this plan and thereby underscoring his own special role in it, the apostle acknowledges God, the source of all understanding and wisdom (11.33–6).

In chapter 6, conclusive evidence is found for another element informing Paul's communication to Rome, namely the "Roman

---

[3] Far more than any other section of Paul's letters; Romans 4 is second at 28 percent and Galatians 3 at only 25 percent.

Factor." A significant emphasis of philosophical Protreptic is the "urging toward virtue" and such Protreptic is often given birth in concrete circumstances of urgency. Chapters 12 and 13 are part of the explicit paranetic section of Romans. Reflecting his perception of Roman concerns, Paul in 12.1–2 admonishes the congregation to pursue rational worship. In Romans 12.3–8 he maintains this focus on rationality and sobriety and advocates virtues that he believes will lead to harmony within the Christian community. In Romans 12.9–21 Paul urges love with respect to both insiders (vv. 9–13) and outsiders (vv. 14–21). In the latter case, the context is clearly that of persecution (vv. 17–21). Given the emphasis on persecution elsewhere in Romans (8.31–9) and in light of 13.1–7, it is most likely that Paul has in mind the past instance of persecution in Rome and the always present danger of a repetition. The specific reference of 13.1–7, especially with respect to taxation in verses 6–7, indicates Paul's knowledge of concrete socio-political conditions in Rome, for at the time of his writing there was widespread social unrest in the capital in reaction to abuses in the system of tax collection. Paul, however, subsumes even fear (vv. 3–4), respect and honour of the authorities (v. 7) under the "command" to love (vv. 8–10). Without compromising his theological integrity, he continues to attempt to present his gospel in a manner least offensive to Jewish Christians and also to affect a political stance that will protect the entire Christian community in Rome. Romans 13.11–14 provides another instance of Paul's subordination of an apocalyptic motif to undergird his insistence on good social conduct and the love of others in the present.

Romans 16 provides additional support for the "Roman Factor." Although a less enthusiastic evaluation is rendered than that of several recent exegetes, it appears that at least a few of the names mentioned in the long list of greetings are of imperial slaves and possibly one of the households mentioned has imperial connections. Paul is responsive to the continuing reverberations from Claudius' expulsion of Christians from Rome some six or seven years before his writing to the Roman Christians and exhibits sensitivity to the community's minority status and its relation to Roman power and ethos. This is not Paul's central concern but it is nevertheless a real factor informing the apostle's communication to Rome.

Conclusion

Romans is undoubtedly a complex work but it has been the working presupposition of this investigation that it is written in a rational manner so as to achieve its author's purpose. Accordingly, an interpretive hypothesis should explain the relationship between the form and the content and how both accord with the proposed audience of the communication as well as the known historical circumstances. The concept of an author's "purpose" is predicated upon an evaluation of the just mentioned factors: form, content, audience, and historical circumstances. The Protreptic has as its primary feature the recommendation of a particular philosophy and way of life. To this end, Protreptics engage in criticism of alternative world views and life styles. The genre or macro-structure of Romans is that of the λόγος προτρεπτικός which was also appropriated by later Christian apologists. Likewise, the analysis of content (of second-century apologetic literature) demonstrated that although criticism of alternative traditions and defense against accusations account for several motifs in apologetic writings, positive or propagandistic motifs are dominant in these writings. The motif analysis of Romans has yielded a preponderant correspondence between apologetic theology and Paul's communication to Rome. Apocalyptic themes, although present in Romans, are subordinated to the primary apologetic orientation. Romans exhibits this emphasis in terms of both structure and content.

The known historical circumstances of Paul's communication to Rome are not without significance in further determining his purpose. Some six or seven years before Romans was written, the emperor Claudius expelled some Christians from the capital, including Prisca and Aquila who were later to provide Paul with shelter in the East. Thus Paul had firsthand reports of this event, which must have been traumatic for the Christian community.[4] Paul's political apologetic in Romans 13.1–7 is not without cause. Moreover, his emphasis on the payment of taxes (vv. 6–7) reflects a current knowledge of affairs in Rome where there is social unrest over abusive taxation at the time of his writing. Further, his knowledge of recent social unrest in Rome and its causes makes it virtually impossible to contend that the apostle is ignorant of the composition of the

---

[4] If the Roman Christians' faith was proclaimed to all the world (1:8), then their encounter with Claudius must surely have been widely discussed among Christians.

Christian community in Rome and the internal problems which it confronts.

The natural conclusion that follows from the emphasis in Romans on many issues of great concern to Jewish Christians but of relatively less interest to Gentile Christians, as well as the extraordinary recourse to biblical modes of argumentation throughout, is that the former are a significant element of the apostle's image of his addressees. It has been demonstrated that the conception of dual audiences, Jewish and Gentile, best accounts for the form and content of Romans. Paul intends to travel to the West and begin his mission in Spain; towards this end he looks forward to receiving assistance from Christians in Rome – the site of the only significant Christian community in the West at the time. Paul, at the very least, hopes to minimize the opposition to his ministry which in the East has often emanated from Jewish Christians. Thus he seeks to explain his gospel and mission in a manner that is the least offensive to them. Paul is aware that acceptance of his own authority and credibility is not to be taken for granted with Roman Christians, especially Jewish Christians. This awareness accounts for the specific emphasis of the apologetic in Romans: the extraordinary extent of the appeals to Scripture, the more nuanced discussion of his position on the Law, the affirmation of the One God, etc. Paul wields the sword of the gospel to cut down the arrogance arising from the cultural and religious presumptions of both *Gentile* and *Jewish* Christians.

Beyond these defensive and critical positions, Paul's primary and positive aim in Romans is to encourage mutual respect between Jewish and Gentile Christians. Theologically, Paul argues that there is one God who justifies both Jews and Gentiles (Rom. 3.29–30); christologically, that Christ has welcomed both Jews and Gentiles (15.7–9); thus Gentile and Jewish Christians (who are both welcomed by Christ and justified by the One God) should love and respect one another. For Paul, the issue of unity is not only social or ecclesiological but also theological and christological. There is a circularity among the three arguments, which is inevitable when a foundational theological and existential commitment is at stake. Paul's call for unity allows and promotes diversity and pluralism within the Roman Christian community. He had also maintained in Galatians that a most significant demonstration of God's activity in Christ is the communion made possible between Jews and Gentiles. Perhaps Paul realized that his own unrestrained polemic in Galatians could only exacerbate tensions between Jewish and Gentile Christians and thus he modified his theological expression so as to better promote the realization that in Christ there is "neither Jew nor Greek." Finally, this investigation leads to the conclusion that Paul disciplined his intellectual energies in Romans through the studied appropriation of the protreptic genre. This conclusion suggests the intriguing possibility, deserving of further exploration, that Paul, who is never quoted by second-century Greek Christian apologists, may nevertheless have had a direct impact on their literary activities and bequeathed to these apologists their most favored literary genre.

APPENDIX: TOPOI IN SECOND-CENTURY CHRISTIAN APOLOGETIC WRITINGS

Defence (against accusations)

		Justin *Apol.*	Athenagoras *Supp.*	Theophilus *ad Autolycum*	Aristides *Apol.*
(a)	moral and criminal charges	I.29.2	XXXI.1-XXXIII.2 XXXV.1–3	III.4,15	XVII.2
(b)	political intrigue	I.11.1–2			
(c)	irrational beliefs and cultic practices	I.13.4	III.1 XXXI		
(d)	atheism I.5.1		I.6.1		

Critiques/polemics (against other traditions)

		Justin *Apol.*	Athenagoras *Supp.*	Theophilus *ad Autolycum*	Aristides *Apol.*
(a)	idols/idol makers	I.9.1–5	XVII.2–4	I.1,9–10 II.3–7 III.3,7	III.2 XIII.2
(b)	gods/mythology	I.54.2–10	VIII.1 XVII.1 XX.1–XXII.8 XXVIII.1–XXX.4		IV–VII VIII–XI XII
(c)	animal worship	I.24.1	I.1–2	I.10	XII.7
(d)	cultic practices	I.13.1	XIV.1–2	III.5	XIII.6 XIV.4

Positive/propagandistic

		Justin *Apol.*	Athenagoras *Supp.*	Theophilus *ad Autolycum*	Aristides *Apol.*
(a)	proof from prophecy	I.30.1–43.8	IX.lf.	I.14 II.9,34,35	
(b)	rewards and punishments	I.8.2–4	XII.1–3 XXXI.2f XXXVI.1–2	I.14	XVI.1–2 XVII.5
(c)	superior morality	I.12.1 I.15.1– 17.4	XXXIV.1f.	III.9–14	XV.3–11 XVI.6
(d)	classical evidence	I.18.3–6 I.20.1– 22.6 I.23.1	V.1–VI.5 XVIII.1– XIX.3 XXXVI.3	II.36–38	

GLOSSARY

apologetic   (1) widely used to refer to the second-century Christian movement of philosophers/writers who defined Christianity in relationship to Graeco-Roman and Jewish traditions; (2) as used in this work it describes the characteristic content and style of argumentation evident in the literature referred to above.

apology   (1) The title of several literary works in antiquity; (2) a genre designation for a type of literature which adduces proof, arguments that contradict charges that are being made.

endeiktikos   According to Philo of Larissa, endeiktikos is one of the two parts comprising the Protreptic and refers to the demonstration of the value and profit of philosophy.

epideictic   In classical rhetorical theory one of three classifications of rhetoric; the discourse of "praise and blame" (the other two are *symboleutic* or *deliberative*, the discourse of advising and *judicial* – the rhetoric of the courtroom). Aristotle said that the purpose of epideictic was to honor or dishonor something or someone.

genre   A type of literature exhibiting characteristic function, form (structure and style) and content.

Protreptic   (1) title to several literary works of the ancient period; (2) genre that invites students to pursue a way-of-life.

protreptikos logos   (see Protreptic) genre encouraging, urging students to adopt or deepen their commitment to a particular way-of-life.

SELECT BIBLIOGRAPHY

Altaner, Berthold, *Patrologie*, Freiburg, Herder, 1978.

Aune, David E., "Romans as a *Logos Protreptikos* in the Context of Ancient Religious and Philosophical Propaganda" in Martin Hengel and Ulrich Heckel (eds.), *Paulus und das antike Judentum*, Tübingen, Mohr/Siebeck, 1992.

Barrett, C. K., *A Commentary on the Epistle to the Romans*, Black's New Testament Commentaries, London, Adam & Charles Black, 1957.

From First Adam to Last, New York, Scribner, 1962.

Barth, Karl, *The Epistle to the Romans*, Edwin C. Hoskyns (tr.), Oxford, University Press, 1935.

Bassler, Jouette M., "Divine Impartiality in Paul's Letter to the Romans," *NovT*, 26 (1984), 43–58.

Bauer, Walter, *A Greek-English Lexicon of the New Testament and Other Early Christian Literature*, Chicago and London, The University of Chicago Press, 1979.

Behm, "θύω", *TDNT*, III (1965), 180–90.

Beker, Christian J., *Paul the Apostle*, Philadelphia, Fortress Press, 1980.

Benke, Stephen, "Pagan Criticism of Christianity during the First Two Centuries A.D.," *ANRW*, II, 23.2 (1980), 1055–118.

Berger, Klaus, *Formgeshichte des Neuen Testament*, Heidelberg, Quelle & Meyer, 1984.

"Hellenistische Gattungun im Neuen Testament," *ANRW*, Part II, vol. 25/2, Berlin & New York, de Gruyter, 1984.

Bertram/Hauck, "μακάριος," *TDNT*, 4 (1967), 362–70.

Betz, Hans Dieter, *Galatians: A Commentary on Paul's Letter to the Churches in Galatia*, Hermeneia, Philadelphia, Fortress, 1979.

Boers, Hendrikus, *Theology Out of the Ghetto*, Leiden, Brill, 1971.

Boobyer, G. H., "Thanksgiving and the Glory of God in Paul," Diss., Leipzig, 1929.

Borgen, Peder, *Bread From Heaven*, 2nd edn, *NovTSup*, 10, Leiden, Brill, 1981.

Paul Preaches Circumcision and Pleases Men, Relieff 8, Dragvoll, University of Trondheim, 1983.

Bornkamm, Günther, "Baptism and New Life in Paul" in *Early Christian Experience*, P. L. Hammer (trans.), New York, Harper & Row, 1969, 71–86.

"Das Doppelgebot der Liebe" in Walther Eltester (ed.), *Neutestamentliche Studien für Rudolf Bultmann*, Berlin, Töpelmann, 1954.

Paul. D. M. Stalker (tr.), New York, Harper & Row, 1971.
"Paulinische Anakoluthe im Römerbrief" in *Des Ende des Gesetses*, Munich, Kaiser, 1953, 76–92.
"Theologie als 'Teufelkunst'" in *Geshichte und Glaube*, vol. 2. Munich, Kaiser 1971, 140–8.
"The Revelation of God"s Wrath, Rom. 1–3" in *Early Christian Experience*, trans. P. L. Hammer, New York, Harper & Row, 1969, 47–70.
Brooten, Bernadette, "Paul's Views on the Nature of Women and Female Homoeroticism," in Clarissa W. Atkinson, Constance H. Buchanan, and Margaret R. Miles (eds.), *Immaculate and Powerful*, Boston, Beacon Press, 1985, 61–87.
Brunner, Emil, *The Letter to the Romans*, trans. H. A. Kennedy, Philadelphia, Westminster, 1959.
Bultmann, Rudolf, *Der Stil der paulinischen Predigt und die kynischstoische Diatribe*, FRLANT, Göttingen, Vandenhoeck & Ruprecht, 1910.
History of the Synoptic Tradition, John Marsh (tr.), New York, Harper & Row, 1976.
Theology of the New Testament, K. Grobel (tr.), 2 vols., New York, Scribners, 1955.
The Problem of Natural Theology in *Faith and Understanding*, New York, Harper & Row, 1969, 313–31.
"The Question of Natural Revelation" in *Essays*, New York, Macmillan, 1955, 90–118.
"ἀλήθεια," *TDNT*, 1 (1964), 238–51.
Burgess, Theodore, "Epideictic Literature," University of Chicago Studies in Classical Philology, 3 (1902), 89–261.
Caird, Edward, *The Evolution of Theology in the Greek Philosophers*, 2 vols., Glasgow, MacLehose, 1904.
Cambier, J., *L'Evangile de Dieu selon l'Epître aux Romains*, StudNeot 3, Bruges, Desclee De Brouwer, 1967.
Chance, J. Bradley, "Paul's Apology to the Corinthians," *Perspectives in Religious Studies*, 9 (1982), 145–55.
Chary, Th., *Les Prophètes et le Culte à partir de L'Exile*, Paris, Tournai Desclee, 1955.
Childs, Brevard S., *Introduction to the Old Testament as Scripture*, Philadelphia, Fortress, 1979.
Collins, John J., *The Sibylline Oracles of Egyptian Judaism*, SBLDS, 13, Missoula, Scholars Press, 1974.
Apocalypse: The Morphology of a Genre, Semeia 14, Missoula, Mt., Scholar's Press, 1979.
"Sibylline Oracles" in James H. Charlesworth (ed.), *The O.T. Pseudepigrapha*, vol. 1, Garden City, Doubleday, 1983.
The Apocalyptic Imagination: An Introduction to the Jewish Matrix of Christianity, New York, Crossroad, 1984.
Conley, T., "Philo's Use of Topoi" in David Winston and John Dillony (eds.), *Two Treatises of Philo of Alexandria*, Brown Judaic Studies 25, Chicago, Scholars Press, 1983, 171–8.
Conzelmann, Hans, "Die Rechfertigungslehre des Paulus. Theologie oder Anthropologie?," *EvTh*, 28 (1968), 389–404.
Heiden–Juden–Christen, Tübingen, Mohr/Siebeck, 1981.

Copleston, Frederick, *A History of Philosophy, Vol. 1: Greece and Rome*, Garden City, Image Books, 1962.

Cranfield, C. E. B., *The Epistle to the Romans*, 2 vols., ICC, Edinburgh, T. & T. Clark, 1980.

Cullmann, Oscar, *The Christology of the New Testament*, rev. edn, Shirley C. Guthrie and Charles A. M. Hall (trs.), Philadelphia, Westminster, 1959.

  Salvation in History, New York, Evanston, Harper & Row, 1967.

Dahl, N. A., "Paul and the Church at Corinth According to 1 Corinthians 1:10 – 4:21" in *Studies in Paul: Theology for the Early Christian Mission*, Minneapolis, Augsburg, (1977), 40–61.

Davies, W. D., *The Gospel and the Land*, Berkeley, University of California Press, 1974.

Dibelius, Martin, "ἐπιγνωσις ἀληθείας" in *Botschaft und Geschichte*, Tübingen, Mohr/Siebeck, 1956, 1–13.

Dirichlet, Gustav L., *De Veterum Macarismis*, Religionsgeschichtliche Versuche und Vorarbeiten 14, Giessen, Topelmann, 1914.

Dodd, C. H., *The Epistle of Paul to the Romans*, MNTC, London, Hodder and Stoughton, 1954.

Doeve, J. W., "Some Notes with Reference to τὰ λόγια τοῦ θεοῦ in Romans 3:2" in Sevenster, J. N. and van Unnik, W. C. (ed.) *Studia Paulina in Honorem J. de Zwaan*, Haarlem (1953) 111–23.

Donfried, Karl P. (ed.), *The Romans Debate*, Minneapolis, Augsburg, 1977.

  (ed.), *The Romans Debate: Revised and Expanded Edition*, Peabody, Hendrickson, 1991.

Drane, J. W., *Paul: Libertine or Legalist?*, London, SPCK, 1975.

Droge, Arthur J., *Homer or Moses: Early Christian Interpretations of the History of Culture*, HUT 26, Tübingen, Mohr-Siebeck, 1989.

Duhring, Ingmar, *Aristotle's Protrepticus: An Attempt at Reconstruction*, Goteberg, Elanders, 1961.

Dumbrell, W. J., "Malachi and the Ezra-Nehemiah Reforms," *Reformed Theological Review*, 35 (1976), 42–52.

Dunn, James D. G., *Romans*, 2 vols., WBC, 38, Dallas, Word Books, 1988.

Elbogen, Ismar, "Studies in the Jewish Liturgy," in Jacob J. Petuchowski (ed.) *Contributions to the Scientific Study of Jewish Liturgy*, New York, Ktav, 1970, 1–51.

Ellis, E. Earle, *Paul's Use of the Old Testament*, Edinburgh, Oliver and Boyd, 1957.

  Prophesy and Hermeneutic, WUNT, 18, Tübingen, Mohr/Siebeck, 1978.

Finkelstein, Louis, "The Origin of the Synagogue" in Joseph Gutman (ed.), *The Synagogue: Studies in Origins, Archaeology and Architecture*, New York, Ktav, 1975, 3–59.

Foester, Werner, "σέβομαι," *TDNT*, 7 (1971), 168–96.

Fowler, Alastair, *Kinds of Literature: An Introduction to the Theory of Genre and Modes*, Cambridge, Harvard, 1982.

Frend, W. H. C., *The Rise of Christianity*, Philadelphia, Fortress, 1984.

Friedrich, Johannes and Wolfgang Pohlmann and Peter Stuhlmacher, "Zur historischen Situation und Intention von Römer 13,1–7," *ZTHK*, 73/2 (1976), 133–65.

Fridrichsen, A., "Der wahre Jude und sein Lob: Röm 2:28f," *Symbolae Arctoae*, 1 (1927), 39–49.

Friedländer, M., *The Jewish Religion*, London, Kegan, Trench, Trübner, 1891.

Geschichte der Jüdischen Apologetik, Leipzig, 1906; Amsterdam, Philo, 1973.

Gaertner, B., *The Areopagus Speech and Natural Revelation*, Carolyn Hannay King (tr.), Uppsala, Almquist & Wiksells, 1955.

Gager, John, *The Origins of Anti-Semitism*, New York and Oxford, Oxford University Press, 1985.

Gamble, Harry, *The Textual History of the Letter to the Romans*, Studies and Documents 42, Grand Rapids, Eerdmands, 1977.

Geffcken, J., *Komposition und Entstehungszeit der Oracula Sibyllina*, Leipzig, J. C. Henrichs, 1902.

Zwei Griechische Apologeten, Leipzig and Berlin, Teubner, 1907.

Georgi, Dieter, *The Opponents of Paul in Second Corinthians*, Dieter Georgi (tr.), rev. edn, Philadelphia, Fortress Press, 1986.

Goeppelt, Leonhhardt, *Typos: Die typologie Deutung des Alten Testaments im Neuen*, BfCTh 2, Reine 43, Gutersloh, 1939, repr. Darmstadt, 1969.

Goodenough, Erwin R., *The Theology of Justin Martyr*, Jena, 1923; Amsterdam, Philo Press, 1968.

An Introduction to Philo Judaeus, 2nd edn, Oxford, Basil Blackwell, 1962.

Goodspeed, E. J., *Die ältesten Apologeten*, Göttingen, Vandenhoeck & Ruprecht, 1914.

A History of Early Christian Literature, rev. Robert M. Grant, Chicago, University of Chicago Press, 1966.

Grant, Robert M., *Gods and the One God*, Philadelphia, Westminster, 1986.

Greek Apologists of the Second Century, Philadelphia, Westminster, 1988.

Griffin, Miriam T., *Nero*, New Haven, Yale University Press, 1985.

Grobel, Kendrick, "A Chiastic Retribution Formula in Romans 2" in *Zeit und Geschichte: Dankesgabe an Rudolf Bultmann zum 80 Geburtstag*, E. Dinkler (ed.), Tübingen, J. C. B. Mohr, 1964, 255–61.

Grafe, E., "Das Verhaeltniss der paulinschen Scriften zur Sapientia Salomonis" in *Theologische Abhandlungen C.v. Weizsaecker gewidmet*, Freiburg i. Br. 1892, 253–86.

Grundmann, "δύναμαι/δύναμις," *TDNT* 2, (1964), 284–317

Guerra, Anthony J., "Romans 4 As Apologetic Theology," *HTR*, 81:3 (1988), 251–70.

"The One God Topos in Spec. Leg. 1.52" in David Lull (ed.), *Society of Biblical Literature 1990 Seminar Papers*, Atlanta, Scholars Press (1990), 148–57.

"Romans: Paul's Purpose and Audience with Special Attention to Romans 9–11," *RB*, 2(1990), 219–37.

"The Conversion of Marcus Aurelius and Justin Martyr: The Purpose, Genre, and Content of the First Apology," *The Second Century*, 9:3 (1992).

Gutbrod, W., "νόμος," *TDNT*, 4 (1967), 1036–91.

Gutman, Joseph, *Synagogues*. New York, Ktav Pub. House, 1975.

Hamlah, Ehrard, "Frömmigkeit und Tugend: Die Gesetzesapologie des

Josephus in c.Ap. 2, 149–295, 220–232" in *Josephus–Studien, Untersuchungen zu Josephus: dem antiken Judentum und dem Neuen Testament*, Göttingen, Vandenhoeck & Ruprecht, 1974.

Hanson, Paul, *The Dawn of Apocalyptic*, rev. ed, Philadelphia, Fortress Press, 1979.

"Apocalypticism," *IDB Supp.* 29, Nashville, Abingdon Press, 1962, 28–34.

Harnack, Adolf, *The Expansion of Christianity in the First Three Centuries*, 2 vols., James Moffatt (tr.), Freeport, Books for Libraries, 1972.

Harris, J. Rendel, *Texts and Studies, no. 1: The Apology of Aristides*, Cambridge, University Press, 1891.

Hartlich, Paul, *De Exhortationum a Greacis Romanisque Scriptarum Historia et Indole*, Leipziger Studien II, 1889.

Hays, Richard, "Psalm 143 and the Logic of Romans 3," *JBL*, 99 (1980), 107–15.

"A Reconsideration of Rom 4:1," *NovT*, 27 (1985), 85–106.

Echoes of Scripture in the Letters of Paul, New Haven, Yale, 1989.

Hengel, Martin, *Judaism and Hellenism*, J. Bornden (ed.), Philadelphia, Fortress, 1981.

Hodgson, Robert, "The Testimony Hypothesis," *JBL*, 98 (1979), 361–78.

Hoenig, Sidney B., "City-Square and Synagogue," *ANRW*, 19.1, 1979.

Hoffken, Peter, "Eine Bemurkung sum religions-geschichtlichen Hintergrund von Dtn. 6,4," *BZ*, 28 (1984).

Hoffman, Lawrence A., "Censoring In and Censoring Out: A Function of Liturgical Language" in Joseph Gutman (ed.), *Ancient Synagogues*, Brown Judaic Studies 22, Chicago, Scholars Press, 1981, 19–37.

Holfelder, Hermann H., "Εὐσέβεια καὶ φιλοσοφία" *ZNW*, 68 (1977), 48–66.

Huby, Joseph, *Saint Paul Epître aux Romains*, VS, 10, Paris, Beauchesne et ses Fils, 1957.

Hurtado, Larry W., *One God, One Lord: Early Christian Devotion and Ancient Jewish Monotheism*, Philadelphia, Fortress, 1988.

Hyldahl, Nils, *Philosophie und Christentum: Eine Interpretation der Einzleitung zum Dialog. Justins*, Acta Theologica Danica 9, Kopenhagen, Munksgaard, 1966.

Isaksson, Abel, *Marriage and Ministry in the New Temple*, ASNU, 24, Uppsala, Lund Gleerup, 1965.

Jervell, Jacob, *Imago dei: Gen 1:26f. in Spätjudentum, in der Gnosis und in der paulinischen Briefen*, Göttingen, Vandenhoeck & Ruprecht, 1960.

"The Letter to Jerusalem" in Karl P. Donfried (ed.), *The Romans Debate*, Minneapolis, Augsburg, 1977, 61–74.

Johnson, E. Elizabeth, *The Function of Apocalyptic and Wisdom Traditions in Romans 9–11*, SBLDS, 109, Atlanta, Scholars Press, 1989.

Jolowicz, H. F., *Historical Introduction to the Study of Roman Law*, Cambridge, University Press, 1952.

Jordan, Mark D., "Ancient Philosophic Protreptic and the Problem of Persuasive Genres," *Rhetorica*, 4 (1986), 309–33.

Käsemann, Ernst, "On the Subject of Primitive Christian Apocalyptic" in

New Testament Questions of Today, W. J. Montague (tr.), Philadelphia, Fortress, 1969, 108–37.

"Justification and Salvation History in the Epistle to the Romans" in *Perspectives on Paul*, Philadelphia, Fortress Press, 1971, 60–78.

Commentary on Romans, Geoffrey W. Bromiley (tr.), Grand Rapids, Eerdmans, 1980.

"An Apologia For Primitive Christian Eschatology" in *Essays on New Testament Themes*, W. J. Montague (tr.), Philadelphia, Fortress Press, 1982, 169–95.

Keck, Leander E., "The Function of Romans 3:10–18 – Observations and Suggestions" in *God's Christ and His People: Studies in Honor of Nils Alstrup Dahl*, Oslo, Universitetsforlaget, 1977, 141–57.

"Jesus in Romans," *JBL*, 108 (1989), 443–60.

Kennedy, George A., *New Testament Interpretation Through Rhetorical Criticism*, Chapel Hill, University of North Carolina Press, 1984.

Klein, Günter, "Römer 4 und die Idee der Heilsgeschichte," *EvTh*, 23 (1963), 424–47.

Kleinknecht, H. "νόμος," *TDNT*, 4 (1967), 1022–35.

Knox, W. L., "Abraham and the Quest for God," *HTR*, 28 (1935), 55–60.

Koester, Helmut, "φύσις," *TDNT*, 9 (1974), 251–77.

Introduction to the New Testament, 2 vols., Philadelphia, Fortress, 1982.

Kuss, Otto, *An die Römer*, vol. I, Regensburg Pustet, 1957.

Lagrange, M. J., *Saint Paul Epître aux Romains*, Paris, J. Gabalda, 1916.

Lanchester, H. C. O., "The Sibylline Oracles" in R. Charles (ed.), *APOT*, vol. 2, Oxford, Clarendon, 1963, 368–406.

Leenhardt, Franz J., *L'Epître de Saint Paul aux Romains*, 2nd edn, CNT, 2.6. Geneve, Labor et Fides, 1981.

Lietzmann, Hans, *An die Römer*, HNT, vol. 8, Tübingen, Mohr/Siebeck, 1928.

Lindars, Barnabas, *New Testament Apologetic*, London, SCM, 1961.

Luedemann, Gerd, *Opposition to Paul in Jewish Christianity*, M. Eugene Boring (tr.), Minneapolis, Fortress, 1989.

Malherbe, Abraham J. "The Apologetic Theology of the Preaching of Peter," *Restoration Quarterly*, 13 (1970), 205–23.

Moral Exhortation: A Greco-Roman Sourcebook, LEC, 4, Philadelphia, Westminster, 1986.

Marmorstein, Arthur, *Studies in Jewish Theology*, Freeport, New World, 1972.

Mceleney, Neil J., "Conversion, Circumcision and the Law," *NTS*, 20 (1973), 319–41.

McKenzie, Steven L. and Howard N. Wallace, "Covenant Themes in Malachi," *CBQ*, 45 (1984), 549–63.

Meeks, Wayne A., *The First Urban Christians: The Social World of the Apostle Paul*, New Haven, Yale, 1983.

Michel, Otto, *Paulus und seine Bibel*, BFCTh, 2/18, 1929, Reprint 1972, Darmstadt, Wissenschaftliche Buchgesellschaft, 1972.

Der Brief an die Römer, 10th edn, MeyerK, 4, Göttingen, Vandenhoeck & Ruprecht, 1955.

Minear Paul, *The Obedience of Faith: The Purpose of Paul in the Epistle to the Romans*, SBT, 2nd Series, London, SCM, 1971.

Moxnes, Halvor, *Theology In Conflict, NovTSup*, vol. 53. Leiden, Brill, 1980.

Munck, Johannes, *Paul and the Salvation of Mankind*, F. Clark (tr.), Richmond, John Knox Press, 1959.

Nickelsburg, George W. E., *Jewish Literature Between the Bible and the Mishnah: A Historical and Literary Introduction*, Philadelphia, Fortress Press, 1981.

Nikiprowetsky, Valentin, *La Troisieme Sibylle*, Paris, Mouton, 1970.

Nilsson, Martin, *A History of Greek Religion*, 2nd edn, F. J. Fielden (tr.), Oxford, Clarendon, 1952.

Norden, Eduard, *Agnostos Theos*, Darmstadt, Wissenschaftliche Buchgesellschaft, 1956.

Nygren, Anders, *Commentary on Romans*, Carl C. Rasmussen (tr.), Philadelphia, Muhlenberg, 1949.

Palmer, D. W., "Atheism, Apologetic and Negative Theology in the Greek Apologists of the Second Century," *VC*, 37 (1983), 234–59.

Pellegrini, M., *Studi su l'antica apologetica*, Rome, Storia e Letteratura, 1947.

Peter, Michal, "Dtn 6,4 – ein monotheistischer Text?," *BZ*, 24 (1980), 252–62.

Peterson, Eric, *Eis theos: Epigraphische, formgeschichtliche und religionsgeschichtliche Untersuchungen*, Göttingen, Vandenhoeck & Ruprecht, 1926.

Petuchowski, Jacob J., *Contributions to the Scientific Study of the Jewish Liturgy*, New York, Ktav, 1970.

   "The Liturgy of the Synagogue" in Jacob Petuchowski and M. Brocke (eds.), *The Lord's Prayer and Jewish Liturgy*, New York, Seabury, 1978, 45–57.

Pfitzer, Victor, *Paul and the Agon Motif, NovTSup*, 16, Leiden, Brill, 1967.

Pierce, C. A, *Conscience in the N.T.*, Chicago, Allenson, 1955.

Quasten, Johannes, *Patrologie*, Freiburg, Herder, 1978.

Rad, Gerhard von, "δόξα," *TDNT*, 2 (1964), 238–42.

   Old Testament Theology, 2 vols., D. M. G. Stalker (tr.), New York, Harper & Row, 1965,

   Deuteronomy, Dorothea Barton (tr.), Old Testament Library, Philadelphia, Westminster, 1966.

Refoule, François, "Et Ainsi Tout Israel Sera Sauvé": Romans 11, 25–32, LD, 117, Paris, Cerf, 1984.

Richard, Earl, "Polemics, Old Testament and Theology: A Study of II Cor 3:1– 4:6," *RB*, 88 (1981), 340–67.

Richardson, Cyril C., *Early Christian Fathers*, New York, Macmillan, 1970.

Rudolph, W., *Kommentar Zum Alten Testament: Haggai, Sacharja 1–9, Sacharja 9–14, Maleachi*, Gütersloh, Gerd Mohn, 1976.

Sanday, W. and A. C. Headlam, *A Critical and Exegetical Commentary on the Epistle to the Romans*, ICC, Edinburgh, T. & T. Clark, 1902.

Sanders, E. P., *Paul and Palestinian Judaism*, 2nd edn, Philadelphia, Fortress, 1977.

Paul, the Law, and the Jewish People, Philadelphia, Fortress, 1983.

Sanneh, Lamin, *Translating the Message: The Missionary Impact on Culture*, ASMS, 13, Maryknoll, Orbis, 1989.

Sasse, "κοσμές," *TDNT*, 3 (1965), 867–98.

Schlatter, Adolf, *Wie sprach Josephus von Gott?*, Gütersloh, Bentelsmann, 1910.

Schlier, Heinrich, *Der Römerbrief*, HThKNT, vol. 6, Freiburg, Herder, 1977.

Schoedel, William R., *Athenagoras: Legatio and De Resurrectione*, Oxford, Clarendon, 1972.

"Apologetic Literature and Ambassadorial Activities," *HTR*, [???] (1989), 55–78.

Schrenk, D. G., "Der Römerbrief als Missionsdokument" in Studien zu Paulus, Zurich, Zwingli, (1954), 81–106.

"γράμμα," *TDNT*, 1 (1964) 761–69.

"πατήρ," *TDNT*, 5 (1967), 945–1022.

Schubert, Paul, *Form and Function of the Pauline Thanksgiving*, Berlin, Topelman, 1939.

Segal, Alan F., *Two Powers in Heaven*, SJLA, 25, Leiden, Brill, 1977.

Shutt, R. J. H., "The Concept of God in the Works of Flavius Josephus," *JJB*, 31 (1980), 171–89.

"Letter of Aristeas" in James H. Charlesworth (ed.), *The Old Testament Pseudepigrapha*, vol. 2., Garden City, Doubleday, 1985, 7–34.

Skarsaune, Oskar, *The Proof from Prophesy, A Study in Justin Martyr's Proof-Text Tradition: Text-Type, Provenance, Theological Profile*, NovTSup, 56, Leiden, Brill, 1987.

Smith, John Merlin Powis, "A Note on Malachi 2:15a.," *AJSL*, 28 (1911), 204–6.

A Critical and Exegetical Commentary on Malachi, ICC, Edinburgh, T. & T. Clark, 1912.

Stanley, D., *Paul and the Language of Scripture*, SNTSMS, 69, Cambridge, University Press, 1992.

Stendahl, Krister, "The Apostle Paul and the Introspective Conscience of the West," *HTR*, 56 (1963), 199–215.

Paul Among the Jews and Gentiles, Philadelphia, Fortress Press, 1976.

Stern, M., *Greek and Latin Authors on Jews and Judaism*, vol. 2. Jerusalem, Israel Academy of Sciences and Humanities, 1974–84.

Stowers, Stanley Kent, *The Diatribe and Paul's Letters to the Romans*, SBLDS, 57, Chico, Scholars Press, 1981.

Letter Writing in Greco-Roman Anitquity, Philadelphia, Westminster, 1986.

Strathman, "λατρεύω," *TDNT*, 4 (1967).

Stuhlmueller, "Malachi," SBL, 87 (1968).

Tcherikover, V., "Jewish Apologetic Literature Reconsidered," *Symbolae R. Taubenschlag Dedicatae*, 3 (1957), 164–78.

Thrall, Margaret E., "The Pauline Use of συνείδησις," *NTS*, 14 (1967–8), 118–25.

Toy, Crawford Howell, *Quotations in the N.T.*, New York, Charles Scribner's Sons, 1884.

van Winden, M., *An Early Christian Philosopher: Justin Martyr's Dialogue with Trypho, Chapters One to Nine*, Philosophia Patrum 1, Leiden, Brill, 1971.

Vaux, R. de and J. T. Milik, *Qumran Grotte 4. DID 6*, Oxford, Clarendon, 1977.

Vermes, Geza, "Pre-Mishnaic Jewish Worship and the Phylacteries from the Dead Sea," *VT*, 9 (1959), 65–72.

"A Summary of the Law by Josephus," *NovT*, 24 (1982), 290–3.

von Arnim, J., *Stoicorum Veterum Fragmenta*, Lipsiae, in aedibus B.G. Teubneri, 1903–24.

von Rad, Gerhard, Deuteronomy, trans. Dorthea Barton, *Old Testament Library*, Philadelphia, Westmister, 1966.

Vuilleumier, René, *Malachie*, CAT 11c, Neuchâtel, Delachaux & Miestle, 1981.

Walter, Nikolaus, *Der Thoraausleger Aristobulos*, Berlin, Akademie, 1964.

Ward, Roy, "The Works of Abraham Jas 2:14–26," *HTR*, 61 (1968), 283–90.

Watson, Francis, Paul, *Judaism and the Gentiles: A Sociological Approach*, SNTSMS, 56, Cambridge, University Press, 1986.

Wedderburn, A. J. T., *The Reasons for Romans*, Edinburgh, T&T Clark, 1988.

Wehofer, Th., *Die Apologie Justins des Philosoher und Martyrers im litear-historischer Beziehung zum erstenmal untersuch*, Roemische Quartal-schritft, Suppl. 6, 1867.

Wilckens, Ulrich, "Zu Römer 3: 21–4:25: Antwort aus G. Klein," *EvTh*, 24 (1964), 586–610.

Der Brief an die Römer, 3 vols., EKKNT, 6, Zurich, Benziger, 1978–82.

Williams, Sam K., *Jesus' Death as Saving Event*, HDR, vol. 2, Missoula, Scholars Press, 1976.

"The 'Righteousness of God' in Romans," *JBL*, 99 (1980), 241–90.

Winckler, H, *Altorientalische Forschungen*, Leipzig, Eduard Pfeiffer, 1899.

Wolfson, Harry Austryn, *From Philo to Spinoza*, New York, Behrman House, 1977.

Wuellner, Wilhelm, "Paul's Rhetoric of Argumentation in Romans: An Alternative to the Donfried-Karris Debate Over Romans" in Karl P. Donfried (ed.), *The Romans Debate*, Minneapolis, Augsburg, 1977, 152–74.

GENERAL INDEX

Abraham
  apologist's use of, 16, 108–12,
    112–13, 114–15, 173
  and Christ, 105, 108, 111, 119
  and Christians, 105, 115–16, 123–24,
    125
  circumcision of, 120–21, 111
  covenant of, 121, 146
  faith of, 104–5, 112, 112–13, 118,
    121–24, 127–28
  as a Gentile/proselyte, 105, 109–10,
    173
  God's blessing to, 121
  God's promise to, 67, 116, 114–15,
    118, 122–23, 144–45, 147
  as Jewish Patriarch, 148, 154
  and Law, 59
  and monotheism, 109–10, 112, 116–17
  New Testament references to, 108
  Paul's use of in Romans, 102, 104–5,
    107–12, 112–25, 127, 173
  sacrifice of Isaac, 142
  and Sarah (birth of Isaac), 115, 123,
    127
  as universal Father figure, 109–10,
    112–13, 117–18, 122, 125, 127
Acts, 114, 168, 150
  Paul in, 50
Adam
  and Christ, 112, 126, 129–31, 173–74
  impact on humanity, 112, 129–31
adoption, 140
Adronicus, 167
Agrippa, Menenius, 159
Alexandria, 19, 60
"Ambrosiaster", 39
animal sacrifice, 158
animal worship, 53–53, 60–61
apocalypticism (see also eschatology)
  in contrast to apologetic, 15, 16, 57
  in Romans, 49, 137, 141, 158, 165,
    176, 177

apologetic literature (see Hellenistic
    Jewish apologetic writings and
    second-century Christian Greek
    apologetic writings)
  in contrast to apocalyptic, 15, 16, 57
  as differing from apology, 2–3
  definition of, 2–3
  political, 18–19, 157, 160, 177
  and Protreptic, 2, 21, 170–71
  purpose of, 19, 65–66
  Romans as, 47–49, 51–60, 65–66, 71,
    76, 102, 108, 113, 123–24, 131–32,
    134, 139, 165, 171–72, 178
  use of Scripture, 71
  universalizing theme of, 112–14
apologist, intent of, 19
apology genre
  as differing from apologetic, 3
  definition of, 2–3, 19
Appeles, 167
Aquila, 161, 167, 168, 177
Aratus, 98
Areopagus speech (in Acts), 50
Aristides
  Apologia, 17
  call to conversion, 18
  ethnological classification, 17, 71
Aristobulus, 82, 98–99, 114
Aristotle, 12, 117
  Protrepticus, 3–4, 9, 12, 141
atheism, 55
  Christians accused of, 16, 20
Athenagoras, 15, 20, 53
Augustus, 113, 127, 163

baptism, 131–32

Christ
  and Abraham, 105, 108–9, 110–11,
    119
  and Adam, 112, 126, 129–31, 174
  and baptism, 132

191

INDEX OF MODERN AUTHORS